Excel Essentials 2019

M.L. HUMPHREY

SELECT TITLES BY M.L. HUMPHREY

EXCEL ESSENTIALS 2019

Excel 2019 Beginner

Excel 2019 Intermediate

Excel 2019 Formulas & Functions

Excel 2019 Formulas and Functions Study Guide

WORD ESSENTIALS 2019

Word 2019 Beginner

Word 2019 Intermediate

POWERPOINT ESSENTIALS 2019

PowerPoint 2019 Beginner

PowerPoint 2019 Intermediate

ACCESS ESSENTIALS 2019

Access 2019 Beginner

Access 2019 Intermediate

CONTENTS

Excel 2019 Beginner

EXCEL ESSENTIALS 2019 BOOK 1

M.L. HUMPHREY

CONTENTS

Introduction

Microsoft Excel is an amazing program and I am so grateful to have learned it because I use it all the time as a small business owner as well as personally.

It allows me to organize and track key information in a quick and easy manner and to automate a lot of the calculations I need.

For example, on a personal level I have a budget worksheet that lets me track whether my bills have been paid, how much I need to keep in my bank account, and where I am financially.

In my professional career I've used it in a number of ways, from analyzing a series of financial transactions to see if a customer was overcharged to performing a text-based comparison of regulatory requirements across multiple jurisdictions.

(While Excel works best for numerical purposes, it is often a good choice for text-based analysis as well, especially if you want to be able to sort your results or filter out and isolate certain results.)

The purpose of this specific guide is to teach you the basics of what you need to know to use Microsoft Excel on a daily basis. By the time you're done with this book you should be able to do over 95% of what you need to do in Microsoft Excel and should have a solid enough grounding in how Excel works and the additional help resources available that you can learn the rest.

The series does continue with *Excel 2019 Intermediate*, which covers more advanced topics such as pivot tables, charts, and conditional formatting, and *Excel 2019 Formulas & Functions*, which goes into more detail about how formulas and functions work in Excel and then discusses about a hundred of those functions, sixty in detail.

You are welcome to continue with those books but you shouldn't have to in order to work in Excel on a daily basis. This book should be enough for that.

It was written specifically for Excel 2019, so all of the screenshots in this book are from Excel 2019 which, as of the date I'm writing this, is the most recent version of Excel.

However, because this book is about the basics of Excel, even if you are working in a different version of Excel most of what we'll cover here should be the same. The basic functions of Excel (like copy, paste, save, etc.) haven't changed much in the twenty-five-plus years I've been using the program.

If you previously purchased *Excel for Beginners* which was written using Excel 2013, most of the content of this book is the same and you probably don't need to buy this book as well.

The visual appearance of Excel 2019 has been changed just enough from the 2013 version to be annoying, so it may help to have the updated screenshots, but don't feel that you need to buy this book to use Excel 2019 if you've already read *Excel for Beginners*.

This book is not a comprehensive guide to Excel. The goal here is to give you a solid grounding in Excel that will let you get started using it without bogging down in a lot of information you don't need when you're getting started.

In this book I will often cover multiple ways of doing the same thing to show you the various options available to you. I may not cover *all* of the possible ways of doing something (I think we're up to five or six ways of doing the same thing on some of this stuff), but I will usually cover at least two ways.

I highly recommend learning any of the control shortcuts that I give you. For example, to copy something you can use the Control key and the C key (which I will write as Ctrl + C). The reason to learn these shortcuts is because they have not changed in all the years I've been using Excel. Which means that even when Microsoft issues the next version of Excel and moves things around a bit (which they will because that's one major way they make money is through new product releases) you'll still know at least one easy way to perform the core tasks.

Also, when in doubt go with the right-click and open a dialogue version of doing something because that too seems to have remained relatively stable over the years and versions of Excel.

If what I just said didn't make sense to you, don't worry. The first thing we're going to do is cover basic terminology so that you know what I'm talking about when I say things.

Alright then. Let's get started with that.

Basic Terminology

First things first, we need to establish some basic terminology so that you know what I'm talking about when I refer to a cell or a row or a column, etc.

Column

Excel uses columns and rows to display information. Columns run across the top of the worksheet and, unless you've done something funky with your settings, are identified using letters of the alphabet. As you can see below, they start with A on the far left side and march right on through the alphabet (A, B, C, D, E, etc.).

If you scroll far enough to the right, you'll see that they continue on to a double alphabet (AA, AB, AC, etc.).

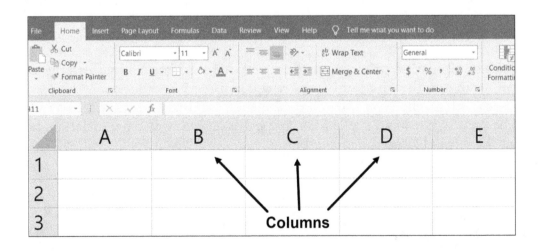

Row

Rows run down the side of the worksheet and are numbered starting at 1 and up to 1,048,576 in Excel 2019.

(Be aware that earlier versions of Excel have less rows in a worksheet so that if you have a lot of data that uses all of the available rows your file may not be compatible with earlier versions of Excel.)

You can click into any cell in a blank worksheet, hold down the ctrl key, and hit the down arrow to see just how many rows your version of Excel has. To return to the first row use the ctrl key and the up arrow.

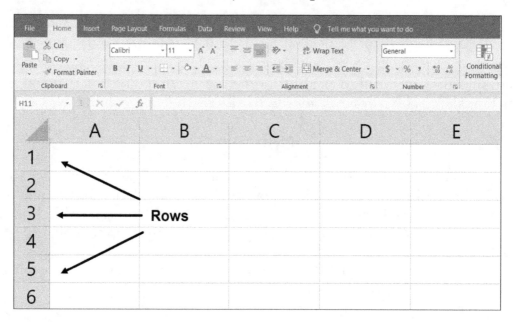

Cell

A cell is a combination of a column and row that is identified by the letter of the column it's in and the number of the row it's in.

For example, Cell A1 is the cell in the first column and the first row of the worksheet. When you've clicked on a specific cell it will have a darker border around the edges like in the image below.

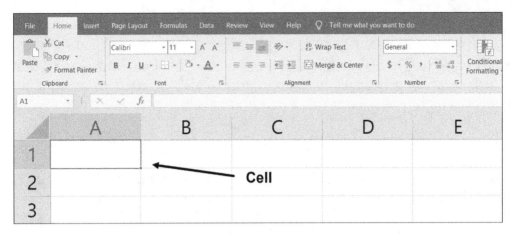

Click

If I tell you to click on something, that means to use your mouse (or trackpad) to move the arrow on the screen over to a specific location and left-click or right-click on the option. (See the next definition for the difference between left-click and right-click).

If you left-click, this selects the item. If you right-click, this generally creates a dropdown list of options to choose from.

If I don't tell you which to do, left- or right-click, then left-click.

Left-click/Right-click

If you look at your mouse or your trackpad, you generally have two flat buttons to press. One is on the left side, one is on the right. If I say left-click that means to press down on the button on the left. If I say right-click that means press down on the button on the right.

(If you're used to using Word you may already do this without even thinking about it. So, if that's the case then think of left-click as what you usually use to select text and right-click as what you use to see a menu of choices.)

Not all track pads have the left- and right-hand buttons. In that case, you'll basically want to press on either the bottom left-hand side of the track pad or the bottom right-hand side of the trackpad.

Spreadsheet

I'll try to avoid using this term, but if I do use it, I'll mean your entire Excel file. It's a little confusing because it can sometimes also be used to mean a specific worksheet, which is why I'll try to avoid it as much as possible.

Worksheet

A worksheet is basically a combination of rows and columns that you can enter data in. When you open an Excel file, it opens to worksheet one.

Excel 2019 has one worksheet available by default when a new file is opened and that worksheet is originally labeled Sheet1.

It is possible to add more worksheets to a workbook (that's the entire Excel file) and we will cover that later. When there are multiple worksheets, the name of the current worksheet is highlighted in white to show that it's in use.

Formula Bar

The formula bar is the long white bar at the top of the screen with the $f\chi$ symbol next to it.

If you click in a cell and start typing, you'll see that what you type appears not only in that cell, but in the formula bar as well. When you input a formula into a cell and then hit enter, the value returned by the formula will be what displays in the cell, but the formula will appear in the formula bar when you have that cell highlighted.

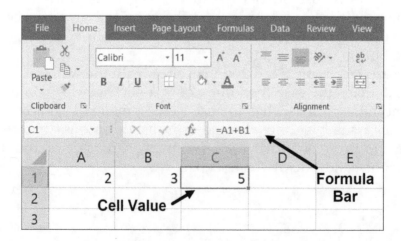

Tab

I refer to the menu choices at the top of the screen (File, Home, Insert, Page Layout, Formulas, Data, Review, View, and Help) as tabs. Note how they look like folder tabs from an old-time filing system when selected? That's why.

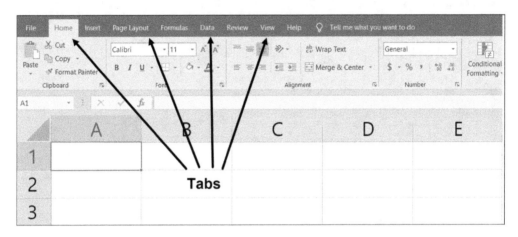

Each menu tab you select will show you different options. On my Home tab I can do things like copy/cut/paste, format cells, edit cells, and insert/delete cells, for example.

Scroll Bar

On the right side and along the bottom of the screen are two bars with arrows at the ends. If you left-click and hold on either bar you can move it back and forth between those arrows. This lets you see information that's off the page in your current view but part of the worksheet you're viewing.

You can also use the arrows at the ends of the scroll bar to do the same thing. Left-click on the arrow once to move it one line or column or left-click and hold to get it to move as far as it can go.

If you want to cover more rows/columns at a time you can click into the blank space on either side of the scroll bar to move an entire screen at a time, assuming you have enough data entered for that.

Using the scroll bars only lets you move to the end of the information you've already entered. You can use the arrows instead of clicking on the scroll bar to scroll all the way to the far end of the worksheet.

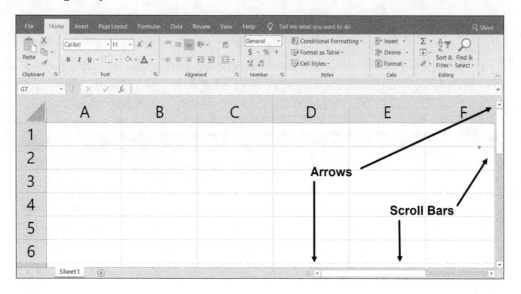

Data

I use data and information interchangeably. Whatever information you put into a worksheet is your data.

Table

I may also refer to a table of data or data table on occasion. This is just a combination of rows and columns that contain information.

This should not be confused with the Word version of a table which is a set aside combination of rows and columns. Even if you create a table in Excel with a border around the edges and nothing else in the document, you're still working in a worksheet that contains a set number of columns and rows that never changes no matter what you do.

Select

If I tell you to "select" cells, that means to highlight them. If the cells are next to each other, you can just left-click on the first one and drag the cursor (move your mouse or finger on the trackpad) until all of the cells are highlighted. When this happens, they'll all be surrounded by a dark box like below.

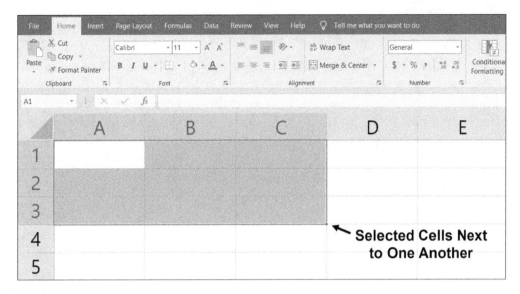

Selected Cells Next to One Another

If the cells aren't next to each other, then what you do is left-click on the first cell, hold down the Ctrl key (bottom left on my keyboard), left-click on the next cell, hold down the Ctrl key, left-click on the next cell, etc. until you've selected all the cells you want.

The cells you've already selected will be shaded in gray. The last cell you selected will be surrounded by a dark border.

In the image below cells A1, C1, A3, and C3 are selected. Cell C3 was selected last.

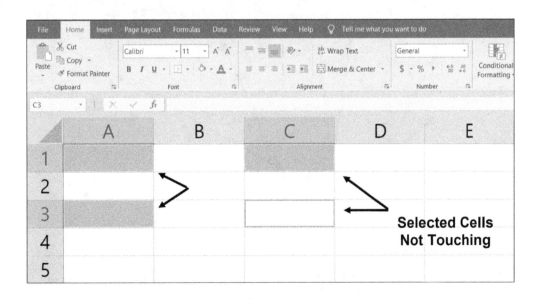

Selected Cells Not Touching

Cursor

If you didn't know this one already, it's what moves around when you move the mouse (or use the trackpad). In Excel it often looks like a three-dimensional squat cross or it will look like one of a couple of varieties of arrow. (You can open Excel and move the arrow to where the column and row labels are to see what I mean.) The different shapes the cursor takes represent different functions that are available.

Arrow

If I say that you can "arrow" to something that just means to use the arrow keys to navigate from one cell to another. For example, if you enter information in Cell A1 and hit Enter, that moves your cursor down to cell A2. If instead you wanted to move to the right to Cell B1, you could do so by using the right arrow.

Dropdown

I will occasionally refer to a dropdown or dropdown menu. This is generally a list of potential choices that you can select from. The existence of the list is indicated by an arrow next to the first available selection. You can see a number of examples in the image below.

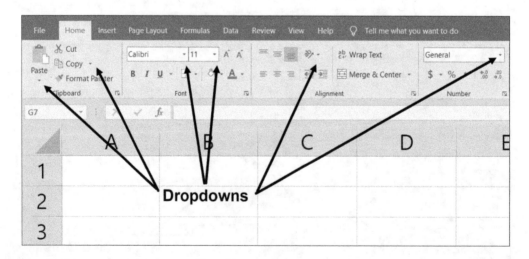

I will also sometimes refer to the list of options you see when you click on a dropdown arrow as the dropdown menu.

Dialogue Box

Dialogue boxes are pop-up boxes that contain a set of available options and appear when you need to provide additional information or make additional choices. For example, this is the Find and Replace dialogue box which appears when you select the Replace option from the Editing section of the Home tab:

Absolute Basics

It occurs to me that there are a few absolute basics to using Excel that we should cover before we get into things like formatting.

Opening an Excel File

To start a brand new Excel file, I simply click on Excel from my applications menu or the shortcut icon I have on my computer's taskbar, and it opens a new Excel file for me.

If you're opening an existing Excel file, you can either go to the folder where the file is saved and double-click on the file name, or you can (if Excel is already open) go to the File tab and choose Open from the left-hand menu.

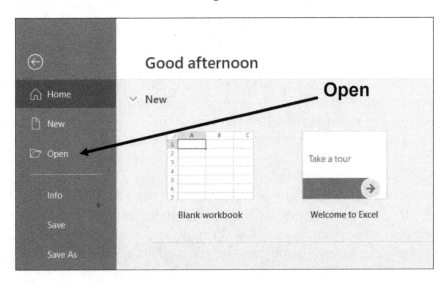

That will show you a list of Recent Workbooks. If it includes the one you're looking for, you can just click on it once and it will open.

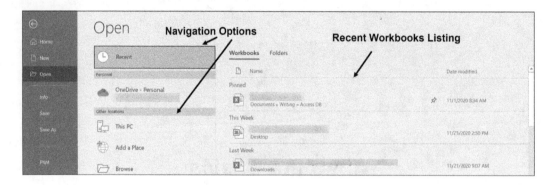

If you don't see the file you're looking for, you can click on the list of navigation options in between the left-hand menu and the list of Recent Workbooks and navigate to where the file is stored. When I click on This PC it gives me a list of recently used folders. If the document I want isn't in one of those folders, I can use the Browse option instead. If you use the cloud, OneDrive is also an option.

Excel may show an error message when you open some files in Excel. The one I usually see is about Excel opening a file in Protected View because it's a file I didn't create.

Don't panic, it's fine. You can see the contents without doing anything or if you need to edit just click on Enable Editing as long as you trust the source of the file.

Saving an Excel File

Excel has two options for saving a file, Save and Save As. If you have an existing file that's already been saved before and no changes to make to its name, location, or type, you can use Ctrl + S or click on the small computer disc image in the top left corner to save the file once more. Simply closing the file will also prompt Excel to ask if you'd like to save your changes to the document.

If the file you are saving is an .xlsx file type, you should really see nothing else at that point. The file is saved when you use Ctrl + S or the disc image or click on Save when you close the file..

If the file you're trying to save is an .xls file type (so an older file type) or another type of file like a .csv file or a .txt file, you may see an additional message when you try to Save about compatibility. The dialogue box that appears will tell you the issue that saving the file as-is will create and you need to decide whether that's okay or whether to go back into the file and fix the issue before saving.

(Usually I can just say continue when this happens because it opened from the old format and is saving to the old format so isn't going to be a huge concern as long as I didn't do some new fancy analysis in the meantime.)

All of the above options will also work for a brand new file, but they will bring up a dialogue box asking what you want to name the file and where you want to save it.

Clicking on More Options from that dialogue box will take you to the Save As screen that can also be reached by clicking on Save As on the left-hand side after clicking on the File tab.

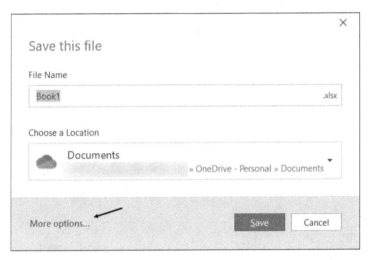

With the Save As option available under the File tab, Excel will ask you to choose which folder to save the file into. You can either choose from the list of recent folders on the right-hand side, or navigate to the folder you want using the locations listing on the left-hand side (OneDrive, This PC, and Browse).

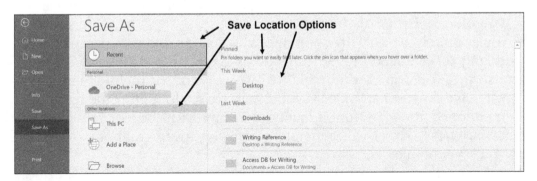

Once you choose Browse or select a folder, a dialogue box will appear where you can name the file and choose its format.

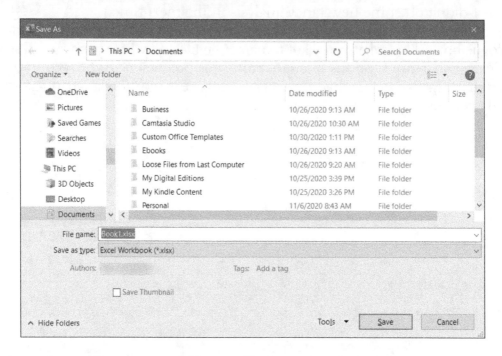

You can also navigate to a different file location at this point if you're more comfortable working in the Save As dialogue box.

To change the file type, click on the dropdown arrow for the option next to Save As Type under the File Name.

The default in Excel 2019 is to save to an .xlsx file type. Know that this file type is not compatible with versions of Excel prior to Excel 2007. At this point you're probably safe working with the default .xlsx file type, but this can be an issue with older versions of the program.

If you routinely work with someone who has an older version of Excel I would highly recommend saving your files as Excel 97-2003 Workbook .xls files instead so that you don't create a file that won't work for them. It's much easier to initially save down to an older version than try to do it after the fact.

As mentioned above, if functionality or content will be lost by saving to the format you chose, Excel will generate a warning message about compatibility when you save the file.

If you have an existing file that you want to rename, save to a new location, or save as a new file type, use the Save As option by going to the File tab and choosing Save As from there.

Deleting an Excel File

You can't delete an Excel file from within Excel. You'll need to navigate to the folder where the file is stored and delete the file there without opening it.

To do this, first, click on the file name. (Only enough to select it. Make sure you haven't double-clicked and highlighted the name which will then try to rename the file.) Then choose Delete from the menu at the top of the screen, or right-click and choose Delete from the dropdown menu.

Renaming an Excel File

You might want to rename an Excel file at some point. You can Save As and choose a new name for the file, but that will mean you now have two versions of the file, one with the old name and one with the new name.

A better option is to navigate to the folder where you have the file saved, click on it once to highlight the file, click on it a second time to highlight the name, and then type in the new name you want to use. If you do it that way, there will only be one version of the file, the one with the name you wanted.

However, if you do rename a file by changing the name in the source folder, know that you can't then access it from the Recent Workbooks listing under Open file. Even though it might be listed there, Excel won't be able to find it because it no longer has that name. (Same thing happens if you move a file from the location it was in when you were last working on it. I often run into this by moving a file into a new subfolder when I suddenly get inspired to organize my records.)

Closing an Excel File

When you're done with Excel you're going to want to close your file. The easiest way to do so is to click on the X in the top right corner of the screen. Or you can use Alt +F4. (If you use Alt+F4 this will only work if the F functions are set up to be the default keys on your keyboard.)

To just close a worksheet but keep Excel open you can use Ctrl + W.

Navigating Excel

The next thing we're going to discuss is basic navigation within Excel. These are all things you can do that don't involve inputting, formatting, or manipulating your data.

Basic Navigation Within A Worksheet

Excel will automatically open into cell A1 of Sheet1 for a new Excel file. For an existing file it will open in the cell and worksheet where you were when you last saved the file. (This means it can also open with a set of cells already highlighted if that's what you were doing when you last saved the file.)

Within a worksheet, it's pretty basic to navigate.

You can click into any cell you can see in the worksheet using your mouse or trackpad. Just place your cursor over the cell and left-click.

From the cell where you currently are (which will be outlined with a dark border), you can use the up, down, left, and right arrow keys to move one cell at a time in any of those directions.

You can also use the tab key to move one cell at a time to the right and the shift and tab keys combined (shift + tab) to move one cell at a time to the left.

To see other cells in the worksheet that aren't currently visible, you can use the scroll bars on the right-hand side or the bottom of the worksheet. The right-hand scroll bar will let you move up and down. The bottom scroll bar will let you move right or left. Just remember that the bars themselves will only let you move as far as you've entered data or the default workspace. You need to use the arrows at the ends of the scroll bars to move farther than that.

For worksheets with lots of data in them, click on the scroll bar and drag it to move quickly to the beginning or end of the data. To move one view's worth at a time, click in the blank gray space around the actual scroll bar.

If you're using the scroll bars to navigate a large amount of data or records, know that until you click into a new cell with your mouse or trackpad you will still be in the last cell where you had clicked or made an edit. So be sure to click into one of the cells you see rather than try to immediately type or to use the tab or arrow keys to navigate. (I run into this frequently when I have Freeze Panes on and then try to use an arrow key to move from the first row of column labels into my data, forgetting that the data I'm actually seeing is hundreds of rows away from that top row. Don't worry, we'll discuss Freeze Panes later.)

F2

If you click in a cell and hit the F2 key, this will take you to the end of the contents of the cell. This can be very useful when you need to edit the contents of a cell or to work with a formula in that cell. I use it often enough that every time I get a new computer I make sure that the F keys are the default rather than the volume controls, etc.

Adding a New Worksheet

When you open a new Excel file in Excel 2019, you'll have one worksheet you can use named Sheet1.

If you need another worksheet, simply click on the + symbol in a circle next to that Sheet1 tab.

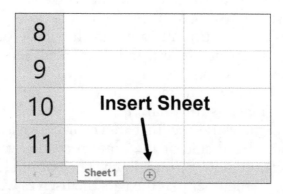

If you already have multiple worksheets in your workbook, the + sign will be located to the right of the last worksheet.

You can also go to the Home tab under the Cells section and left-click the arrow under Insert and then select Insert Sheet from the dropdown menu there.

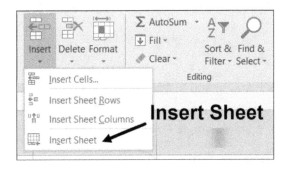

Deleting a Worksheet

Sometimes you'll add a worksheet and then realize you don't want it anymore. It's easy enough to delete. Just right-click on the name of the worksheet you want to delete and choose the Delete option from the dropdown menu (which will actually drop upward.)

If there was any data in the worksheet you're trying to delete, Excel will give you a warning message to that effect in a dialogue box.

If you don't care, click Delete. If you do care and want to cancel the deletion, click Cancel.

Another way to delete a worksheet is to go to the Cells section in the Home tab, left-click on the arrow next to Delete, and choose Delete Sheet from the dropdown menu there.

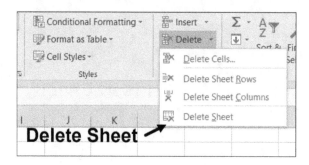

Be sure you want to delete any worksheet you choose to delete, because you can't get it back later. This is one place where undo (which we'll discuss later) will not work.

Basic Navigation Between Worksheets

Once you have multiple worksheets in your workbook, you can navigate between them by either clicking on the name of the worksheet you want at the bottom of the screen or by using Ctrl + Page Up to move one worksheet to the left or Ctrl + Page Dn to move one worksheet to the right.

The Ctrl shortcuts do not loop around, so if you're at the first worksheet and want to reach the last one you need to use Ctrl + Page Dn to move through all of the other worksheets to get there.

Or you could just click onto the last one like I do and skip the ctrl shortcut.

If you have too many worksheets to see their names on one screen, use the arrows at the left-hand side of the worksheet names or the … at the ends (when visible) to see the rest. The … will take you all the way to the beginning or the end.

Insert a Cell in a Worksheet

Sometimes you will just want to insert one cell or a small handful of cells into your worksheet. This will happen when you already have data entered into the worksheet and realize that you need to put additional data in the midst of what you already have entered.

(Because, remember, Excel worksheets have a fixed unchanging number of cells based upon the numbers of rows and columns they contain. So inserting a cell isn't really inserting a cell so much as telling Excel to move all of your information from that point over or down to make room for the new cell or cells.)

To insert a cell or cells, select the cell or cell range where you want to insert your new blank cells, right-click, and choose Insert from the dropdown menu.

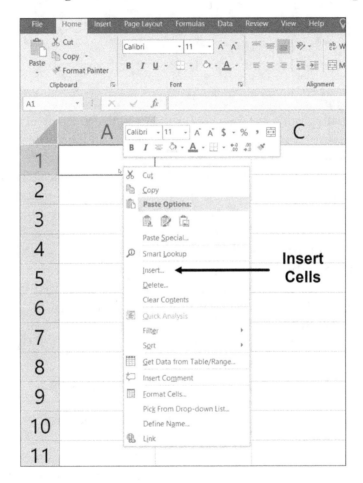

You'll be given four choices, Shift Cells Right, Shift Cells Down, Entire Row, and Entire Column. (See dialogue box screenshot on next page.)

Shift Cells Right will insert your cell or range of cells by moving every other cell in that row or rows to the right to make room for the new cell or cells.

Shift Cells Down will insert your cell or range of cells by moving every other cell in that column or columns down to make room.

Entire row will insert an entire new row at that point.
Entire column will insert an entire new column at that point.

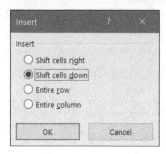

If you have a range of cells selected when you choose entire row or entire column then that number of rows or columns will be inserted. So, select three rows and choose entire row and three new rows will be inserted. Select three columns and choose entire column and three new columns will be inserted.

(Be sure that the cells you select and the option you choose make sense given the other data you've already entered in the worksheet. Sometimes I find that I need to actually highlight a larger range of cells and insert cells for all of them in order to keep the rest of my data aligned.)

You can also highlight the cell or cells where you want to insert and then go to the Cells section of the Home tab where it says Insert and choose Insert Cells from the dropdown to bring up the Insert dialogue box. Just clicking on Insert instead of using the dropdown menu will automatically insert a cell or cells by moving everything down.

There is also a control shortcut for this one (Ctrl+Shift+=) but I never use it.

Insert a Column or Row

From the above discussion you can see that it's also possible to insert an entire row or column into your existing data.

The easiest way to do so is to select the row or column where you want your new row or column to go, right-click, and choose Insert from the dropdown menu.

(To select a row or column you just click on either the letter of the column or the number of the row. You'll know it worked if all cells in that row or column are then shaded gray showing that they've been selected.)

For columns, when a new column is inserted all of your data will shift to the right one column. For rows all of your data will shift down one row. So data in Column C will move to Column D and data in Row 2 will move to Row 3.

As we saw above, you can also just right-click in a single cell, choose Insert, and then choose Entire Row or Entire Column from the Insert Dialogue Box.

Another option is to click in a cell or highlight the row or column where you want to insert and then go to the Cells section of the Home tab and use the Insert dropdown to choose Insert Sheet Rows or Insert Sheet Columns.

Delete a Cell in a Worksheet

Deleting a cell or range of cells in a worksheet is a lot like inserting one. Select the cell or cells you want to delete, right-click, and choose Delete from the dropdown menu.

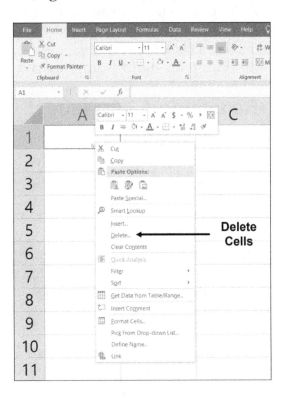

Next, choose whether to shift cells up or left, keeping in mind that when you remove a cell everything will have to move to fill in the empty space it leaves.

Double-check to make sure that deleting that cell or range of cells didn't change the layout of the rest of your data. (I sometimes find I need to delete more than one cell to keep things uniform.)

(Note that you can also delete an entire row or column this way as well just like you could with inserting.)

Another option is to highlight the cell(s) you want to delete, and then go to the Cells section of the Home tab where it says Delete and choose the delete option you want from there. Just clicking on Delete will shift the remaining data upward one row. Using the dropdown to choose Delete Cells will open the Delete dialogue box which gives you the option to shift the remaining data to the left.

Delete a Column or Row

Same as with inserting a column or row. The easiest option is to highlight the entire row or column you want to delete, right-click, and select Delete.

You can also highlight the row or column and then go to the Cells section of the Home tab where it says Delete and choose the delete option you want from the dropdown there. Or you can click into one cell, right-click, select Delete, and then choose Entire Row or Entire Column from the dialogue box.

Renaming A Worksheet

The default name for worksheets in Excel are Sheet1, Sheet2, Sheet3, etc. They're not useful for much of anything, and if you have information in more than one worksheet, you're going to want to rename them to something that lets you identify which worksheet is which.

If you double left-click on a worksheet name (on the tab at the bottom) it will highlight in gray and you can then delete the existing name and replace it with whatever you want by simply typing in the new worksheet name.

You can also right-click on the tab name and choose Rename from the dropdown menu and it will highlight the tab name in gray and let you type in your new name that way as well.

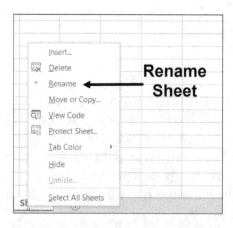

A worksheet name cannot be more than 31 characters long, be blank, contain the forward slash, the back slash, a question mark, a star, a colon, or brackets (/ \ ? * : [ ]), begin or end with an apostrophe, or be named History.

Don't worry about memorizing that. In Excel 2019 it won't let you type the prohibited characters or let you type more characters than the limit allows.

Moving or Copying Worksheet

There may be times that you want to move a worksheet around, so change the order of the worksheets in a workbook or even move that particular worksheet into a new Excel workbook. I've also on more than one occasion wanted to take a copy of a worksheet in one workbook and put that copy into a different workbook.

To move a worksheet within an Excel workbook, click on the name of the worksheet you want to move, hold down that click, and drag the worksheet to the new position you want for it. While you're dragging you should see what looks like a little piece of paper under your cursor arrow. This shows you where you're dragging the worksheet to. Once it's where you want it, just release the click and it should drop into the new position.

To move a worksheet to a new workbook or to copy one to a new workbook is basically the same. Right-click on the worksheet name and choose Move or Copy from the dropdown menu.

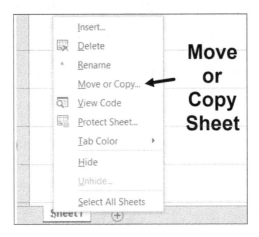

This will open the Move or Copy dialogue box. There are three options available in the dialogue box. The first is "To Book" which is where you select the file you'd like to move your worksheet to. If you're just copying the worksheet and keeping that copy within the current workbook, then leave this option alone. If you want to move or copy the worksheet to a new workbook, then use the dropdown menu to select that new workbook. Your options will consist of all of the workbooks you have open at the time as well as an option to create a new workbook.

The second choice you have is where to place the copied or moved worksheet. This is in a box labeled Before Sheet and it will list all of the current worksheets in the selected workbook. Choose the (move to end) option to place the worksheet at the end.

If you are copying the worksheet and not just moving it, so you want the original version to stay where it is but to use a copy in either that workbook or another, be sure to check the Create a Copy checkbox at the bottom.

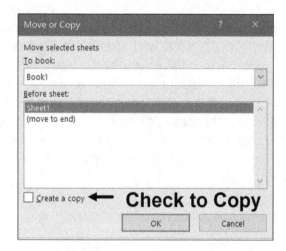

Click OK when you're done and the worksheet will be moved or copied.

Inputting Your Data

At its most basic, inputting your data is very simple. Click in the cell where you want to input information and type. But there are some tricks to it that you'll want to keep in mind.

First, let's take a step back and talk about one of the key strengths of using Excel and that's the ability to sort or filter your data. For example, I publish books, and every month I get reports from the places where my books are published listing all of the sales of my books at those locations. But what if I only care about the sales of book A? How can I see those if I have a couple hundred rows of information about various books in the report they've given me?

Well, if the site where I sold those books is nice and helpful and they understand data analysis, they've given me my sales listings in an Excel worksheet with one header row at the top and then one row for each sale or for each book. If they've done that, then I can very easily filter my data on the title column and see just the entries related to a specific title. If they haven't, then I'm stuck deleting rows of information I don't need to get to the data I want.

Which is all a roundabout way of saying that you can input your data any way you want, but if you follow some key data principles you'll have a lot more flexibility in what you can do with that data once it's entered.

Those principles are:

1. Use the first row of your worksheet to label your data.

2. List all of your data in continuous rows after that first row without including any subtotals or subheadings or anything that isn't your data.

3. To the extent possible, format your data in such a way that it can be analyzed. (So rather than put in a free-text field, try to use a standardized

list of values instead. See below. Column E, which uses a 1 to 5 point ranking scale, is better for analysis than Column D, which is a free text field where anyone can say anything.)

4. Standardize your values. Customer A should always be listed as Customer A. United States should always be United States not USA, U.S.A., or America.

5. Store your raw data in one location; analyze or correct it elsewhere.

I get into all of this much more in a book called *Data Principles for Beginners*, but that's the basic gist of how to best store data in an Excel worksheet if you're planning to do any analysis on it.

Here's an example of how it looks.

	A	B	C	D	E	F	G	H
1	Customer Name	Invoice	Date	Customer Feedack	Customer Satisfaction Score		Row 1 Identifies	
2	Customer Name A	$110	1-Jan	asbasbdasdas	1		Contents	
3	Customer Name B	$125	15-Feb	asdas	1			
4	Customer Name C	$150	7-Apr	kjjkhj	1		Other Rows	
5	Customer Name D	$225	21-Jan	adsas	4		Contain Data	
6	Customer Name E	$250	10-Sep	aiasdasd	5			

This is for data analysis, but there are many ways in which I use Excel that don't require that kind of analysis so don't follow those types of rules. My budgeting worksheet, for example, is not meant to be filtered or sorted. It's a snapshot of information that summarizes my current financial position. But my worksheet that lists all vendor payments for the year? You bet it's formatted using this approach.

So before you enter any data into your Excel file, put some time into thinking about how you want to use that data.

Is it just a visual snapshot? If so, don't worry about structuring it for sorting or filtering.

Will it be hundreds of rows of values that you want to summarize or analyze? If so, then arrange it in the way I showed above. You don't have to have Row 1 be your column headings (although it does make it easier), but wherever you do put those headings, keep everything below that point single rows of data that are all formatted and entered in the same way so that they can be compared to one another.

Okay?

Now that we've gotten that out of the way, let's discuss a few quick tricks that will make entering your data and analyzing it easier, starting with Undo and Redo.

Undo

If you enter the wrong information or perform the wrong action and want to easily undo it, hold down the Ctrl key and the Z key at the same time. (Ctrl + Z) You can do this multiple times if you want to undo multiple actions, although there are a few actions (such as deleting a worksheet) that cannot be undone.

You can also click on the left-pointing hooked arrow at the very top of the Excel workbook to undo an action. It's located in the Quick Access Toolbar right above the File and Home tabs next to where you can click on the disc image to save a file.

Clicking on the dropdown arrow next to the undo arrow will give you a list of all of the actions that you can undo at that point in time. You can then select the first action or a series of actions from there. If you want to undo something you did four actions ago, you have to undo the last three actions as well.

Undo is a life saver. If you only remember one control shortcut, make it this one. Ctrl + Z is your friend.

Redo

If you mistakenly undo something and want it back, you can hold down the Ctrl key and the Y key at the same time to redo it. (Ctrl + Y)

In the Quick Access Toolbar there is an arrow that points to the right that will be available if you just undid something which you can click on as well instead of using the control shortcut.

If you undo multiple actions at once, you can redo all of them at once as well using the Quick Access Toolbar. But again, if you want to redo actions 1, 2, and 4 you will also have to redo action 3. You can't pick and choose.

Auto-Suggested Text

If you've already typed text into a cell, Excel will suggest that text to you in subsequent cells in the same column.

For example, if you are creating a list of all the books you own (something I once tried to do and gave up after about a hundred entries), and in Cell A1 you type "science fiction", when you go to Cell A2 and type an "s", Excel will automatically suggest to you "science fiction". If you don't want to use that suggestion, then keep typing. If you do, then hit enter.

This is very convenient because instead of typing fifteen characters you only have to type one, but it only works when you have unique values for Excel to identify. If you have science fiction/fantasy and science fiction as entries in your list then it's not going to work because Excel waits until it can suggest one single option. So you'd have to type "science fiction/" before it made any suggestions in that scenario

Also, if there are empty cells between the entries you already completed and the one you're now completing and you have no other columns with completed data in them to bridge that gap and let Excel know the cells are related, Excel won't make a suggestion.

(Which means if you're going to use Auto-Suggested text it helps to have a column next to where you're inputting your data that is a numbered entries column that will let auto-complete work even if you're not entering your data row by row but are instead jumping around a bit.)

Another time this doesn't work is if you have a very long list that you've completed and the matching entry is hundreds of rows away from the one you're now completing.

Excel also doesn't make suggestions for numbers. If you have an entry that combines letters and numbers, it won't make a suggestion until you've typed at least one letter from the entry.

Despite all these apparent limitations, auto-suggested text can be very handy to use if you have to enter one of a limited number of choices over and over again and can't easily copy the information into your worksheet. It's also helpful to factor this in when deciding what your values will be. For example, I have a book *Excel for Beginners* and a book *Excel for Beginners Quiz Book*. Rather than list them that way in my advertising tracker where I have to make manual entries I list the quiz book as *Quiz Book: Excel for Beginners*. This lets me just type E or just type Q and have Excel complete the rest of both titles for me.

(We're not going to get into it in this book, but if you do have a limited list of values that you want available to enter and can't use auto-suggested text because maybe it's Widget1 and Widget2 so it won't help, then one alternate workaround would be to set up Data Validation with a list of values. Data Validation is covered in *Excel 2019 Intermediate*.)

Alright. Next.

Copying the Contents and Formatting of One Cell To Another

Copying the contents and formatting of a cell to another is something you will probably need to do often. And it is very easy to do.

First, highlight the information you want to copy, next, hold down the Ctrl and C keys at the same time (Ctrl + C), and then go to the cell where you want to put the information you copied and hit Enter.

If you want to copy the information to more than one location, instead of hitting Enter at the new cell, hold down the Ctrl and V keys at the same time (Ctrl + V) to paste.

If you use Ctrl + V, you'll see that the original cell you copied from is still surrounded by a dotted line which indicates that the information you copied is still available to be pasted into another cell. You can see this by clicking into another cell and using Ctrl + V again. It will paste the information you copied a second time.

Another way to copy is to select your information and then right-click and choose Copy from the dropdown menu. You can then use Enter, Ctrl + V, or right-click and choose Paste from the dropdown menu to paste the information.

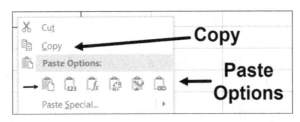

For a basic copy of the information choose the first option under Paste Options which is a clipboard with a blank piece of paper. Hold your cursor over it and you should see it described as Paste (P).

Once you're done pasting the values into new cells and want to do something else, just hit the Esc key. This will remove the dotted line from around the cell you were copying and ensure you don't accidentally paste it somewhere else. Typing text into a new cell also works to turn off the copy/paste that you've initiated.

(When in doubt in Excel using Esc is very helpful. It's kind of like an Undo function when you haven't yet done anything but have started something you don't want to finish.)

In the Clipboard section of the Home tab you can also find another set of Copy and Paste options (as well as Cut which we're about to discuss), but I almost never use them because these are tasks where learning your control shortcuts will save you a lot of time.

So, Ctrl + C to Copy, Ctrl + V to Paste, and, as we're about to learn, Ctrl + X to Cut. Memorize those and learn to use them. Trust me.

Moving the Contents of a Cell

To move selected information rather than just copy it, select the information, type Ctrl and X at the same time (Ctrl + X), click on the new location, and hit Enter or type Ctrl + V.

Unlike with copying, you can only move the contents of a cell to one new location. Once you hit Enter or use Ctrl + V that information will have moved and you cannot paste it anywhere else without first copying it from the new location.

Another option for moving your information is to highlight the information you want to move, right-click, and choose Cut from the dropdown menu and then paste your cell contents in the new location.

Copying the contents of a cell (Ctrl + C) is different from cutting and moving the contents of a cell (Ctrl + X), because when you copy the contents of a cell, (Ctrl + C), they remain in their original location. When you move the contents of a cell, (Ctrl + X), you are removing them from their original location to place them in their new location.

Note that I've been talking about Copying or Cutting information rather than cells, because you can actually click into a specific cell, highlight just a portion of the content of that cell and Copy or Cut that portion only. You do this by clicking into the cell and then going to the Formula Bar to highlight the text you want, or by clicking on a cell and then using F2 to access the contents of that cell and then the arrow keys and the Shift key to highlight the text you want.

Copying Versus Moving When It Comes to Formulas

If you're dealing with text, copying (Ctrl + C) or cutting the text (Ctrl + X) doesn't really change anything. What ends up in that new cell will be the same regardless of the method you use.

But with formulas, that's not what happens.

With formulas, moving the contents of a cell (Ctrl + X) will keep the formula the exact same as it was. So if your formula was =A2+B2 it will still be =A2+B2 in the new cell.

Copying the contents of a cell (Ctrl + C) will change the formula based upon the number of rows and columns you moved. The formula is copied relative to where it originated. If your original formula in Cell A3 is =A2+B2 and you copy it to Cell A4 (so move it one cell downward) the formula in Cell A4 will be =A3+B3. All cell references in the formula adjust one cell downward.

If you copy that same formula to Cell B3 (so one cell to the right) the formula in B3 will be =B2+C2. All cell references in the formula adjust one cell to the right.

If this doesn't make sense to you, just try it. Put some sample values in cells A2 and B2 and then experiment with Ctrl + C versus Ctrl + X.

Also, there is a way to prevent a formula from changing when you copy it using the $ sign to keep the cell references fixed. We'll talk about that next.

Copying Formulas To Other Cells While Keeping One Value Fixed

If you want to copy a formula while keeping the value of one or more of the cells fixed, you need to use the $ sign.

A $ sign in front of the letter portion of a cell location will keep the column the same but allow the row number to change. ($A1)

A $ sign in front of the number portion of a cell location will keep the row the same but allow the column to change. (A$1)

A $ sign in front of both the column and row portion will keep the referenced cell exactly the same. ($A$1)

This will be discussed in more detail in the manipulating data section because where it really comes up is in mathematical calculations and functions.

Paste Special

I often want to take values I've calculated in Excel and just keep the end result without keeping the formula. For example, with my advertising in the UK the values are reported to me in that currency (GBP) but I want to convert them to my currency (USD). Once I've done that, I don't need to keep the calculation because the only thing that matters for my purposes is the end value in my currency.

Other reasons to use Paste Special include wanting to copy the contents of a cell but not keep the formatting from that cell. Also, I use it to turn a series of values that are displayed across columns into a series of values that are displayed across rows, or vice versa.

The first thing to know about Paste Special is that you can only use it if you've copied (Ctrl + C) the contents of a cell or cells. It doesn't work with Cutting (Ctrl + X).

To Paste Special use the dropdown option for pasting or the dropdown option in the Clipboard section of the Home tab. You cannot use the Ctrl shortcut to paste.

So, right-click where you want to Paste and go to Paste Options or click on the dropdown arrow under Paste in the Clipboard section of the Home tab. You should see options that look like this:

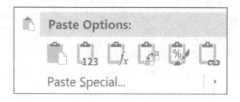

In my opinion, not all of these choices are useful. So I'm just going to highlight two of them for you.

Paste Values, the second option above which has the 123 on its clipboard, is useful for when you want the results of a formula, but don't want the formula anymore. I use this often.

It's also useful when you want the contents of a cell, but would prefer to use the formatting from the destination cell(s). For example, if you're copying from one Excel file to another.

Another way I use it is when I've run a set of calculations on my data, found my values, and now want to sort or do something else with my data and don't want to risk having the values change on me. I highlight the entire data set, copy, and then paste special-values right over the top of my existing data. (Just be sure to type Esc after you do this so that the change is fixed in place.)

Paste Transpose, the fourth option with the little arrow arcing between two pairs of cells, is very useful if you have a row of data that you want to turn into columns of data or vice versa. Just highlight the data, copy, paste-transpose, and it will automatically paste a column of data as a row or a row of data as a column.

Just be sure before you paste that there isn't any data already there that will be overwritten, because Excel won't warn you before it overwrites it.

There are more paste options available than just the six you can see above. If you click on where it says Paste Special you'll see another dropdown menu to the side with eight more options, and if you go to the bottom of that breakout menu and click on Paste Special again, it will bring up the Paste Special dialogue box which allows you to pick and choose from the various paste options. The dropdown available from the Clipboard section of the Home tab is the same as the Paste Special dropdown list of options and you can also bring up the dialogue box from there by choosing Paste Special at the bottom.

Displaying The Contents Of A Cell As Text

Excel likes to change certain values to what it thinks you meant. So if you enter June 2015 into a cell, it will convert that entry to a date even if you intended it to be text. To see this, type June 2015 in a cell, hit enter, click back into the cell, and you'll see in the formula bar that it says 6/1/2015 and it displays as Jun-15 in the cell.

Excel also assumes that any entry that starts with a minus sign (-), an equals sign (=), or a plus sign (+) is a formula.

To keep Excel from messing with your entries, you can type a single quote mark (') before the contents of the cell. If you do that, Excel will treat whatever you enter after that as text and will keep the formatting type as General.

So if you want to have June 2015 display in a cell in your worksheet, you need to type 'June 2015.

If you want to have

- Item A

display in a cell, you need to type it as:

'- Item A

The single quote mark is not visible when you look at or print your worksheet. It is only visible in the formula bar when you've selected the impacted cell.

Entering a Formula Into a Cell

The discussion just above about displaying the contents of a cell as text brings up another good point. If you want Excel to treat an entry as a formula, then you need to enter the equals (=), plus (+), or negative sign (-) as your first character in the cell. So, if you type

1+1

in a cell, that will just display as text in the cell. You'll see

1+1

But if you type

+1+1

in a cell, Excel will treat that as a formula and calculate it. You'll see 2 in the cell and

=1+1

in the formula bar.

Same with if you type

$$=1+1$$

It will calculate that as a formula, display 2 in the cell, and show

$$=1+1$$

in the formula bar.
If you type

$$-1+1$$

in a cell it will treat that as a formula adding negative 1 to 1 and will show that as 0 in the cell and display

$$=-1+1$$

in the formula bar.

Best practice is to use the equals sign to start every formula since Excel converts it to using the equals sign anyway.

Including Line Breaks Within a Cell

I sometimes need to have multiple lines of text or numbers within a cell. So instead of a, b, c, I need

a
b
c

You can't just hit Enter, because if you do it'll take you to the next cell. Instead, hold down the Alt key at the same time you hit Enter. This will create a line break within the cell.

Deleting Data

If you enter information into a cell and later decide you want to delete it, you can click on that cell(s) and use the delete button on your computer's keyboard. This will remove whatever you entered in the cell without deleting the cell as well.

You can also double-click into the cell or use F2 to get to the end of the contents in the cell and then use your computer's backspace key to delete out the contents of the cell from the end. If you double-click and end up somewhere in the middle of the cell you can use the delete key to delete text to the right of your cursor.

Deleting the contents of a cell does not remove its formatting. To delete the contents of a cell as well as its formatting, go to the Editing section of the Home tab, click on the dropdown next to the Clear option, and choose Clear All.

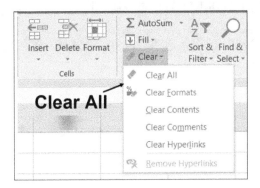

Find and Replace

Sometimes you have a big worksheet and you need to find a specific entry. An easy way to do this is to use the Find option. The easiest way to access it is to type Ctrl and F at the same time (Ctrl + F). This opens the Find dialogue box. Type what you're looking for into the "Find what" field and hit enter.

The other way to access Find is through the Editing section of the Home tab. The Find & Select option has a dropdown menu that includes Find.

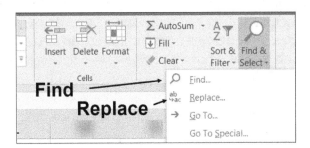

The default is for find to look in formulas as well, so if you search for "f" and have a formula that references cell F11, it will hit on that as much as it will hit on the cell that actually contains the letter f in a word.

You can change this setting under Options where it says Look In at the bottom left. Change the dropdown from Formulas to Values.

If you're looking for something in order to change it, you can use Replace instead. Type Ctrl and H (Ctrl + H) at the same time (or just Ctrl + F and then click over to the Replace tab), or you can access it through the Editing section of the Home tab.

When the Replace dialogue box opens, you'll see two lines, "Find what" and "Replace with." In the "Find what" line, type what you're looking for. In the "Replace with" line, type what to replace it with.

Be VERY careful using Replace.

Say you want to replace "hat" with "chapeau" because you've suddenly become pretentious. If you don't think this through, you will end up replacing every usage of hat, even when it's in words like "that" or "chat". So you'll end up with "tchapeau" in the middle of a sentence instead of "that" because the hat portion of "that" was replaced with "chapeau". (This probably happens in Word more than in Excel, but it's still something to be aware of.)

Replace is good for removing something like double spaces or converting formatting of a particular value, but otherwise you might want to use find and then manually correct each entry to avoid inadvertent errors.

You can get around some of these issues by clicking on Options and then using the checkboxes that let you Match Case or Match Entire Cell Contents Also, that brings up a Format dropdown that lets you search by pretty much any formatting you want such as italics, bold, underline, cell color, border, font, alignment, etc.

Searching by format can come in really handy when you need to, for example, replace italics with bold or change out a font that you used. But again, Find and Replace is used more with Microsoft Word than with Microsoft Excel in my experience.

Copying Patterns of Data

Sometimes you'll want to input data that repeats itself. Like, for example, the days of the week. Say you're putting together a worksheet that lists the date and what day of the week it is for an entire year. You could type out Monday, Tuesday, Wednesday, Thursday, Friday, Saturday, Sunday, and then copy and paste that 52 times. Or…

You could take advantage of the fact that Excel can recognize patterns. With this particular example, it looks like all it takes is typing in Monday. Do that and then go to the bottom right corner of the cell with Monday in it and position your cursor so that it looks like a small black cross. Left-click, hold that left-click down, and start to drag your cursor away from the cell. Excel should auto-complete the cells below or to the right of the Monday cell, depending on the direction you move, with the days of the week in order and repeating themselves in order for as long as you need it to.

If you're dealing with a pattern that isn't as standard as days of the week sometimes it takes a few entries before Excel can identify the pattern.

For example, if I type 1 into a cell and try to drag it, Excel just repeats the 1 over and over again. If I do 1 and then 2 and highlight both cells and start to drag from the bottom of the cell with the 2 in it, then it starts to number the next cells 3, 4, 5 etc.

You'll see the values Excel suggests for each cell as you drag the cursor through that cell, but those values won't actually appear in those cells until you're done highlighting all the cells you want to copy the pattern to and you let up on the left-click. (If that doesn't make sense, just try it a few times and you'll see what I mean.)

	E	F	G	H
1	Customer Satisfaction Score			**Excel**
2		1	1	**Copying**
3		1	2	**a Pattern**
4		1		**Into**
5		4		**Three**
6		5		**Cells**
7		3		

(You can combine Excel's ability to copy patterns with the AutoFill option by double-clicking in the bottom right-hand corner instead. This only works for columns and when your current column is next to a column that already has values in it for all the rows where you want to copy your pattern. (See the Manipulating Your Data section for more detail on AutoFill.)

Freeze Panes

If you have enough information in a worksheet for it to not be visible in one page, there's a chance you'll want to use freeze panes. What it does is freezes a row or rows and/or a column or columns at the top and side of your page so that even when you scroll down or to the right those rows or columns stay visible. So if you have 100 rows of information but always want to be able to see your header row, freeze panes will let you do that.

To freeze panes, go to the Window section of the View tab and click on the arrow under Freeze Panes.

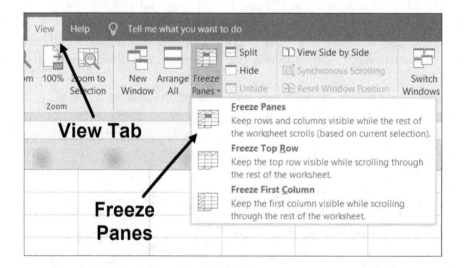

It gives you three options: Freeze Panes, Freeze Top Row, and Freeze First Column.

Those second two are pretty obvious. Choose "Freeze Top Row" and you'll always see Row 1 of your worksheet no matter how far down you scroll. Choose "Freeze First Column" and you'll always see Column A of your worksheet no matter how far to the right you scroll. When you use either of those options you are limited to just that one option, top row or first column.

However, the first option, Freeze Panes gives you the ability to freeze any number of rows AND columns at the same time. You just have to choose your cell first before choosing your freeze panes option.

So if I click on cell C4, which has three rows above it and two to the left, and then choose Freeze Panes, Excel will keep the top three rows AND the left two columns of my worksheet visible no matter where I scroll in the document.

For example, if you had customer name, city, and state in your first three columns and wanted to be able to see that information as you scrolled over to see other customer data, you could.

Or say your worksheet has a couple of rows of descriptive text and then the real row labels begin in row 5, you can click in Cell A6, choose to freeze panes, and those top five rows will always stay visible.

Freeze panes is very handy when dealing with large amounts of data. Just be careful that you don't accidentally lose where you are. If you click into a frozen row or column and then arrow down or over from there, it will take you to the next row, not the data you're seeing on the screen. So if you were looking at row 10,522 and you had the top row frozen and clicked into Row 1 for some reason and then arrowed down from there it would take you to Row 2 not Row 10,522 which is what you see on the screen. (It happens to be something I do often, so figured it was worth mentioning.)

Another thing to be cautious about with freeze panes is that you don't freeze so many rows and columns that you can't see any new data. But that would probably take quite a lot to make happen. But if you are arrowing down or to the right and can't see any new data, you just keep seeing what's already on the screen, that could be the cause.

To remove freeze panes, you can go back to the View tab and the Freeze Panes dropdown and you'll now see that that first option has become Unfreeze Panes. Just click on it and your document will go back to normal. Use that option regardless of whether you initially choose freeze panes, freeze top row, or freeze first column.

Formatting

If you're going to spend any amount of time working in Excel then you need to learn how to format cells, because inevitably your column won't be as wide as you want it to be or you'll want to have a cell with red-colored text or to use bolding or italics or something that isn't Excel's default.

That's what this section is for. It's an alphabetical listing of different things you might want to do. You can either format one cell at a time by highlighting that specific cell, format multiple cells at once by highlighting all of them and then choosing your formatting option, or format just a portion of the contents of a cell by selecting the specific text you want to format and then choosing your formatting option.

There are four main ways to format cells in Excel 2019.

The first is to use the Home tab and click the option you want from there.

The second is to right-click and select the Format Cells option from the dropdown menu which will bring up the Format Cells dialogue box.

The third is to right-click and select an option from what I refer to as the mini formatting menu (pictured below) which is located either just above or just below the dropdown menu and looks like a condensed version of the Home tab options.

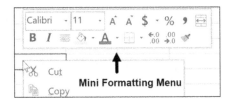

The fourth option is to use control shortcuts. These are available for some of the key formatting options such as bolding (Ctrl + B), italicizing (Ctrl + I), and underlining (Ctrl + U).

For basic formatting, I use the control shortcuts or the Home tab. If you're new to Excel you may want to use the mini formatting menu instead of the Home tab. (I don't use it because it didn't exist when I was learning Excel and it doesn't save so much time that I found it worth learning.)

For less common formatting choices, you will likely need to use the Format Cells dialogue box instead.

Aligning Your Text Within a Cell

By default, text within a cell is left-aligned and bottom-aligned. But at times you may want to adjust this. I often will center text or prefer for it to be top-aligned because it looks better to me that way when I have some column headers that are one line and others that are multiple lines.

To change the alignment in a cell or range of cells, highlight the cell(s) you want to change, and go to the Alignment section on the Home tab. There are a total of six choices which make nine possible combinations as shown below.

The six choices are on the left-hand side of the Alignment section and represented visually.

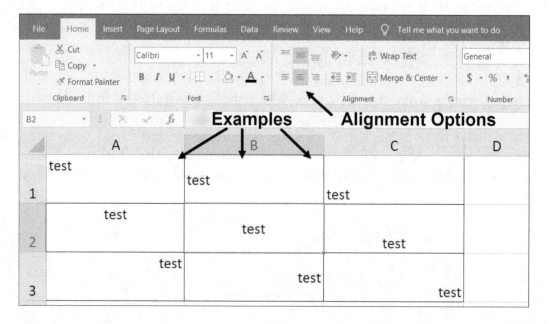

The first row has the top aligned, middle aligned, and bottom aligned options. You can choose one of these three options for your cell.

The second row has the left-aligned, centered, and right-aligned options. You can also choose one of these three options for your cell.

So you can have a cell with top-aligned and centered text or top-aligned and right-aligned text or bottom-aligned and centered text, etc. The image on the opposite page includes an example of the nine possible combinations.

You can also change the direction of your text so that it's angled or vertical.

To do so from the Home tab, click on the arrow next to the angled "ab" in the top row of the Alignment section and select one of the pre-defined options listed there.

You can choose Angle Counterclockwise, Angle Clockwise, Vertical Text, Rotate Text Up, and Rotate Text Down. (The last option, Format Cell Alignment, will bring up the Format Cells dialogue box.)

Another way to change the text alignment within a cell(s) is to highlight your cell(s) and then right-click and choose Format Cells from the dropdown menu. This will also bring up the Format Cells dialogue box. You can then go to the Alignment tab to see your available choices.

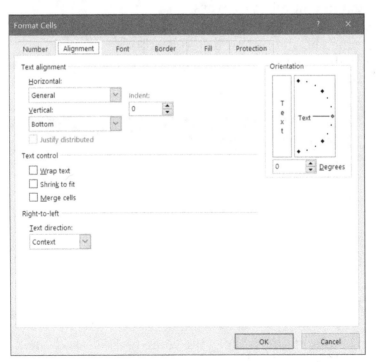

Choose from the Horizontal and Vertical dropdown menus to change the basic alignment of your text (Top, Center, Bottom, Left, Right, etc.).

The dropdown menus do have a few additional choices (like Justify and Distributed), but you generally shouldn't need them. And be wary of Fill which it seems will repeat whatever you have in that cell over and over again horizontally until it fills the cell. (Remember, if you do something you don't like, Ctrl + Z is your friend.)

On the right-hand side of the dialogue box you can also change the orientation of your text to any angle you want by entering a specified number of degrees (90 to make it vertical) or by moving the line within the Orientation box to where you want it. This is generally how I choose to angle text since I usually want an angle of about 30 degrees instead of the default choice in the Home tab which is 45 degrees.

If all you want to do is center your text, you can also use the third option in the bottom row of the mini formatting menu.

Bolding Text

You can bold text in a number of ways.

First, highlight the content you want bolded and then type Ctrl and B (Ctrl + B) at the same time. This is my preferred method.

Second, highlight your content and click on the large capital B in the Font section of the Home tab or in the bottom left row of the mini formatting menu.

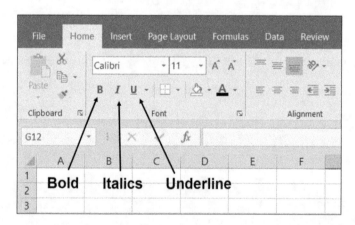

Third, you can highlight the cell(s) you want to bold and then right-click and choose Format Cells from the dropdown menu. Once you're in the Format Cells dialogue box, go to the Font tab and choose Bold from the Font Style options.

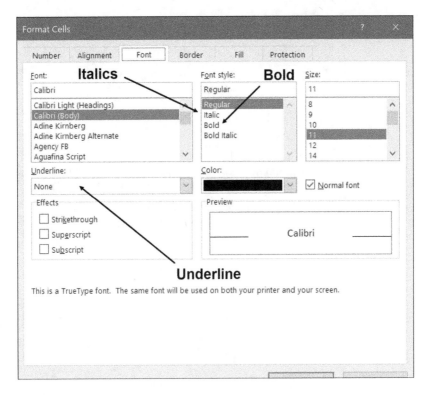

If you want text that is both bolded and italicized, choose Bold Italic.

To remove bolding from text or cells that already have it, highlight the bolded portion and then type Ctrl + B or click on the large capital B in the Font section of the Home tab or the mini formatting menu.(If you happen to highlight text that is only partially bolded you may have to do it twice to remove the bold formatting since the first time it will apply it to the rest of the text.)

Borders Around Cells

It's nice to have borders around your data to keep the information in each cell distinct, especially if you're going to print your document.

There are two main ways to add borders around a cell or set of cells. First, you can highlight the cells you want to place a border around and then go to the Font section on the Home tab and choose from the Borders dropdown option. It's a four-square grid with an arrow next to it that's located between the U used for underlining and the color bucket used for filling a cell with color.

Click on the arrow next to the grid to see your available options, and then choose the type of border you want.

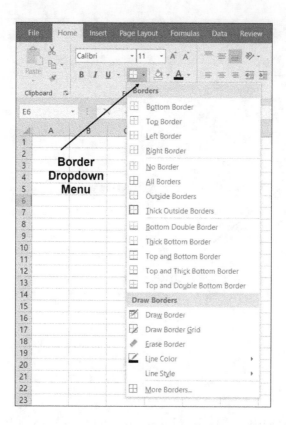

If you just want a simple border all around the cells and between multiple cells click on the All Borders option.

To adjust line thickness or line colors use the options in the Draw Borders section at the bottom, but be sure to choose your colors and line style *before* you choose your border type because the color and line type you choose will only apply to borders you draw after that.

You can also combine border types to get the appearance you want. For example, you could choose All Borders for the entire set of cells and then Thick Box Border to put a darker outline around the perimeter.

Your second choice for adding a border to your cells is to highlight the cells where you want to place a border and then right-click and select Format Cells from the dropdown menu.

When the Format Cells dialogue box appears, go to the Border tab and choose your border style, type, and color from there. (See image on next page.)

There are three Preset options at the top. If you want a basic outline or inside lines, just click on that option. To clear what you've done and start over you can select None from the Presets section.

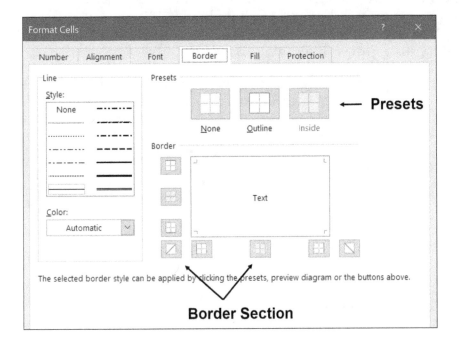

The Border section of the dialogue box allows you to pick and choose which lines you want to have in your cells, including diagonal lines. Simply click on the choice(s) you want.

You will see a preview of how it will appear in that Text box in the center section of the dialogue box.

You can click on more than one of the lines in the Border section. So you could have, for example, a top and bottom border, but nothing else.

If you want to change the style of a line or its color from the default, you can do so in the Line section on the left-hand side, but be sure to do so before you select where you want your lines to appear.

If you forget to change the style or color first, change it then just select the line placement again and it will apply the new style and/or color.

The fact that it works this way allows you to have multiple line styles or colors on a single cell which can come in handy at times.

Coloring a Cell (Fill Color)

You can color (or fill) an entire cell with almost any color you want. To do this, highlight the cell(s) you want to color, go to the Font section of the Home tab, and click on the dropdown arrow for the paint bucket that has a colored line under it. (The color will be bright yellow by default but will change as you use the tool.) You can also use the mini formatting menu where the fill color icon is the fourth in the bottom row.

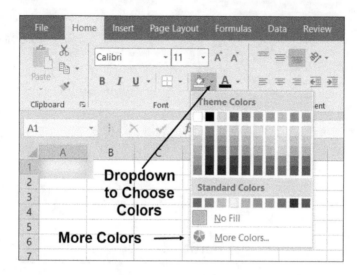

Either option will bring up a dropdown menu with 70 different colors to choose from, including the theme colors which consist of ten columns of color with six shades per color.

If you want to use any of the seventy colors you can see in the dropdown, just click on it.

If none of those colors work for you, or you need to use a specific corporate color, click on More Colors at the bottom of the dropdown menu.

This will bring up a Colors dialogue box. The first tab of that box looks like a honeycomb and has a number of colors you can choose from by clicking into the honeycomb.

The second tab is the Custom tab. It has a rainbow of colors that you can click on and also allows you to enter specific RGB or HSL values to get the exact color you need. (If you have a corporate color palette, they should give you the values for each of the corporate colors.)

On the Custom tab, you can also click and drag the arrow on the right-hand side to darken or lighten your color.

With both tabs, you can see the color you've chosen in the bottom right corner. If you like your choice, click on OK. If you don't want to add color to a cell after all, choose Cancel.

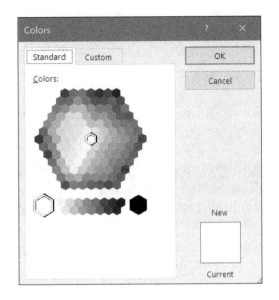
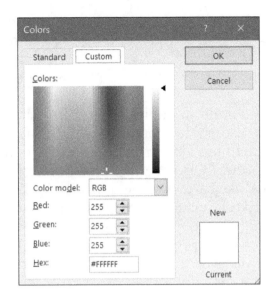

Column Width (Adjusting)

If your columns aren't the width you want, you have three options for adjusting them.

First, you can right-click on the column and choose Column Width from the dropdown menu. When the box showing you the current column width appears, enter a new column width.

Second, you can place your cursor to the right side of the column name—it should look like a line with arrows on either side—and then left-click and hold while you move the cursor to the right or the left until the column is as wide as you want it to be.

Or, third, you can place your cursor on the right side of the column name and double left-click. This will make the column as wide or as narrow as the widest text currently in that column. (Usually. Sometimes this one has a mind of its own.)

To adjust all column widths in your document at once, you can highlight the entire worksheet and then double-left click on any column border and it will adjust each column to the contents in that column. (Usually. See comment above.)

To have uniform column widths throughout your worksheet, highlight the whole worksheet, right-click on a column, choose Column Width, and set your column width. Highlighting the whole worksheet and then left-clicking and dragging one column to the desired width will also work.

(We cover it later, but to select the entire worksheet you can click in the top left corner at the intersection of the columns and rows. Or you can use Ctrl + A.)

Currency Formatting

In addition to applying basic formatting like bold, italics, and underline, Excel can also apply more complex formatting such as currency formatting or date formatting. The first of these we're going to cover is currency formatting. There are actually two default options for formatting numbers in Excel so that they look like currency notation such as $25.00. They are Accounting and Currency.

Excel defaults to the Accounting option which places the $ sign to the left-hand side of the cell even when the numbers don't fill the cell.

I tend to prefer the Currency option which keeps the $ sign with the numbers but that's because I'm usually only using this for a small range of values that are about the same size.

To apply the default Accounting format to your cells, highlight them, and then go to the Number section of the Home tab or the mini formatting menu, and click on the $ sign.

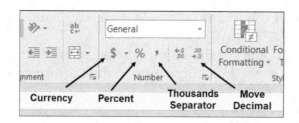

You can also use the dropdown menu in the Number section of the Home tab (which by default shows General) to choose either the Currency or Accounting format.

The final formatting option is to highlight the cell(s), right-click, choose the Format Cells option from the dropdown menu, go to the Number tab of the Format Cells dialogue box, and choose either Currency or Accounting from there.

Date Formatting

Excel can also format your entries as dates. Doing so will allow Excel to use those dates in calculations. But sometimes Excel has a mind of its own about how to format dates.

For example, if I type in 1/1 for January 1st, Excel will show it as 1-Jan and immediately turn it into a date in the current year. It may means the same thing as what I wanted, but if I'm going to display a current year date I would rather it display as 1/1/2020. That means I need to change the formatting.

One option is to click on the cell(s) with your date in it, go to the Number section on the Home tab, click on the dropdown menu, and choose either Short Date or Long Date.

If you select a cell or range of cells where the first cell already has a number in it, you will see examples of what the format will look like when you choose it. In the example above it's showing what the number 25 will look like in each format.

I prefer Short Date because I don't really need to see the day of the week named as well, which is what Long Date does.

Another option, and the one I probably use more for this, is to highlight your cell(s), right click, choose Format Cells from the dropdown menu, go to the

Number tab of the Format Cells dialogue box, and choose your date format from there by clicking on Date and then selecting one of the numerous choices it provides.

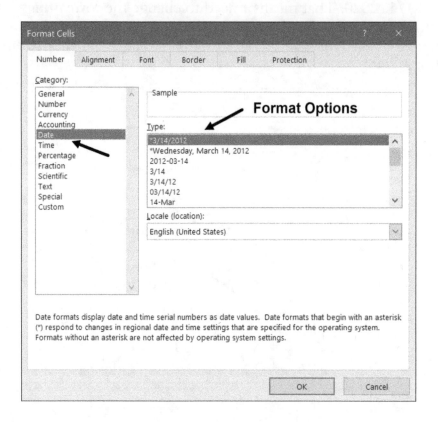

Keep in mind when selecting date formats that different countries write dates in different ways. So in the United States if I write 3/1/20 that means March 1, 2020 but in other countries that can mean January 3, 2020. You can see that the first couple of date options listed in the dialogue box will adjust for regional differences on different computers, but sometimes it's better to choose a spelled-out date to avoid any confusion.

And, just to reiterate because it's been an issue for me in the past, as mentioned above, Excel will always assign a year to a date no matter what you have it display or what information you provide. Always. So if that matters to you, be sure to control that information yourself.

Font Choice and Size

In Excel 2019 the default font choice is Calibri and the default font size is 11 point. You may have strong preferences about what font you use or work for a company that uses specific fonts for its brand or just want some variety in terms of font size or type within a specific document. In that case, you will need to change your font.

There are multiple ways to do this.

First, you can highlight your selection, go to the Font section on the Home tab, and select a different font or font size from the dropdown menus there.

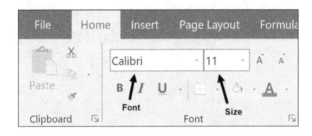

You also have the option there to increase or decrease the font one size at a time by clicking on the A's with little arrows off to the right-hand side of the dropdowns.

The same choices are also available on the left side of the first row of the mini formatting menu.

You can also highlight the cells or text you want to change, right-click, and choose Format Cells from the dropdown menu, and then go to the Font tab and choose your Font and Size from the listed values there. (I almost never find myself needing to use this option since the Home tab is so convenient.)

With any of the above options you can also choose a font size that isn't listed by clicking into the font size box and typing the value you want. So if you want a font size of 13 or 15, etc. you can just type it in.

Font Color

The default color for all text in Excel is black, but you can change that if you want or need to. (For example, if you've colored a cell with a darker color you may want to consider changing the font color to white to make the text in that cell more visible.)

You have multiple options here as well.

First, you can highlight the cells or the specific text you want to change, go to the Font section on the Home tab, and click on the arrow next to the A with a line under it. (The line is red by default but changes as you use this option.)

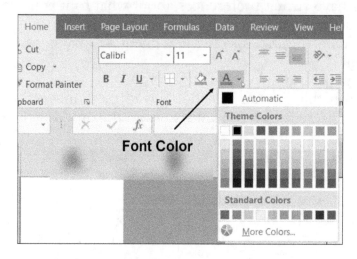

You can then choose from one of the 70 colors that are listed, and if those aren't enough of a choice you can click on More Colors and select your color from the Colors dialogue box. (See Coloring a Cell for more detail about that option.)

Second, you can use the fifth option in the bottom row of the mini formatting menu.

Third, you can highlight your selected text, right-click and choose Format Cells from the drop-down menu, go to the Font tab of the Format Cells dialogue box, and then click on the dropdown menu under Color which will bring up the same seventy color options and the ability to choose More Colors and add a custom color instead. Again, not an option I use often since the Home tab option is so convenient.

Italicizing Text

To add italics to a selection, highlight your selection and hold down the Ctrl key and the I key at the same time. (Ctrl + I)

Or you can highlight what you want italicized, and click on the slanted I in the Font section on the Home tab (see image under the Bolding description) or the bottom row of the mini formatting menu.

Another option is to highlight your selection, right-click, choose Format Cells from the dropdown menu, go to the Font tab of the Format Cells dialogue box, and choose Italic from the Font Style options.

As mentioned before, you can italicize just part of the text in a cell by only selecting that portion and then using one of the methods above.

To remove italics from text or cells that already have it, you follow the exact same steps. (Highlight your selection and then type Ctrl + I or click on the slanted I in the Font section on the Home tab or the mini formatting menu.) You may need to do it twice if your selection was not fully italicized already.

Merge & Center

Merge & Center is a specialized command that can come in handy when you're working with a table where you want a header that spans multiple columns of data.

If you're going to merge and center text, make sure that the text you want to keep is in the top-most and left-most of the cells you plan to merge and center. Data in the other cells that are being merged will be deleted. (You'll get a warning message to this effect if you have values in any of the other cells.)

You can merge cells across columns and/or down rows. So you could, for example, merge cells that span two columns and two rows into one big cell while keeping all of the other cells in those columns and rows separate.

To merge and center, highlight all of the cells you want to merge. Next, go to the Alignment section of the Home tab and choose Merge & Center. You can also find the Merge & Center option in the top right corner of the mini formatting menu.

Choosing Merge & Center will combine your selected cells into one large cell and center the contents from the topmost, left-most cell that was merged across the selection and then bottom-align the remaining text.

The Home tab also has a dropdown menu that includes additional options.

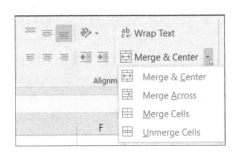

Merge Across will merge the cells across each individual row of the selected range rather than create one giant merged cell.

Merge Cells merges the cells into one cell but places the resulting text in the bottom right corner instead of the center.

Also, if you ever need to unmerge merged cells (like I do with one of my sales reports I receive) you can do so by selecting the Unmerge Cells option from the Merge & Center dropdown in the Home tab.

You can also Merge Cells by highlighting the cells, right-clicking, selecting the Format Cells option, going to the Alignment tab in the Format Cells dialogue box, and then choosing to Merge Cells from there. If you choose that option, you have to center the text separately.

A quick warning: Don't merge and center your cells if you plan to do a lot of data analysis with what you've input because it will mess with your ability to filter, sort, or use pivot tables. It's really for creating a finalized, pretty-looking report.

Number Formatting

Sometimes when you copy data into Excel it doesn't format it the way you want. For example, I have a report I receive that includes ISBN numbers which are 10- or 13- digit numbers. When I copy those into Excel, it sometimes displays them in Scientific number format (9.78E+12) as opposed to as a normal number.

To change the formatting of your data to a number format, you have a few options.

First, you can highlight the cell(s) and go to the Number section of the Home tab. From the drop-down menu choose Number. (Sometimes General will work as well.)

That will then convert your entries to numbers with two decimal places but no commas. So 100.00 instead of 100.

You can also click on the comma right below the dropdown to create a number with two decimal places and commas separating the thousands, hundred thousands, millions, etc.

You can then use the zeroes with arrows next to them that are located right below the drop-down box to adjust how many decimal places to display.

The one with the right-pointing arrow will reduce the number of decimal places. The one with the left-pointing arrow will increase them.

Second, the mini formatting menu has an option to format a cell as a number with commas for the thousands, hundred thousands, millions, etc. and will display with two decimal places.

To use it, select your cell(s), right-click, and from the mini formatting menu click on the comma in the top row on the right.

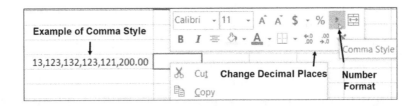

To adjust your decimal places then click on the zeroes with arrows under them in the bottom row. You can see an example of what the default looks like on the left-hand side of the image above.

Finally, you can highlight the cell(s), right-click, select Format Cells from the dropdown, go to the Number tab in the Format Cells dialogue box, choose Number on the left-hand side listing, and then in the middle choose your number of decimal places and how you want your negative numbers to display.

If I'm working with negative numbers a lot I'll use this option so that I can display my negative numbers either as red text or with ( ) around them.

You can also choose whether to use a comma separator or not here by checking the box that says "Use 1000 Separator".

Percent Formatting

To format numbers as a percentage, highlight the cell(s), and click on the percent sign in the Number section of the Home tab or in the top row of the mini formatting menu.

This one will take the number 5 and turn it into 500% or the number 0.1 and turn it into 10%, for example, so be sure your numbers are formatted to work as percentages.

You can also highlight the cell(s), right-click, select Format Cells from the dropdown, go to the Number tab, of the Format Cells dialogue box choose Percentage on the left-hand side, and then in the middle, choose your number of decimal places.

Row Height (Adjusting)

If your rows aren't the correct height, you have three options for adjusting them.

First, you can right-click on the row you want to adjust, choose Row Height from the dropdown menu, and when the box showing you the current row height appears, enter a new row height.

Second, you can place your cursor along the lower border of the row number until it looks like a line with arrows above and below. Left-click and hold while you move the cursor up or down until the row is as tall as you want it to be.

Third, you can place your cursor along the lower border of the row, and double left-click. This will fit the row height to the text in the cell. (Usually.)

To adjust all row heights in your document at once you can highlight the entire worksheet and then double-left click on any row border and it will adjust each row to the contents in each individual row. (Again, usually. It doesn't work particularly well for cells with lots and lots of text in them.)

To have uniform row heights throughout your worksheet, you can highlight the whole sheet, right-click on a row, choose Row Height and set your row height that way or select the entire worksheet, left-click on the border below a row, and adjust that row to the height you want for all rows.

As mentioned above, to select all rows at once you can use Ctrl + A or you can click in the corner at the intersection of the rows and columns.

Underlining Text

You have three options for underlining text.

First, you can highlight your selection and type Ctrl and U at the same time. (Ctrl + U). This is the easiest method and the one I use most often.

Second, you can highlight your selection and click on the underlined U in the Font section on the Home tab. (See the Bolding section for a screen shot.)

Third, you can highlight the selection, right-click, choose Format Cells from the dropdown menu, go to the Font tab of the Format Cells dialogue box, and choose the type of underlining you want (single, double, single accounting, double accounting) from the Underline drop down menu.

As noted above, you can apply formatting to just part of the text in a cell by clicking into the cell, highlighting the portion of the text that you want to underline, and then applying your chosen format.

To remove underlining from text or cells that already have it, highlight the text or cells and then use one of the above options.

Wrapping Text

Sometimes you want to read all of the text in a cell, but you don't want that column to be wide enough to display all of the text in a single row. This is where the Wrap Text option becomes useful, because it will keep your text within the width of the column and display it on multiple lines by "wrapping" the text.

To Wrap Text in a cell, select the cell(s), go to the Alignment section of the Home Tab, and click on the Wrap Text option on the right-hand side in the Alignment section.

Or you can highlight the cell(s), right-click, choose Format Cells from the dropdown menu, go to the Alignment tab in the Format Cells dialogue box, and choose Wrap Text under the second section, Text Control.

You will likely have to adjust the row height after you do this to see all of the text. The double-click method to auto-adjust your row height will generally work here, but if you have lots of text Excel has a limit to how much it will auto-adjust the height of a row and you may have to click and drag to get the row height you need.

* * *

One final trick that I use often, probably more in Word than in Excel, but that's still handy to know:

Format Painter
(Or How To Copy Formatting From One Cell To Another)

In addition to the specific formatting options discussed above, if you already have a cell formatted the way you want it to, you can take the formatting from that cell to other cells you want formatted the same way.

You do this by using the Format Painter

First, highlight the cell(s) that have the formatting you want to copy. (If the formatting is identical across all cells then just highlight one cell.)

Next, click on the Format Painter which is either located in the bottom right corner of the mini formatting menu or in the Clipboard section of the Home tab. It looks like a little paint brush. (I call it format sweeping because it always looked like a little broom to me, but given the name it's obviously a paint brush.)

Finally, select the range of cells where you want to copy the formatting.

The contents of the destination cells will remain the same, but the font, font color, font size, cell borders, italics/bolding/underlining, text alignment and text orientation will all change to match that of the cell that you took the formatting from.

As I alluded to above, you can select a range of cells and take their formatting and apply it to another range of cells. So I can have the first cell be bold, the second be italic, the third be red, etc. and I can select that cell range and then use Format Painter to apply that same different formatting across as many cells as I swept the formatting from.

If you do that, you can just click into the first cell of the range where you're applying the formatting. Excel will change the formatting of X number of cells where X is the original range of cells you chose your formatting from.

You need to be careful using the Format Painter because it will change *all* formatting in your destination cells.

So, if the cell you're copying the formatting from is bolded and has red text, both of those attributes will copy over even if all you were trying to do was copy the bold formatting. This is more of a problem when using the tool in Word than in Excel, but it's still something to watch out for especially if you have borders around cells. If you, for example, copy formatting from a cell that's in the center of a formatted table to a cell that's on the edge of that table you could end up removing the edge border.

(If that sounds confusing, just play around with it a bit and you'll see what I'm talking about.)

Also, the tool copies formatting to whatever cell you select next, which can be a problem if the cell you're copying from isn't near the one you're copying to. I sometimes have the temptation to use the arrow keys to move to the cell where I want to place the formatting, but that obviously does not work because the minute I arrow over one cell the formatting transfers to that cell.

To avoid this issue, click directly into the cell where you want to transfer the formatting.

(And remember, that Ctrl + Z is your friend if you make a mistake.)

Also, if you have more than one isolated cell that you need to apply formatting to, you can double-click the Format Painter instead of single clicking and it will continue to copy the formatting of the original cell to every cell you click in until you click on the Format Painter again or hit Esc. (You'll know the tool is still in operation because there will be a little brush next to your cursor as you move it around.)

If you format sweep, realize you made a mistake, and then use Ctrl + Z to undo, you'll see that the cell(s) you were trying to take formatting from will be surrounded by a dotted border as if you had copied it. Hit the Esc key before you continue. Otherwise you risk copying the contents of that cell or cells to a new one if you click in another cell and hit Enter.

(Not a common problem, but one to be aware of.)

Manipulating Your Data

Once you've entered your data into a worksheet, you are then ready to work with that data by filtering it, sorting it, and performing calculations on it.

This section will walk you through the basics of selecting, sorting, filtering, and analyzing your data. I'm just going to touch on formulas and the most essential functions, but this series does have an entire book (*Excel 2019 Formulas and Functions*) that is devoted to the topic if you find that you need or want to know more. Also, PivotTables and charts can be very useful for data analysis, but those are covered in *Excel 2019 Intermediate* because the goal in this book is to firmly ground you in the basics.

So, let's start with a few quick tricks for selecting your data that you want to analyze.

Select All

I mentioned this already in the formatting chapter when we discussed changing row height and column width, but I want to cover it again. If you want to select every single active cell in a worksheet, you can use Ctrl + A. (To select all of the rows and columns in a worksheet you may need to apply it more than once because it may just select your cells with data in them the first time.)

As mentioned above, it can be helpful when trying to adjust the row height or the column width in an entire worksheet quickly.

I also use it to copy the entire contents of a worksheet at once.

I will often combine Select All with Paste Special – Values onto the same worksheet. This is a simple way to remove any formulas from the worksheet as well as any PivotTables.

Another way to select all of the cells in your worksheet is to click in the small box at the intersection of the rows and columns labels. It does the exact same thing as Ctrl + A.

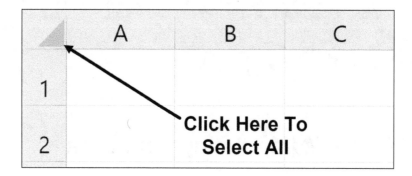

One caution when selecting all is that you don't then do something like apply borders to the entire worksheet. This can mess with your file size as well as printing because Excel stores that information for all of those cells even if you don't have any information in them. So don't do that. If you do so accidentally, you can Undo or select all and then go to the Clear dropdown in the Editing section of the Home tab and choose Clear Formats.

Select A Row

I often will want to select a row of data in my worksheet To do so, click on the row number on the left-hand side. (You may have to do it twice to select the row)

All of the cells in that row except the first one should turn gray to show that they've been selected.

Be careful about applying formatting if you do this, because you will rarely need to format an entire row and doing so can mess with printing.

To select more than one row, you can select left-click on the first row you want and then hold that down as you drag the mouse up or down to select more rows.

If the rows you need are not touching, use the Ctrl key as you click on each row number. You can also click on one row, hold down the shift key and click at the end of the range you select to select all of the rows in between.

Select A Column

Selecting a column works just like selecting a row. Click on the letter of the column you want to select. (You may have to do so twice to actually select the cells)

When the column is selected all cells in that column will be shaded gray except for the first one. You can select multiple columns by clicking and dragging, using the control key as you click on each one you want, or using the shift key to select a range of columns.

Again, selecting columns is useful for copying the data in a column or when writing a formula that references the values in a column, but don't apply formatting to the entire column.

Select A Range of Cells

It's very easy to select an entire table of data as long as it has a header row that labels all of the columns and an identifier column that has a value in it for every row of the table. (This helps define the range of columns and rows in the table.)

To do so, click in the top left corner of your data and then while holding down the Shift and Ctrl keys use the down arrow key followed by the right arrow key to highlight all of your cells in the table. (You can also arrow right and then down.)

Once the cells are selected, you can then apply all the formatting you want to that range of cells or copy it, etc.

What is happening when you do this is that you are telling Excel to start where you are and go in the direction of the arrow you used and select all of the cells it finds that have content in them until it reaches one that doesn't and then stop.

Because we were talking about a table that had column labels and row labels that selects the entire range of the table, even the blank cells within the table.

Sometimes your data won't be that neatly arranged and there will be gaps. If that happens, just keep arrowing in the direction you wanted until you reach the end of your data.

Also, I tell you to start in the top left corner of your data because that's the easiest way to make sure you select it all, but you can do this from any point. The only problem is you can go left OR right but not left AND right. Same with up and down. You can go up OR down but not up AND down. So start in a corner.

Being able to select a data range is very helpful when it comes to sorting and filtering. I can usually get away with just selecting all, but there are times when it is better to select a specific range of cells.

Also, selecting a range of cells comes in very useful when you don't want to bring over header information from another worksheet but just want the data.

Reach The End Of A Data Range

What if you want to reach the end of your data but you don't want to select it?

You can do so with just the Ctrl key and the arrows. Using Ctrl and an arrow will take you to the cell in that direction that is the last cell with something in it before an empty cell.

Depending on how your data is set up, that may not be the absolute end. But if your data is set up cleanly where it's all labeled and kept together Ctrl + an arrow key should take you to the edge of your existing data. You can then use the arrow key one more time from there to get to an empty cell.

Sorting

Now that we know how to select a range of data, let's talk about sorting.

Sorting allows you to take a data set and display it in a specific order. For example, chronologically by date, in increasing or decreasing value, or alphabetically.

Excel also allows you to sort at more than one level at a time. So you can sort by date and then by customer name and then by transaction value, for example. This would put all April 12th orders together and then all orders by each customer together, making them easy to locate.

Okay, so how do you do this?

First, select all cells that contain your information, including your header row if there is one.

(If you set your data up with the first row as the header and all of the rest as data, you can use Ctrl + A or click in the top left corner to select all.)

If you have a table of data that starts lower down on the page or that has a summary row or that is followed by other data that you don't want to use, then you need to be careful to only select the cells you want to work with.

Be very careful also to keep your data together. What I mean by that is, say you want to sort by date and customer name, but you have ten other columns of data related to each transaction by each customer on each day. You need to select all twelve columns of data even though you're only sorting on two of those columns.

If you don't do that then Excel will sort the two columns you selected but leave the other ten columns in their original position. That will mean that Customer Jones's July 3rd transaction information is now listed as Customer Smith's August 5th transaction.

So always, always before you sort make sure that all of your related data has been selected.

Once you've selected your data, go to the Editing section of the Home tab. Click on the arrow for Sort & Filter and then choose Custom Sort.

Your other option is to go to the Data tab and click on the Sort option there.

You can also right-click and choose Sort and then Custom Sort from the dropdown menu. All three options will open the Sort dialogue box.

The first choice you need to make is to indicate whether or not your data has headers. In other words, does the first row of your data contain column labels?

If so, click on that box in the top corner that says, "My data has headers." If you indicate that there is a header row, it will not be included in your sort and will remain the first row of your data.

When you do this, you'll see that your Sort By dropdown now displays your column labels.

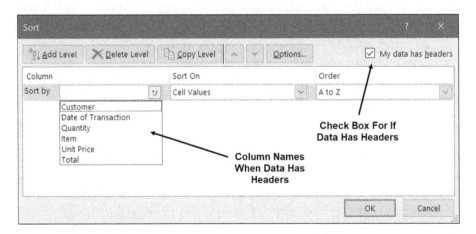

If you don't check this box, the dropdown will show generic column names (Column A, Column B, etc.) and *all* of your data will be sorted, *including* the first row.

Sometimes Excel tries to decide on its own whether there are headers or not and is wrong, so always make sure that your Sort By choices make sense given the data you selected, and that you check or uncheck the "My data has headers" box to get the result you want.

The next step is to choose your sort order.

What is the first criteria you want to sort by? In the examples I've mentioned above it would be date because I want all of my data grouped by date first and then I'll sort by customer name. But if you cared more about looking up information by customer name first and then by date of transaction you'd want to choose customer name for your first Sort By option.

Whatever that primary criteria is, choose that column from the Sort By dropdown menu.

Next, choose how to sort that column of data. You can sort on cell values, cell color, font color, or conditional formatting icon.

I almost always use values but if you were working with a data set where you'd used conditional formatting (which is discussed in detail in *Excel 2019 Intermediate*) you could, for example, sort by font color and have all of your overdue payments listed first.

After you choose what to sort on, then you can choose what order to use for your sort.

For text it's usually going to be A to Z to sort alphabetically but you can also choose Z to A to sort in reverse alphabetical order.

The third option, Custom List, is very useful for when you have text entries that should be in a specific order but that order is not alphabetical. I use this for when I have data broken down by month. I can choose Custom List and then in the Custom Lists dialogue box there are two month-based sort options. (As well as two day-of-the-week-based sort options.)

The Custom Lists dialogue box also allows you to create a brand new sort order with the NEW LIST option.

For date fields, your sort choices are Oldest to Newest, Newest to Oldest, and Custom List.

For numbers your short choices are Smallest to Largest, Largest to Smallest, and Custom List.

That's the first sort order and often it will be all you need. For example, if you just want your data sorted by month. If that's the case, click OK in the bottom right corner of the Sort dialogue box.

If, however, you want to use a second sort criteria, so sort first by date and then by customer, you need to add another level to your sort. You do this by clicking on Add Level and then repeating the same process for the next row of choosing your Column, Sort On criteria, and Order.

If you ever add a level you don't need, highlight it by clicking on the words "sort by" or "then by" on the left-hand side of the row, and then choose Delete Level from the list of options at the top of the dialogue box.

If you have listed out multiple levels to sort by but then decide that they should be sorted in a different order, you can select one of the levels and use the arrows at the top of the dialogue box to move that level up or down.

The default is to sort your data from top to bottom, so in rows.

Row 2 (assuming you have a header in Row 1) will be the first entry based on your sort criteria, Row 3 will be the second, etc.

You can click on Options in the Sort dialogue box, however, if you want to sort across columns instead.

(I think I've only ever needed to do that once. But just spitballing here, if I had, for example, a table of information and had listed student names across my columns and wanted those sorted alphabetically so that Column B was Anna and Column C was Bob, etc. I could use this option to make that happen.)

Options is also where you can do a case-sensitive sort, but I've never found myself needing to do that.

When you're done with all of your sort options, click OK.

(If you change your mind about performing a sort, click Cancel.)

Immediately check your results. Look across an entire row of data and ask if that still makes sense. Did you properly select and sort the data so that all of Customer Smith's transaction information stayed together?

If not, use Ctrl + Z to undo and try again because if you save the file with a bad sort order it's done for. You'll have to go back to your original raw data and start over. (Assuming you were smart enough to save your raw data in one location and do any analysis work in another. Which you should always, always do. As discussed previously and in *Data Principles for Beginners*.)

One final note about sorting, Excel also offers quick-sort options (the ones that say Sort A to Z or Sort Z to A) which are basically options to sort in ascending or descending order based upon the cell you're in at the time you make the selection.

Theoretically these options identify your data range, figure out if you have a header or not, and then sort based on the column you chose. But be wary when using them. Sometimes they work great, most times they sort in the wrong order for me or on the wrong column or miss that I have a header row.

Filtering

Okay. Now on to filtering which is also incredibly useful. I often won't need to permanently change the order of my data, I just want to see a subset of my data that meets a certain criteria. For example, I only want to see sales for Title A or Author B.

Filtering allows me to do that without having to sort.

This works best with a data table that has continuous and labeled columns and continuous rows.

If you have non-continuous columns, you need to manually select all of your columns when you choose to filter in order for the filter option to show for all of them. Otherwise, Excel will only show the filter option for the column in which you were clicked at the time you turned on filtering as well as for any columns that are connected to that column.

This sounds confusing, so let me show you what I mean.

	A	B	C	D	E	F	G
1	Customer	Date of Transaction		Quantity	Item	Unit Price	Total
2	Richard Martinez	4/7/2016		20	Whasit	$ 1.50	$ 30.00
3	Richard Martinez	3/7/2016		10	Who knows what	$ 3.50	$ 35.00
4	Albert Jones	9/1/2015		3	Whatchamacallit	$ 15.00	$ 45.00
5	Albert Jones	8/30/2015		10	Widget	$ 25.00	$250.00
6	Albert Jones	8/1/2015		1	Widget	$ 20.00	$ 20.00
7	Albert Jones	8/1/2015		1	Other	$ 5.00	$ 5.00
8							

Here I have six columns of data, but I have a blank column in Column C so that the data is not continuous. When I click into Cell A1 and turn on filtering, it only turns on filtering for Columns A and B. (You can tell filtering is on by looking at those little arrows in the corners in Cells A1 and B1.)

Because Column C was blank, Excel didn't know to also turn on filtering for Columns D, E, F, and G. I can work around this by turning off filtering, selecting Cells A1 through G1 and turning filtering back on. That will apply filtering to all of the columns.

Or I can make my life simpler and simply not have the blank column in the middle of my data in which case when I click into Cell A1 (or any of the cells in Row 1) filtering will be available for all of the columns of data.

If for some reason you don't want to filter starting at the top row of your data, you can highlight a row of data that is not at the top of the range and Excel will apply the filtering options starting at the highlighted row. (Usually for me what happens is I do that accidentally and notice that the filtering is in Row 3 where my data is instead of Row 1 where my header row is and I have to go turn off filtering and reapply it at Row 1.)

To apply filtering, click into the appropriate spot in your data, and then in the Editing section of the Home tab, click on the arrow next to Sort & Filter and choose Filter.

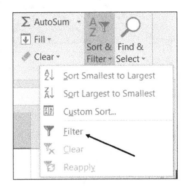

Once you turn on filtering you should see small gray arrows in the bottom right corner of each cell in your header row. (Like on the previous page with Customer and Date of Transaction in Cells A1 and B1.)

Filtering in Excel has evolved over the years, which means the complex type of filtering we're about to discuss was not always available in prior versions of Excel. So if you filter a file and try to share that with someone using an older version of Excel it may do weird things. Namely, they won't be able to remove or adjust your filtering easily. (Easy way to deal with that is never save your data in a filtered form.)

Okay, so let's talk filtering options. Once you have filtering turned on, you can click on that little arrow in the corner at the top of a column and it will bring up a dropdown menu that has a variety of options for you to use to filter the contents of your data table. (See the next page for an example.)

The very top options in that dropdown are sort options.

The first filter option, Filter by Color, will generally be grayed out unless you have different font colors or fill colors in your data.

If you have used different font or fill colors, you can hold your cursor over where it says Filter by Color and it will then give you additional options to Filter by Cell Color or Filter by Font Color.

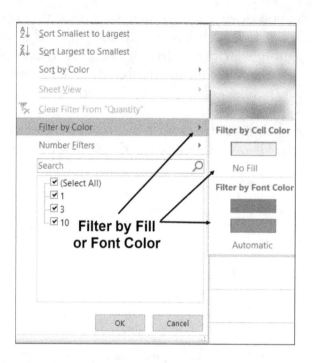

These options will only show the font or fill colors you've used in your data. If you want cells that are the standard color or the standard fill you can choose the No Fill or the Automatic filtering choices.

After the filter by color choices, there is another set of filter options that will be named based upon the type of data in that column. Above you can see that the next option is Number Filters, but you may also see Date Filters or Text Filters.

Holding your cursor over this option will show filter criteria for that type of data. For numbers you'll see choices such as Equals, Greater Than, Between, etc. For dates you'll see Before, After, Tomorrow, Today, etc. For text you'll see Begins With, Contains, etc.

I find these options to be useful when there are a large number of individual entries that all differ slightly from one another but that I want to include in my display. So if I want all of my Excel books, for example, I can use a Contains filter and look for entries with "Excel" in them. That's much easier than going through and checking boxes to select each title individually.

The filter approach I probably use the most, though, is the final option which is the checkbox option. You can see above and on the next page that the dropdown will list the possible values for that column with checkboxes next to each value. You can select one or more of the values in that list by checking or unchecking the box next to each value.

If you just want one value and there are a number of choices, click in that Select All box at the top to unselect everything and then go back and click on the entries you want. It's much faster than unchecking everything one box at a time.

You also have the option to use the Search field that's directly above the checkboxes. Excel will filter your data down to just those entries that contain the search term and then you can refine from there if you need to.

When cells in your worksheet are filtered, the row numbers in your worksheet will be colored blue, and you'll see that the row numbers skip since some rows won't be displayed. (In the screenshot below, Row 2 is not displayed because it had a date in April 2016 and I unchecked that box.)

Columns where filtering is in place will show a funnel instead of an arrow on the gray dropdown next to the column name.

To remove filtering from a specific column, click on the gray arrow, and select Clear Filter from [Column Name] in the dropdown menu.

To remove all filtering you've applied to a worksheet, go to the Editing section of the Home tab, click on Sort & Filter, and then choose Clear. This will leave the filtering option in place but remove all filters.

To remove filtering altogether, go to the Editing section of the Home tab, click on Sort & Filter, and click on Filter.

Some of this can also be done through right-click and using the dropdown available on the worksheet. If you're clicked into a cell and want to filter by that value or fill color or font color, you can right-click, move your cursor to the Filter option, and then choose Filter by Selected Cell's Value, Color, Font Color, or Icon. That will perform the filter task you wanted as well as turning on filtering for that range of cells.

Once filtering is on, you can also right-click, go to Filter, and choose to clear the filter from a specific column.

Because the right-click option is somewhat limited, I tend to just use the Editing section of the Home tab.

* * *

Basic Math Calculations

Alright, that was sorting and filtering. Now let's talk basic math calculations in Excel. I'm going to cover addition, subtraction, multiplication, and division.

Let's start with doing each of those tasks using standard math notation.

In Excel these are referred to as calculation operators, but you'll probably recognize them as the way you used to write an equation in math class.

For addition, you use a plus sign (+). For subtraction, you use a minus sign (-). For multiplication you use an asterisk (*). For division, you use a forward slash (/).

To perform one of these basic calculations in a cell in Excel, click into the cell where you want to perform the calculation, type an equals sign, type the first value you want to use, type the calculation operator for the calculation you want to perform (+ - * /), and then type the second value you want to use. Hit Enter. You will see the result of that calculation in the cell and if you go back to the cell you'll see your equation in the formula bar.

So, for example:

=23+23

would add 23 and 23 and when you hit enter you would see a value of 46 in that cell.

=23/23

would divide 23 by 23 and you would see a value of 1 in that cell after you hit enter.

=4*5

would return a value of 20.

And

$$=10\text{-}2$$

would return a value of 8.

If that's all that Excel could do it wouldn't be very useful. About as useful as a calculator. The power that Excel has is that it can perform those same calculations by using cell references. So rather than type in 23, you can have the value 23 in a cell and point Excel at that cell to retrieve the value for you.

That still doesn't sound too exciting until you realize that you can combine that task with copying formulas which means you can write a simple formula that says add this cell in Column A to that cell in Column B and then copy that one formula you wrote a hundred thousand times with a single click, and have Excel add those two cells in those two columns for all hundred thousand rows of your data in less than a minute.

But to make that happen requires using cell notation instead of numbers.

The easy way to use cell notation is to let Excel do it for you by simply clicking on the cells you want as you build your formula.

So you click in the cell where you want your calculation, type an equals sign, click on the cell that contains the first value you want to use in your calculation, type your calculation operator (+ - * /), and then click on the cell that contains the second value you want to use in your calculation, and then hit enter.

Excel will build your formula for you and write the name of the cell you click on each time into your formula.

You can even see if the correct cells were used by going back to the cell where you did the calculation and double-clicking on it. Excel will show you the formula it wrote and highlight all of the cells it used in the formula as well as color code each cell and cell reference in the formula. Cell A2 will be blue and the text A2 in the formula will also be blue, for example, so you can see exactly where each value was used.

Which is great, but I like to understand how to do it myself so I can better troubleshoot issues. So let's cover how that works real quick.

First, a quick refresher about how you reference a cell. A cell is the intersection of a row and a column and is always written with the column identifier first. So if I write A1 that means the cell that's at the intersection of Column A and Row 1. (You don't have to include Cell when you write this in a formula because that's implied.) Likewise, B2 is the cell that is at the intersection of Column B and Row 2.

To reference more than one cell at a time, you need to use either a colon (:) or a comma (,).

A comma (,) written between two cell references means "and.". So

$$A1,B3$$

means Cells A1 and B3.

A colon (:) written between two cell references means "through". So

$$A1:B3$$

means all cells in Columns A and B and all cells in those columns that are in Rows 1, 2, and 3.

Likewise,

$$D24:M65$$

means all cells in Columns D through M and in Rows 24 through 65.

To reference an entire column, you just leave out the row numbers. So

$$B:B$$

means all of the cells in Column B. And

$$B:C$$

means all of the cells in Columns B and C.

To reference an entire row you leave out the column letters. So

$$2:2$$

means all of the cells in Row 2. And

$$2:10$$

means all of the cells in Rows 2 through 10.

Putting that together with what we discussed earlier about using calculation operators, the following are how you would write addition, subtraction, multiplication, and division of values in Cells A1 and B1:

$$=A1+B1$$

$$=A1-B1$$

$$=A1*B1$$

$$=A1/B1$$

Remember from math class that with addition and multiplication order isn't going to matter, A1+B1 and B1+A1 give you the same result. But with subtraction and division, which value is listed first will impact the result you get. A1-B1 and B1-A1 are different equations.

Which is why there is no shortcut, quickie way to subtract or divide multiple values in Excel. But for addition and multiplication there are. You can use what are called functions to sum or multiply any number of cells that you want.

The function you use for addition is SUM. The function you use for multiplication is PRODUCT. (I often use SUM, I rarely use PRODUCT although I do use one we won't cover here that is SUMPRODUCT that combines the two.)

If you're going to use a function for a calculation, you click into the cell, type your equals sign, then type the function you want and an opening paren, then you type your cell references or highlight the cells you want, then type a closing paren and hit enter.

This table shows how to use the operators when just using two values and how to use the functions or operators when dealing with multiple values:

	With Two Values In Cells A1 and B1	With Six Values In Cells A1, B1, A2, B2, A3, and B3
Addition	=A1+B1	=SUM(A1:B3)
Subtraction	=A1-B1	=A1-B1-A2-B2-A3-B3
Multiplication	=A1*B1	=PRODUCT(A1:B3)
Division	=A1/B1	=A1/B1/A2/B2/A3/B3

A few more comments:

With addition, there are two other tricks to know.

First, if you don't care about recording the value you calculate, you can simply highlight the cells you want to add together and then look in the bottom right corner of the worksheet. It should show you the average, the count, and the sum of the cells you have highlighted.

Second you can use the AutoSum option in the Editing section of the Home Tab to add either a row or column of values without having to type in the formula. This is basically just another way to have Excel create your formula for you.

To use it, click into the empty cell at the end of your range of values and then click on the AutoSum icon which looks like the mathematical sum function (a big pointy E-like shape). Excel will then create and display a SUM function for you and highlight the cells it thinks you wanted to add.

The AutoSum option stops at blank cells, so if you need to sum across a blank space, you'll need to edit the formula for it to work properly, but it can be a nice way to get a quick start on writing your formula.

(You'll note that there's a dropdown there as well, so you can also use it for Average, Count Numbers, Max, and Min.)

Complex Formulas

Excel can handle incredibly complex formulas. You just have to make sure you write them properly so that Excel knows which functions to perform first.

Put something in parens and Excel will do that before anything else. Otherwise it will follow standard mathematical principles about which actions to perform in which order.

According to the Excel help documentation (under Operator Precedence), Excel will first combine cells (B1:B3 or B1,B2), then create any negative numbers (-B1). Next it will create percents, then calculate any exponentials (B2^2), then do any multiplication and division, then do any addition and subtraction, then concatenate any values, and then do any comparisons last.

All of this, of course, at least in the U.S., is done from left to right in a formula.

So, basically, Excel calculates starting on the left side of the equation and moves to the right, doing each of those steps above in that order throughout the entire formula before circling back to the start and doing the next step. Which means that multiplication and division are done first and then addition or subtraction.

Of course, anything in parens is treated as a standalone equation first. So if you have =3*(4+2), Excel will add the 4 and the 2 before it does the multiplication.

Basically, if you're going to write complex formulas they're definitely doable but you should be very comfortable with math and how it works. Also, be sure to test your equation to make sure you did it right. I do this by breaking a formula into its component steps and then making sure that my combined equation generates the same result.

Other Functions

We briefly discussed SUM and PRODUCT, but Excel has hundreds of available functions that can do all sorts of interesting things and not just with numbers.

To see what I'm talking about, go to the Formulas tab. There are seven different subject areas listed there (Financial, Logical, Text, Date & Time, Lookup & Reference, Math & Trig, and More Functions which shows an additional six categories). Click on each of those dropdowns and you'll see twenty-plus functions for each one.

But how do you know if there's a function that does what you want to do? For example, is there a function for trimming excess space from a string of values? (Yes. It's called TRIM.) Or for calculating the cumulative principal paid on a loan between two periods? (Yes.)

So how do you find the function you want without hovering over each function to see what it does because the names by themselves are certainly no help?

The simple way is to go to the Formulas tab and click on Insert Function. This will bring up the Insert Function dialogue box which includes a search function. Type a few words for what you're looking for.

For example, if I want to calculate how many days until some event occurs and I want to have this formula work no matter what day it is when I open my worksheet, then I need some way to set a value equal to today's date whatever day today is. So I search for "today" and get a function called TODAY that it says "Returns the current date formatted as a date." Perfect.

Once you've found a function you like, select it and click on OK. Excel will take you back to the worksheet and show you a Function Arguments dialogue box that tells you what inputs are needed to create that particular function.

If the function doesn't require any arguments, like TODAY doesn't, it will just let you know that and insert the function into your selected cell.

Sometimes selecting a function this way, even if you know what it does, is helpful because it shows you what order you need to put the information in and what form it needs to take. But you can also see this to a lesser degree when you start to type the function into your cell. Once you type the opening paren it will show you the components you need and their order. (Very helpful for things like SUMIF and SUMIFS that have different orders even though they do similar things.)

As mentioned before, *Excel 2019 Formulas and Functions*, which is 200 pages long, is going to be the best resource if you really want to dig in on how formulas and functions work.

Copying Cells With Formulas in Them

One of the nice things about working with formulas in Excel is that you don't have to type them over and over and over again. You can type a formula once and if you need to use it again, simply copy it to a new cell.

There are some tricks to copying formulas. So let's walk through those.

By default, formulas are relative. Meaning that if you have a formula that says

$$=B1+C1$$

and you copy it (Ctrl + C) over to the right one cell it will become

$$=C1+D1$$

See how the column value for each referenced cell changed by one column? If you copy that same formula down one cell from the original location it will become

$$=B2+C2$$

See how the row number for each referenced cell changed by one?

This is great when you have rows and rows of data with everything located in the same position and want to perform the exact same calculation on each of those rows. You can simply copy the formula and paste it down the entire column and it will perform that calculation on each and every row.

But sometimes you just want to move the calculation. Say it's in Cell B2 now and you want to put it in Cell A10. That's when you need to cut the formula (Ctrl + X) instead of copy it. By cutting and moving the formula, it stays the exact same. If it said =B1+C1 before it still will after you paste it into the new location..

Another way to do this is to click into the cell, highlight all of the text in the cell, copy it, and tab (or Esc) out of the cell, and then click on the new location and paste it that way.

(If you click into the cell, highlight all of the text, and try to click on where you want to paste it, you'll end up replacing your existing text in the source cell with a reference to the cell you clicked into.)

What if you want to copy the formula, but you want to keep some portion of it fixed? Say either the row reference, the column reference, or the reference to an entire cell. (Useful when calculating different scenarios where you build a table with different values for variable x in one row and different values for variable y in one column and then calculate what value you get for each combination of x and y. So, hourly pay and hours worked, for example.)

You can fix a portion of a cell reference by using the $ sign. (We discussed it earlier with respect to inputting data, but I'll run through it again here.)

To fix the reference to a cell, put a $ sign before both the letter and the number in the cell name. So cell B2 becomes $B$2 in your formula.

If you reference a cell that way ($B$2), no matter where you copy that formula to it will continue to reference that specific cell.

This is useful if you have a constant value in your formula. So say you're selling widgets and they're all priced at $100. You might list Widget Price at the top of your worksheet and put 100 in a cell at the top and then calculate how much each customer owes by multiplying their units purchased by that fixed value in that cell.

If you want to keep just the column the same, but change the row reference, then put the dollar sign in front of the letter only. So $B2 when copied would become $B3, $B4, etc. no matter where you copy that formula to it's always B.

If you want to keep the row the same, but change the column reference, you'd put the dollar sign in front of the number only. So B$2. When copied, that portion of the formula would change to C$2, D$2, etc. but the 2 would never change.

One more thought about copying formulas. I usually just highlight all of the cells where I want to copy the formula to and then paste, but there's a shortcut that you can sometimes use that's faster when you have many many rows of data.

If you have a formula in a cell and want to copy it downward and the column where that cell is located is touching another column of data that has already been completed (so you have a full column of data next to the column where you want to put your formula), you can place your cursor on the bottom right corner of the cell with the formula and double-left click. This should copy the formula down all of your rows of data.

It doesn't work if the other column of data hasn't been filled in yet. Excel only knows how far to copy the formula based on the information in the other column. But it can be a handy shortcut in a table with lots of completed information where you're just adding a calculation.

Okay. So that was manipulating data, let's now talk about how to print when you have a finished product that's ready to go.

Printing

You might not think that printing needs its own section, but it definitely does. Not because clicking on Print is so hard to do, but because you need to format your data well to get it to print well. If you just hit print without thinking about how that information in your worksheet will appear on a printed page, you'll likely end up with pages and pages worth of poorly-formatted garbage.

Now, it's possible you have no intent of printing anything (I never print my budget spreadsheet) in which case, skip this section. But if you are going to print, let's try and waste as little paper as possible.

First things first. To print, go to the File tab and select Print.

Typing Ctrl and P at the same time (Ctrl + P) will also take you to the print screen.

You should see a number of print options in the center of the screen and a preview section on the right-hand side.

If everything looks good, you can just click on the big Print button right there at the top and be done with it.

Sometimes that's the case if you're printing a small amount of data, but usually I find I need to make adjustments, especially if I have enough information that it carries over to additional pages.

Let's walk through all of the options you have with respect to printing, but first let me just show you what the print screen will look like:

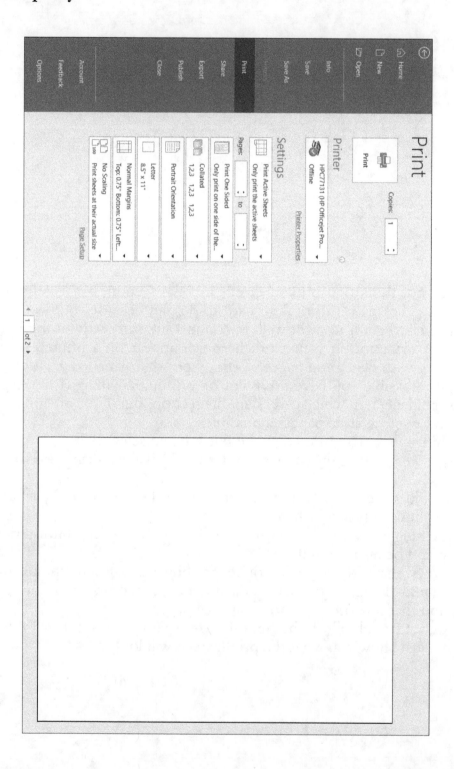

You can see in the image that you have a number of print options listed underneath the text Print and then on the right-hand side you have a print preview of what your document will look like on a page-by-page basis.

(In this case, mine is blank but you can see at the bottom where it says 1 of 2 and you can arrow to a second page.)

Let's walk through each of those options starting with the image of a printer right under the text Print.

Print

Once you're ready to print your page, you can click on the button on the top left with the image of a printer that says Print and your document will print.

Copies

To the right of that image where it says Copies is where you specify how many copies to print. If you want to print more than one copy, change that number by either using the up and down arrows or by clicking into the box and typing in a new value.

Printer

It should display your computer's default printer here, but if you want to use a different printer than that one, click on the arrow next to the printer name and choose from the listed options. If the printer you want isn't listed, choose Add Printer.

Print Active Sheets / Print Entire Workbook / Print Selection

The default is Print Active Sheets. This will generally be the worksheet you were working in when you chose to print.

However, you can select more than one worksheet by holding down the Control key and clicking on multiple worksheet names. (When you do this, you'll see that the names of all of your selected worksheets are highlighted, not just one of them.) If you do this before you choose to print, then when you do Print Active Sheets it will print all of the worksheets you've selected.

I would only print multiple worksheets if you're satisfied that each one is formatted exactly the way you want it formatted.

Also, choosing to print more than one sheet at a time either with Print Active Sheets or Print Entire Workbook, results in strange things happening to your headers and footers. For example, your pages will be numbered across worksheets. If you mean each worksheet to be a standalone report with numbered pages specific to that report, then you need to print each worksheet separately.

As I just alluded to, the Print Entire Workbook option prints all of the worksheets in your workbook. Print Selection allows you to just print a highlighted section of a worksheet or worksheets.

(I happened to have three worksheets selected at once and then highlighted the first twenty cells in one of those worksheets and when I went to Print Selection Excel printed those twenty cells in *each* of those three worksheets.)

Pages

Just below the Print Active Sheets option is a row that says Pages and has two boxes with arrows at the side. You can choose to just print a specific page rather than the entire worksheet by using the options here. To figure out which page to print, look at your preview. To specify the pages numbers either use the up and down arrows or click into the boxes and type in your value(s) using commas between page numbers.

Print One Sided / Print on Both Sides (long edge) / Print on Both Sides (short edge)

The default is to just print on one side of your paper. If you have a printer that can print on both sides of the page you can change your settings to do so. You want the long-edge option if your layout is going to be portrait-style and the short-edge option if your layout is going to be landscape-style. (See below.)

Whether or not you have the option to choose to print on both sides will depend on the printer you have selected. I have occasionally printed to PDF and then come back to print in Excel and found that I couldn't print on both sides because my printer had been changed to the PDF option and I had forgotten to change it back.

Collated / Uncollated

This only matters if what you're printing has more than one page and if you're printing more than one copy.

In that case, you need to decide if you want to print one full copy at a time x number of times or if you want to print x copies of page 1 and then x copies of page 2 and then x copies of page 3 and so on until you've printed all pages of your document. In general, I would choose collated (one copy at a time), which is also the default. The uncollated option (one page at a time) could be good for handouts.

Portrait Orientation / Landscape Orientation

You can choose to print in either portrait orientation (with the short edge of the page on top) or landscape orientation (with the long edge of the page on top). You can see what difference it will make by changing the option in Excel and looking at your print preview.

Which option you choose will likely depend on how many columns of data you have.

Assuming I'm dealing with a normal worksheet with rows of data listed across various columns, my goal is to fit all of my columns on one page if possible. Sometimes changing the layout to landscape allows me to do that because it allows me to have more columns per page than I'd be able to fit in portrait mode.

If I have just a few columns of data, but lots of rows I'll generally stick with portrait orientation instead.

You'll have to decide what works best for you and your specific situation.

Letter / Legal / Statement / Etc.

This is where you select your paper type. Unless you're in an office, chances are you'll leave this exactly like it is. I'm sure my printer could print on legal paper, but I don't have any for it to use so it's a moot point for me. In the U.S. the default is. 8.5"x11" but I assume that overseas it is A4 or some other regional standard.

Normal Margins / Wide Margins / Narrow Margins / Custom Margins

I would expect you won't use this often, but if you need to then this would be where you can change the margins on your document. The normal margins allow for .7" on each side and .75" on top and bottom. If you have a lot of text and need just a little more room to fit it all on one page, you could use the narrow margin option to make that happen. I generally adjust my scaling instead although that does change the text size which changing the margins will not do.

No Scaling / Fit Sheet on One Page / Fit All Columns on One Page / Fit All Rows on One Page/ Custom Scaling Options

I use this option often when I have a situation where my columns are just a little bit too much to fit on the page or my rows go just a little bit beyond the page. If you choose "Fit All Columns on One Page" that will make sure that all of your columns fit across the top of one page. You might still have multiple pages because of the number of rows, but at least everything will fit across the top.

Of course, depending on how many columns you have, this might not be a good choice. Excel will make it fit, but it does so by decreasing your font size. If you have too many columns you're trying to fit on one page your font size may become so small you can't read it.

So be sure to look at your preview before you print. (And use Landscape Orientation first if you need to.)

Fit All Rows on One Page is good for if you have maybe one or two rows too many to naturally fit on the page.

Fit Sheet on One Page is a combination of fitting all columns and all rows onto one page. Again, Excel will do it if you ask it to, but with a large set of data you won't be able to read it.

Custom Scaling brings up the Page Setup dialogue box. This is often where I will go to adjust my scaling for a document because it has the most flexibility. You can specify exactly how many pages to scale by in each direction. (We'll talk about that more below.)

Page Setup

The Page Setup link at the very bottom of the Print Screen Options gives you access to even more print options by opening the Page Setup dialogue box.

A few things to point out to you that I find useful:

1. Scaling

On the Page tab you can see the scaling option once more in the second section of the box where it says Scaling.

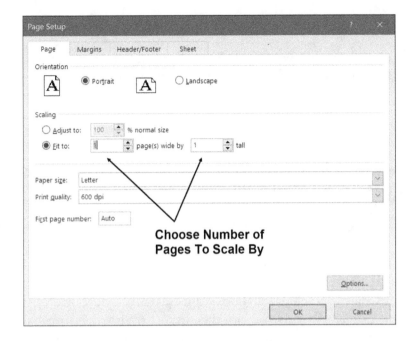

The nice thing here is that you can fit your information to however many pages across by however many pages long. You're not limited to 1 page wide or 1 page tall.

So say you have a document that's currently one page wide and four pages long but the last page is just one row. You can scale that document in the Page Setup dialogue box so that the document that prints is one page wide by three pages long and that last row is brought up onto the prior page.

2. Center Horizontally or Vertically

On the Margins tab there are two check boxes that let you center what you're printing either horizontally or vertically on the page, or both.

I will often choose to center an item horizontally if there aren't many columns.

3. Header/Footer

We're going to talk about another way to do this in a moment, but if you want to set up a header and/or a footer for your printed document you can do so on the Header/Footer tab.

The dropdown boxes that say (none) include a number of pre-formatted headers and footers for you to use. So if you just want the page number included, there should be a pre-formatted one that you can select via the dropdown options.

Same with including the worksheet name or file name in the header or footer. As you look at each one it will show you examples of the actual text that will be included. You also have the option of customizing either the header or footer.

4. Sheet

The sheet tab has a couple of useful options, but I'm going to show you a different way to set these options through the Page Layout Tab.

Page Layout Tab

If you exit out of the File tab go back to your worksheet by clicking the little arrow in the top left corner of the screen or using Esc, you'll see that one of the tabs you have available to use is called Page Layout. There are certain attributes that I set up here *before* I print my documents. (Or that I come back here to set up if I forget before I try to print, which is more often the case.)

Let's walk through them.

(Also, note that you can change margins, orientation, and size here just as easily as in the print preview screen.)

1. Print Area

If you only want to print a portion of a worksheet, you can set that portion as your print area by highlighting it and then clicking on the arrow next to Print Area and choosing Set Print Area in the Page Setup section of the Page Layout tab.

Only do it this way (as opposed to highlighting the section and choosing Print-Selection) if it's a permanent setting. Because once you set your print area it will remain set until you clear it. You can add more data to your worksheet but it will never print until you change your print area or clear that setting and it's easy to forget you've done that and then not be able to figure out why the whole document won't print for you.

I use this setting when I have a worksheet that either has extra information I don't want to print or where the formatting extends beyond my data and Excel keeps trying to print all those empty but formatted cells. (Sometimes removing that extra formatting is more of a hassle than it's worth and using print area is a quick workaround.)

2. Breaks

You can set where a page break occurs in your worksheet. So say you have a worksheet that takes up four pages and you want to make sure that rows 1 through 10 are on a page together and then rows 11 through 20 are on a page together even though that's not how things would naturally fall.

You can set a page break to force that to happen by clicking in a cell in your worksheet and then going to Breaks and choosing Insert Page Break from the dropdown menu. This will insert a page break above the cell where you clicked and to the left of the cell.

You can see where the breaks are located because Excel will insert a solid line through your worksheet above your selected cell and, if it wasn't the first column, to the left of your selected cell. It's not terribly easy to see in the worksheet itself, but if you go to print and look at the preview you'll see that your information is now broken into new pages at the place or places where you inserted the break(s).

To remove a page break, click into the cell below it or to the right of it and go to Breaks in the Page Setup section of the Page Layout tab and choose Remove Page Break. You can also choose Reset All Page Breaks.

Personally, I find page breaks a challenge to work with, so I usually try to get what I need some other way.

3. Print Titles

This is the one we came here to discuss. I find Print Titles incredibly valuable. When you click on this option you'll see that it brings up the Page Setup dialogue box and takes you to the Sheet tab. The top section of the Sheet tab lets you choose rows to repeat at the top of every page or columns to repeat at the left. This is invaluable. If you learn nothing else about printing, learn this.

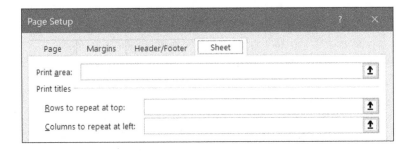

Why? Say you have a worksheet with a thousand rows of data in it that will print on a hundred pages. How do you know what's in each column on each page? You need a header row. And you need that header row to repeat at the top of each and every page.

"Rows to repeat at top" is where you specify what row(s) is your header row. Click in that box and then click on the row number in your worksheet that you want to have repeat at the top of each page. Excel will do its thing and put $1:$1 or whatever row reference it needs to for you. (You can also just type this same information in from the Print screen if you remember cell notation. Just use $ signs and your row or row numbers that you want. So $1:$3 would repeat Rows 1 through 3 on every page.)

To set a column(s) you want to repeat on the left-hand side of each page, such as a customer name or student name or record number, click in the box that says "Columns to repeat at left", and then click on the letter for the column(s) you want to repeat on each page. Again, Excel will do its magic and convert that to cell notation for you. But, again, you can write it yourself I you want, too by using $ and the letter for the column. So, $C:$C would repeat the values in Column C on every page.

Do be careful if you're going to choose more than one row or column to repeat that you don't end up selecting so many rows or columns to repeat that you basically just print the same thing over and over and over again. You need to leave room for the rest of the data in your worksheet.

Conclusion

Alright, so there you have it. A beginner's guide to Excel. This wasn't meant to be a comprehensive guide to Excel, but to instead give you the basics you need to do 95% of what you'll ever want to do in Excel. I hope it did that.

If something wasn't clear or you have any questions, please feel free to reach out to me at mlhumphreywriter@gmail.com.

As I mentioned previously, the next book in this series is *Excel 2019 Intermediate* which covers more advanced topics such as charts, pivot tables, conditional formatting, subtotaling and grouping data, and limiting the set of values that can be entered into a cell.

There is also *Excel 2019 Formulas and Functions* which gets much more in depth about how formulas and functions work in Excel and then goes one-by-one through about sixty functions in detail while covering approximately one hundred functions total.

But you can also just research specific topics on your own. The Microsoft website has a number of tutorials and examples that I think are very well-written and easy to follow at www.support.office.com. I usually find what I need there with a quick internet search for something like "bold text Excel 2019" and then choose the Microsoft support link to take me directly to the page I need.

The help available directly in Excel 2019 is excellent as well. Click on the Help tab and then click on the blue circle with a question mark that says Help. This will bring up a search box on the right-hand side of the screen where you can type in the topic that you need to know more about.

Another source of more information is to simply hold your mouse over the tasks listed on the various tabs. This will usually show a brief description of what that item does. A lot of the descriptions also have a "tell me more" link at the bottom of the description that will take you directly to the help screen related to that item. (The Format Painter on the Home tab is a good example of this. Just hold your cursor over it to see what I'm talking about.)

Your final option is to wade into the mess that is online help forums. I generally recommend against asking your own question in those forums because I find they're full of people who are rude if you don't ask your question in just the right way and provide every little piece of detailed information when you originally ask your question. How can a new user know what they don't know or what they need to provide to get their answer, right, so it always annoys me to see that.

But sometimes finding where someone else asked your question already and seeing what the answer was can be very helpful. Forums are best for the "is this possible" type of question rather than the "how does this work" type of question. Microsoft is very good at providing enough help on how things work that you can find that on their website or in the Excel help tab. But they are less helpful at telling you whether you can do something.

Again, if there's something specific you want to know, just ask. Happy to help if I can.

And thanks for reading this guide. Excel is an incredibly powerful tool and now that you have the foundation you need to use it effectively, I hope you see that.

Excel 2019 Intermediate

EXCEL ESSENTIALS 2019 BOOK 2

M.L. HUMPHREY

CONTENTS

CONTENTS (CONT.)

Introduction

This book is the second book in the Excel Essentials 2019 series.

In the first book of the series, *Excel 2019 Beginner*, we covered almost all of what you need to know to work in Excel on a daily basis such as how to open, close, and save files, how to input data, how to format it, some basic ways to manipulate your data such as filtering and sorting, and how to print the results.

(So if you don't know those things, start there first.)

In this book we're going to take the next step and learn very useful ways to work in Excel that you probably won't need on a day-to-day basis but that will come in incredibly handy when you do need them. Things like conditional formatting, PivotTables, and charts as well as a few other little tips and tricks I've learned along the way such as removing duplicate values, converting text to columns, and limiting allowed inputs in cells.

What we will not cover here, because it's covered in the third book in this series, is functions. *Excel 2019 Formulas and Functions* covers more functions than you probably ever wanted to know about. (Approximately a hundred of them.) So if your real interest is in how to use functions in Excel, that's the book you want.

I'd highly recommend mastering the content of *Excel 2019 Beginner* before reading this book or the formulas and functions one (although if you've learned it elsewhere that works, too), but once you're comfortable in Excel *Excel 2019 Intermediate* and *Excel 2019 Formulas and Functions* can be read in any order and are written to be standalone books.

Also, as I did in *Excel 2019 Beginner*, at the end I'll discuss how to find the answer when you want to do something I haven't covered. There are a number of excellent help resources out there that you should be able to use once you have a solid understanding of how Excel works and therefore what's possible.

I should note here as well that even after three books we will not have covered everything you can do in Excel. For example, I'm not going to try to teach you how to use macros because you can really mess things up if you get them wrong and most people will never need them. Also, I'm not going to talk about VBA or how to use Excel to create a database. But I can also tell you that in over twenty-five years of using Excel I've rarely if ever needed any of that.

So the goal of this series is not to cover every single solitary thing you could ever want to know about Excel. It's to give you the information you need to use Excel on a regular basis with as little extraneous information as possible.

Okay?

One other note. While this book contains a large number of screenshots to show you what I'm talking about this is not a book that contains exercises for you to do. This book should be self-contained so that you can read it on your commute or wherever you have time to read it. For me with Excel often the key is simply knowing that something can be done and then playing around to make it happen once that time comes.

Finally, this book is written specifically for users of Excel 2019. If you're using an older version of Excel it is possible that there will be certain things that do not work the same way in your version or that only exist in Excel 2019. Now that we're moving into intermediate-level topics this becomes much more likely.

(I did write a book called *Intermediate Excel* that is still available and was written using Excel 2013. That book was written to be generally applicable to all versions of Excel from Excel 2007 onward and covers most of the same material as this book if that's an issue for you.)

Alright. Let's get started. First we'll do a quick review of basic terminology and then we'll dive into the fun stuff with conditional formatting.

Basic Terminology

Most of the terminology I use is pretty standard but I think I do have a few quirks in how I refer to things, so be sure to do a quick skim of this section just to make sure we're on the same page. This is meant to be a refresher only. These terms were initially taught in *Excel 2019 Beginner*.

Column

Excel uses columns and rows to display information. Columns run across the top of the worksheet and, unless you've done something funky with your settings, are identified using letters of the alphabet.

Row

Rows run down the side of the worksheet and are numbered starting at 1 and up to a very high number. In Excel 2019 that number is 1048576.

Cell

A cell is a combination of a column and row that is identified by the letter of the column it's in and the number of the row it's in. For example, Cell A1 is the cell in the first column and first row of a worksheet.

Click

If I tell you to click on something, that means to use your mouse (or trackpad) to move the cursor on the screen over to a specific location and left-click or right-click on the option. (See the next definition for the difference between left-click and right-click).

If you left-click, this generally selects the item. If you right-click, this generally creates a dropdown list of options to choose from. If I don't tell you which to do, left- or right-click, then left-click.

Left-click/Right-click

If you look at your mouse or your trackpad, you generally have two flat buttons to press. One is on the left side, one is on the right. If I say left-click that means to press down on the button on the left. If I say right-click that means press down on the button on the right. (If you're used to using Word or Excel you may already do this without even thinking about it. If that's the case then think of left-click as what you usually use to select text and right-click as what you use to see a menu of choices.)

Spreadsheet

I'll try to avoid using this term, but if I do use it, I'll mean your entire Excel file. It's a little confusing because it can sometimes also be used to mean a specific worksheet, which is why I'll try to avoid it as much as possible.

Worksheet

This is the term I'll use as much as possible. A worksheet is a combination of rows and columns that you can enter data in. When you open an Excel file, it opens to Sheet1.

Workbook

I don't use this term often, but it may come up. A workbook is an Excel file and can contain multiple worksheets. The default file type for an Excel 2019 workbook is a .xlsx file type.

Formula Bar

This is the long white bar at the top of the screen with the fx symbol next to it.

Tab

I refer to the menu choices at the top of the screen (File, Home, Insert, Page Layout, Formulas, Data, Review, View, and Help) as tabs. Note how they look like folder tabs from an old-time filing system when selected? That's why.

Data

I use data and information interchangeably. Whatever information you put into a worksheet is your data or data set.

Select

If I tell you to "select" cells, that means to highlight them. Same with text.

Arrow

If I say that you can "arrow" to something that just means to use the arrow keys to navigate from one cell to another.

Cell Notation

We may end up talking about cell ranges in this book. Excel uses a very specific type of cell notation. We already mentioned that a cell is referenced based upon the letter of its column and the number of its row. So A1 is the cell in Column A and Row 1. (When used as cell notation you don't need to include Cell before the A1.)

To reference a range of cells Excel uses the colon (:) and the comma (,). A colon between cells means "through". So A1:B25 means all of the cells between Cell A1 and Cell B25 which is all of the cells in Columns A and B and Rows 1 through 25. A comma means and. So A1,B25 would be Cells A1 and B25 only.

When in doubt, go into Excel, type = and the cell range, hit enter, and then double-click back into that cell. Excel will highlight all of the cells in the range you entered.

Dialogue Box

I will sometimes refer to dialogue boxes. These are the boxes that occasionally pop up with additional options for you to choose from for a particular task.

Paste Special – Values

Paste Special - Values is a special type of pasting option which I often use to remove formulas from my data or to remove a pivot table but keep the table it created. If I tell you to Paste Special - Values that means use the Values paste option which is the one with a 123 on the clipboard.

Dropdown

I will occasionally refer to a dropdown or dropdown menu. This is generally a list of potential choices that you can select from if you right-click on your worksheet or on one of the arrows next to an option in the tabs at the top. For example, if you go to the Home tab and click on the arrow under Paste, you will see additional options listed in a paste dropdown menu.

Task Pane

I am going to call the separate standalone pane that appears on the right-hand side of the screen on occasion a task pane. These appear for PivotTables, charts, and the Help function.

Conditional Formatting

Alright then. Let's dive right in with a conversation about conditional formatting.

What is it and why would you want to use it?

At its most basic, conditional formatting is a set of rules you can apply to your data that help you see when certain criteria have been met.

I, for example, use it in my budget worksheet where I list my bank account values. I have minimum balance requirements on my checking and savings accounts, so both of the cells where I list those minimum required balances are set up with conditional formatting that will color those cells red if the balance in either account drops below the minimum requirement.

This helps remind me of those requirements, because I'm not always thinking about them when I move money around.

Another example of how to use conditional formatting would be if you track payments people owe you in Excel. You could either set up conditional formatting to flag when a payment is more than 30 days past its due date or when the date is outside of a specified range.

Conditional formatting is also useful when you have a set of data and want to easily flag certain results as good or bad. In my prior career I had to look for customer transactions where the customer paid a commission of over 5%. Sometimes there were thousands of lines of data, but I could have set up a conditional formatting rule that shaded any value over 5% red which would have made it very easy to scan my results and see the ones that were too high.

Even better, you can actually combine conditional formatting with filtering so that you first apply your conditional formatting (in this case turning all values over 5% red) and then your filter the data using Cell Color or Font Color so that you're only seeing the rows with data that was flagged.

The easiest way to see how conditional formatting works is to walk through an example. So let's do that.

Highlight Cells Rules

One of my favorite things to create in Excel is a two-variable analysis grid. This takes one item, say price, and puts it across the top of a table. And then takes another item, say units sold, and puts that down the side of the table. The center of the table is then a calculation of the result for all possible combinations of your two variables.

Here is one I already built that calculates the amount earned at various combinations of price and units sold.

		Price				
		$1	$2	$3	$4	$5
Units	10	$10	$20	$30	$40	$50
	25	$25	$50	$75	$100	$125
	100	$100	$200	$300	$400	$500
	500	$500	$1,000	$1,500	$2,000	$2,500

See the prices along the top and the units along the side and how at the intersection of each price and unit combination the value is the price multiplied times the number of units?

Now. Let's say that you need to earn at least $500 in order to make a profit on selling whatever this product is. There are a number of ways to do that. You could sell 500 units for $1. You could sell 100 units for $5.

It's possible to just look through the values and manually identify the ones that are over $500, but this is where conditional formatting can be incredibly helpful.

We're now going to apply shading to those calculated values so that we can quickly and easily see each value that is $500 or more.

First step, highlight the cells we want to apply our formatting to.

Next, we go the Styles section of the Home tab and click on the arrow under Conditional Formatting to see the dropdown menu.

We're going to choose the first option in that dropdown which is Highlight Cells Rules. If you hold your mouse over that text it will bring up a secondary dropdown menu with a large variety of choices.

Specifically, you can choose from Greater Than, Less Than, Between, Equal To, Text That Contains, A Date Occurring, and Duplicate Values. There's also a More Rules option at the bottom that will bring up the New Formatting Rule dialogue box. But for now we're going to choose Greater Than.

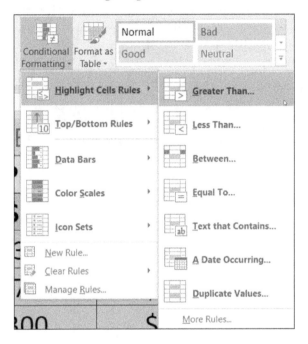

This brings up the Greater Than dialogue box which has two inputs. On the left-hand side you specify the value that you want to use for your greater than condition and on the right-hand side you choose the type of format you want to apply to your cells if that condition is met.

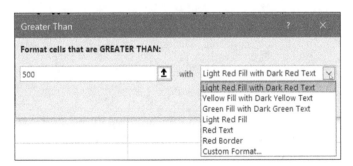

In the screenshot above I have actually made an error in what I chose. Because this is a GREATER THAN condition which means if I enter 500 then only values above 500 will be formatted the way I want. What I need to enter is 499.99 instead.

You can't see it here, but as you enter your values in the dialogue box and choose your formatting Excel will apply that formatting to the worksheet so you can see what the result is going to be before you give the final OK. In a scenario like this one where I want to flag the good results I usually use the Green Fill with Dark Green Text option because green = good, red = bad, at least in the U.S.

For a basic, simple analysis like this one the Light Red Fill with Dark Red Text and the Green Fill with Dark Green Text options usually do all you need. But there is a Custom Format option at the bottom of that dropdown that will let you apply pretty much any formatting you want via the Format Cells dialogue box.

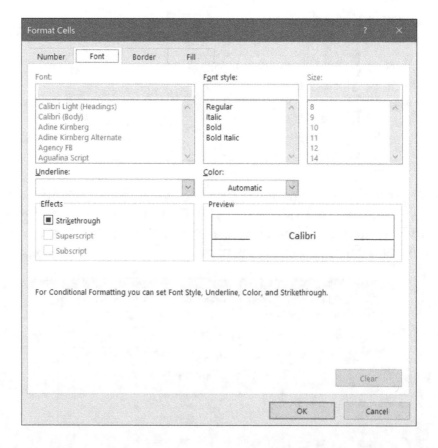

Font and Font Size are grayed out, but borders, fill color, font style, number format, etc. are all available.

I was just able to choose to format my text with a purple font and in italics. But let's just change that back to Green with Green and click OK.

Here we are:

		Price				
		$1	**$2**	**$3**	**$4**	**$5**
Units	**10**	$10	$20	$30	$40	$50
	25	$25	$50	$75	$100	$125
	100	$100	$200	$300	$400	$500
	500	$500	$1,000	$1,500	$2,000	$2,500

Compare this to our earlier version of the grid and you can see that there are now six cells that have shading on them. (And if this were in color you'd see that they are green with green text.)

All six of those cells meet our condition of being equal to or greater than $499.99. Now,with a simple glance we can see what combinations of price and units get us to our goal.

The other options in that Highlight Cells Rules dropdown work basically the exact same way. Each one you select will bring up a dialogue box where you input your parameter and select your formatting. The only real difference is what type of analysis it's doing. (Greater Than, Less Than, etc.)

The duplicate values option is a little weird because it doesn't discriminate between different values. In our sample data table we have two cells with a value of $50, two cells with a value of $100, and two cells with a value of $500. If I select the cells in my data table and tell Excel to highlight duplicate values, this is what I get:

		Price				
		$1	**$2**	**$3**	**$4**	**$5**
Units	**10**	$10	$20	$30	$40	$50
	25	$25	$50	$75	$100	$125
	100	$100	$200	$300	$400	$500
	500	$500	$1,000	$1,500	$2,000	$2,500

Even though there are three separate values that are duplicated, all six cells with duplicate values are formatted the exact same way.

115

I personally don't find that tremendously useful because I then still have to distinguish between the $50, $100, and $500 values. Most times when I'm looking for duplicates it is so I can eliminate one (or more) entry with the same value.

The date option is a bit odd as well because you can't specify a date or date range to use. It only lets you flag a date occurring yesterday, today, tomorrow, in the last seven days, last week, this week, next week, last month, this month, or next month.

Depending on what you want to use it for, those options could be very useful or very limited.

Top/Bottom Rules

The next set of conditional formatting rules you can use are called Top/Bottom Rules.

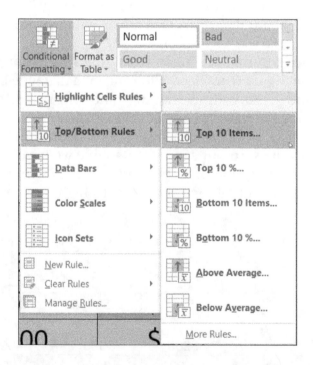

With the Top/Bottom Rules, you can format values that fall in the top X of your range (like top 10), the bottom X of your range, the top X% of your range, the bottom X% of your range, above the average for the range, or below the average for the range.

(While the options are labeled Top 10 Items, Top 10%, etc. when you click on them you'll see that you can adjust the number to whatever you want to use.)

For example, here is the Top 10 items dialogue box.

In the screenshot above you can see that I've changed the value so that it will format the top 16 values instead of the top 10. You can use the arrows there next to the number or click into the box and type in the number you want.

As with the Highlight Cells Rules you have the same set of preset dropdown format options or can choose Custom Format at the bottom of the list.

Data Bars

Data bars are where things start to get interesting. Up until now you could have technically gone through and manually formatted your data to get the same effect as the highlight cells rules or the top/bottom rules.

(It would be a bad idea, because conditional formatting adjusts with your data whereas manually doing that exact same formatting to flag values only works if your data never changes again. But technically they'd *look* the same in that moment in time.)

Data bars, however, place a bar in each cell where the length of the bar is determined by how big the value in that cell is compared to all other values in the selected range.

Your options in the secondary dropdown menu are mostly just formatting-related options. You can choose different default colors, namely blue, green, red, orange, light blue, and purple. And you can choose between a solid bar and a gradient bar.

The easiest way to see the difference between the solid and the gradient option is to look at it. So let's do that. In the screenshot below the gradient option is on the left-hand side and the solid option is on the right-hand side. Both of these were done in the "light blue" color.

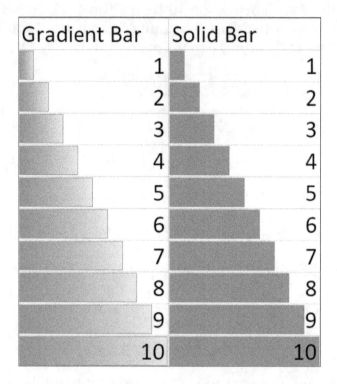

With data bars you can change the settings so that only the bar shows and the number is hidden, but we'll talk about that in a moment after we talk about Color Scales and Icon Sets.

Color Scales

Color Scales is one I actually use quite often. I have an Excel spreadsheet that shows the amount of revenue I've earned each month as well as the amount I've spent on ads each month and for each of those columns I have color scales applied that quickly show me the months where I either earned the most or spent the most.

So what do color scales do? They color a cell a shade of color along a spectrum based upon the relative value in that cell compared to the rest of the range.

Just like with data bars, the secondary dropdown menu on this one is basically preset color choices. You have red/yellow/green, red/white/green, red/white/blue, shades of red, shades of green, and green/yellow and you can choose those to go in either direction.

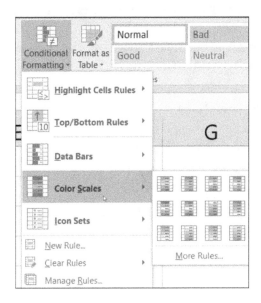

What I mean by that is that you can, for example with the red/yellow/green option shade the smallest values red and the largest values green or you can shade the smallest values green and the largest values red. It all depends on what is "good" or "bad" in your particular scenario.

I will add a comment here to be careful about color-coding when your color choices are arbitrary. For example, that red/white/blue option is meaningless to me. Red and green are commonly used together to represent "bad" and "good" results but when you replace green with blue my mind does not automatically assume that blue is bad so then I'm left looking at shaded cells and wondering what to make of it.

In another scenario I saw recently someone had used shading that was applied to values ranging from -100 to 100. Zero was neutral, -100 was good, 100 was bad. But they had used just one color so it was all shades of red which made the zero results, which were neutral, look like they were bad results. In that example, the green/yellow/red scale or something like it would've been a better choice.

We'll get into customization in a moment, but this is one where I like to choose a custom color to use for my scales just because I find the default choices of red and green boring.

Another thing to keep in mind with this one is that you may have to change your font color for the larger values because black text does not always show well with the darker cell shading.

Real quick, here is an example of the difference between the white-red color scale option and the red-white color scale option. As you can see, the white-red option made the cell with a value of 10 in it the white cell and the red-white option made the cell with a value of 1 in it the white cell.

White-Red	Red-White
1	1
2	2
3	3
4	4
5	5
6	6
7	7
8	8
9	9
10	10

Icon Sets

Your last option is Icon Sets which are an interesting one because they insert a symbol into each cell based on its relative value within the range. You can see your icon choices in the secondary menu after you select Icon Sets.

There are a number of icon sets to choose from that will group your data into three-part, four-part, or five-part categories and will use various shapes such as arrows, circles, etc. to do so.

In the following screenshot I've used four of the options to show you how they differ based upon shape and number of levels. I've labeled each column according to the description that Excel uses. (You can see the name Excel has assigned to each icon set by holding your mouse over it in the secondary dropdown menu.)

Five Quarters		4 Ratings		3 Triangles		3 Symbols Circled	
○	1	◢	1	▼	1	⊗	1
○	2	◢	2	▼	2	⊗	2
◔	3	◢	3	▼	3	⊗	3
◔	4	◢	4	▬	4	!	4
◑	5	◢	5	▬	5	!	5
◑	6	◢	6	▬	6	!	6
◕	7	◢	7	▬	7	!	7
◕	8	◢	8	▲	8	✓	8
●	9	◢	9	▲	9	✓	9
●	10	◢	10	▲	10	✓	10

So a wide variety of choices.

In Excel 2019 if you use icon sets on your data you can then filter your data by each icon. It's under the Filter By Color option. Pull up the secondary menu there and you'll see your icons listed as filter choices under the heading Filter by Cell Icon.

Customization

What we just walked through are the defaults. But you can customize your data ranges and your formats much more than that.

If you want to use Data Bars, Color Scales, or Icon Sets but you want to set absolute limits for when a format is applied (as opposed to letting Excel look at the data and divide it evenly), you can do so by applying default rules and then choosing Manage Rules from the Conditional Formatting dropdown in the Styles section of the Home tab. This will bring up the Conditional Formatting Rules Manager.

The dialogue box will default to Current Selection and only show you the rules that exist for that cell or range of cells, but you can change the dropdown to This Worksheet to see all of the rules that exist in your worksheet.

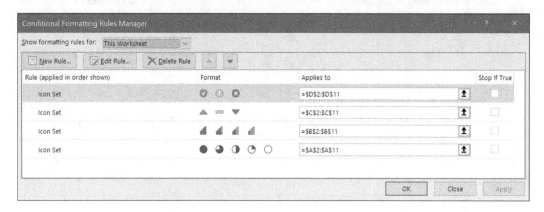

In the screenshot above I have four sets of conditional formatting rules in this worksheet, each applied to a different range of cells.

Note that you can apply more than one conditional formatting rule to a specific cell. When you do that, you can tell Excel by checking the checkboxes on the right-hand side to stop if one of the rules is true and then not apply the rest of the rules.

You can also change the order of your rules using those arrows in the section directly above the rule listing. Just click on the rule you want to move first.

In the past I've had conditional formatting rules where I wanted different formatting on different value ranges and so I had a rule that was >100, say, and then a rule that was >50, etc. Because of how they were written, with that > operator and the overlap in potential results where a value of 150 would be both >100 and >50, the order of the rules mattered.

In this scenario that we're looking at here, it doesn't. There's no overlap across the cell ranges.

So back to customization.

Choose the rule you want to customize, click on its row, and then choose Edit Rule. That will bring up the Edit Formatting Rule dialogue box which will already be completed with the defaults that Excel chose for you when your initially created the rule.

Let's look at an example.

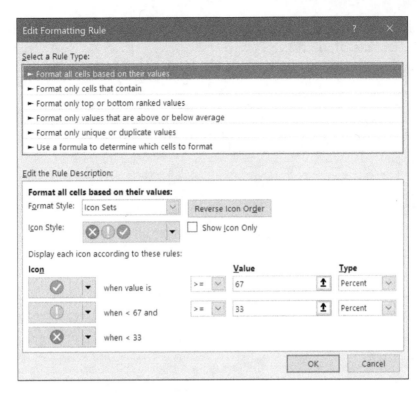

So you can see here that I've chosen an icon set rule that has three categories, the X, the exclamation mark, and the checkmark. Because of that Excel has divided my results on a percent basis where the bottom third of the values are the X, the next third are the exclamation mark, and the final third are the checkmark.

I can change this. So let's say that I want absolute values. Anything 6 and above gets a checkmark, anything under 2 gets an X, and anything in between gets the exclamation mark.

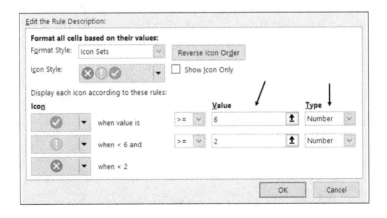

I do that by changing the Type dropdown from Percent to Number and then entering my values of 6 and 2.

Now the criteria are applied on an absolute value basis. This is the result:

3 Symbols Circled
⊗ 1
❗ 2
❗ 3
❗ 4
❗ 5
✓ 6
✓ 7
✓ 8
✓ 9
✓ 10

See the difference? There's now only one X in the whole table because there's only one value below 2 and the 6 and 7 values now have a check next to them instead of an exclamation mark.

Be careful of your edge cases. In this scenario the 6 and the 2.

Because I used >= as my rule for both, that meant that the 2 value was not given an X. If I'd wanted values of 2 or less to be an X, then I would've needed to change that option to > only. (That's the only other choice you have.)

I usually forget to pay attention to that and have to go back and fix it later. If you're like me, be sure to always test those values in your data when you set up your conditional formatting.

In the Edit Formatting Rule dialogue box you can also change the icon set you're using or, actually, change anything about your conditional formatting.

Here's the top portion of that dialogue box:

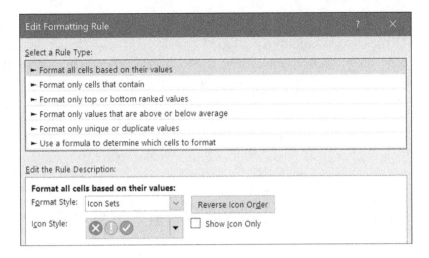

First, see at the bottom where it says Icon Style and there's a dropdown? You can click there and select any of the other icon set options.

To the right of that is a checkbox where you can click to Show Icon Only. This will keep the shapes or the bars or whatever, but it will hide the actual value.

Above that you can reverse the icon order so that the value that was "bad" before is now "good."

And then above that if you read those options in Select Rule Type you'll see that you can change this conditional formatting rule to any of the other options. For example, the third option there, format only top and bottom ranked values is the Top/Bottom Rules.

The dropdowns we walked through before were the shortcuts that Excel has put in place to make it easy to do the most common formatting. But here you have almost complete control.

Remove Conditional Formatting

What do you do if you've added conditional formatting and you want to remove it? You can go back to the Conditional Formatting dropdown and choose Clear Rules from the bottom section. This will show you a secondary dropdown that says Clear Rules from Selected Cells or Clear Rules from Entire Sheet. (There are two other options there about clearing rules from tables or PivotTables that will only be available if that applies in your situation.)

If you've selected the cells with the formatting that you want to remove, just choose Clear Rules from Selected Cells.

If you're not sure where you have conditional formatting and want it all removed from the worksheet you can choose Clear Rules from Entire Sheet.

The other option is to select Manage Rules. This brings up the Conditional Formatting Rule Manager and you can then see all rules that exist for that selection or any worksheet in the entire file. To remove one of those rules, click on the rule to select it and then click Delete Rule from the section above the rules.

Extend a Covered Range of Cells

There are probably other ways to do this, but when I have a range of cells that have conditional formatting on them and I add to the values but my new values are not included in the formatting range, I go to the Manage Rules option to fix this.

It's tempting to think that you can use the Format Painter to do this—just click on one of the cells with your conditional formatting and then click on the new cell range. But the problem with doing so is that Excel treats those new cells as a new range. So the formatting transfers, but the range you had before and the new range are evaluated separately.

For an absolute value scenario like the one we created above, that's not a problem. For a relative value scenario, it is. See here:

▭	5	⚠	5
▲	6	✓	6
▲	7	✓	7
▼	8	✓	8
▭	9	✓	9
▲	10	✓	10

What I did for both of these columns is remove the conditional formatting from the cells for 8, 9, and 10 and then reapplied it using Format Painter.

The example on the left is one where the conditional formatting rule is relative. The bottom 1/3 of values get a down arrow, the middle 1/3 get a bar, and the top 1/3 get an up arrow.

You can see here that 8, 9, and 10 were treated as their own group for purposes of assigning an icon which is why the 8 has a down arrow and the 9 has a bar even though they are in a column of numbers ranging from 1 through 10.

The column on the right is the one we edited earlier where we had absolute values in our criteria. Any value 6 or above got a checkmark. Using Format Painter in this scenario worked because the criteria are absolute.

Rather than go through that mental gymnastics, I just always use the Manage Rules option to extend my cell range. Although that can have its issues as well.

To do this, go to the Conditional Formatting dropdown in the Styles section of the Home tab and choose Manage Rules. This will let you see each rule and the cell range it applies to. (In the Applies To column.)

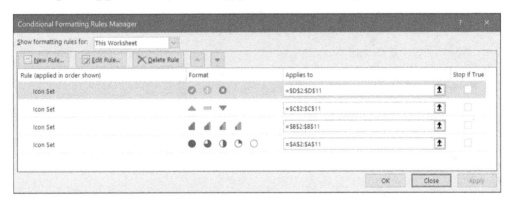

If you're just extending a range, click into that box, backspace to delete the current last row value and type in the new row value and then hit enter. If you want to put a second, non-continuous cell range, you can do so by using a comma and typing in the new range.

This approach works well as long as you don't try using the arrow keys. Click into that box and use the arrow key and Excel tries to be helpful and gives you the next cell in your worksheet from the one you had selected when you opened the dialogue box. It basically erases what was already in there and replaces it with a cell selection you don't want.

(Ctrl + Z , undo, is your friend when things like that happen.)

There is also an arrow with a bar under it at the end of the listed cell range. You can click on that and it will show you in the worksheet which cells the formatting currently applies to. You can then click into your worksheet and highlight the cells you want it to apply to and you'll see a small dialogue box that updates with the new range. Hit enter when you're done with your selection and it will update.

Okay, so that was probably more than you ever wanted to know about conditional formatting. Now on to something much simpler: Inserting Symbols.

Insert Symbols

This doesn't come up often, which is why I included it in this book instead of the beginner book. But I do occasionally want to insert a symbol into a field. For example, maybe I want to use the € sign for Euros or the £ sign for British Pounds. There are shortcuts you can type that will insert them, but I don't do it often enough to know them.

Another time I've used symbols is in my tracking of my short story submissions where I used stars and exes to indicate which stories had received personal rejections from a market and which had received form rejections.

Inserting a symbol is a very straight-forward process. You can either insert a symbol into its own cell or as part of text within a cell. Like this:

	A
1	It cost €25
2	☺

In Cell A1 I typed text and then inserted the Euros symbol. In Cell A2 I just inserted a smiley face symbol.

Once a symbol is there, you can treat it just like text and change the font size or the font color. DO NOT change the font, though. For a lot of these that's what determines the symbol you're seeing. For example, that smiley face symbol is actually what a capital J looks like in the Wingdings font.

So how do you do this? How do you insert a symbol?

Simple.

First, click into the cell or the portion of the cell where you want to add the symbol.

Next, go to the Insert tab and click on Symbol in the Symbols section on the right-hand side. This will bring up the Symbol dialogue box:

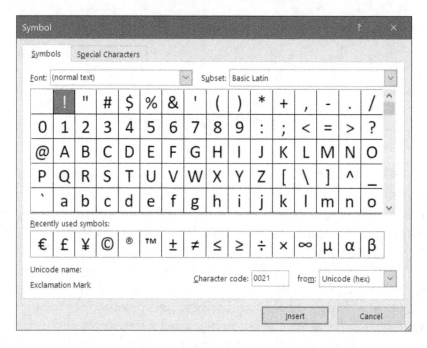

If you've recently used the symbol you're looking for it will be under Recently Used Symbols at the bottom of the dialogue box. By default this section contains some commonly use symbols that you can see above.

Otherwise, you can scroll through the displayed letters and symbols until you find the one you want. That subset dropdown menu will let you narrow the results down if you already have an idea where the symbol you want is located.

Another option is to change the font dropdown to find a font that has a lot of shapes or symbols in it. The most common for that are Wingdings, Wingdings 2, and Wingdings 3.

There is also a Special Characters tab that you can click on at the top where you can find things like the copyright symbol, trademark symbol, and section symbol.

When you find what you're looking for, click on the symbol so that it's highlighted and then click on Insert at the bottom of the dialogue box. In the cell where you inserted the symbol you will now see the symbol.

One more thing to note is that in the Excel worksheet the symbol will appear like what you saw in the Symbol dialogue box, but in the formula bar it will appear as the character it is in that particular font, if applicable.

So here I have the smiley face next to a trademark symbol. You can see that in the cell. In the formula bar above it you can see the capital J for the smiley face and the trademark symbol for the trademark. And above that you can see that this is the Wingdings font being used in this cell.

That's it. It's that simple. Just remember that a lot of the symbols you'll insert are driven by the font choice, so if you do insert symbols into your file be very careful about using the Format Painter or selecting all and changing the font, because you may end up erasing any symbol you inserted and be left with weird letters or other characters in the midst of your text instead.

Hide Rows or Columns

We'll jump into PivotTables in a minute, but first I want to cover another easy little trick you may need, which is how to hide rows or columns. This can come in very useful at times.

For example, I have an advertising tracker that I use where I have to input various values like the title, the advertiser I used, the amount spent, and then the results information. I want all of that information, but it comes from different sources so sometimes I'm inputting information in Columns C and M but not any of the columns in between. Being able to hide those columns so that I can jump straight from Column C to Column M saves me a lot of time and effort.

(I also sometimes use grouping data for this one, we'll cover that one next.)

Another way to use this is if you enter information into a worksheet that you need in that worksheet, say for calculation purposes, but you don't need to see it all the time. You can just hide the rows with that data in them.

Use hide when it's more of a permanent solution, use group when it's temporary or you expect to repeatedly hide and unhide the row or columns. Also, I use hide when I already have group on a set of rows or columns and need to hide a subset of them.

So how do you do this? First, select the column(s) or row(s) you want to hide, right-click and choose Hide from the dropdown menu. Excel will hide that column(s) or row(s) and you will now see that your column lettering or row numbering skips the hidden column(s) or row(s).

In the below screenshot you can see that I've hidden Column B and I've hidden Row 2. If you recall, filtering will do this as well where it skips a row number, but the way to tell which one is in place is to look at the color of the row numbers. With filtering, they are colored blue, with hiding a row, they are not.

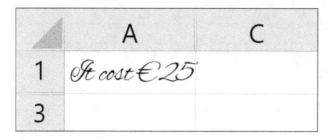

Also, with hiding you'll see that little double line between the row or column identifiers that indicates at least one row or column is hidden. (This will look the same regardless of the number of rows or columns you've hidden.)

To unhide a column(s) or row(s) you've hidden, select the columns or the rows on either side of the hidden column(s) or row(s). So above I'd select Columns A and C or Rows 1 and 3. Right-click and choose Unhide from the dropdown.

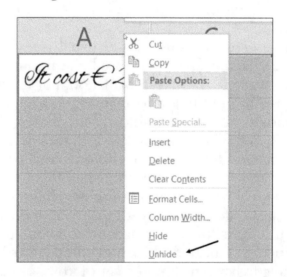

One thing to keep in mind when unhiding column(s) or row(s) is that it will unhide all of the hidden columns or rows between those two columns or those two rows. So if you've hidden Columns B, C, D, and E, for example, when you select Columns A and F and choose Unhide all four columns will be unhidden.

There is no way that I'm aware of to just unhide Column B or Column D and leave the others hidden. Even if each one was hidden individually, they all unhide as a group.

Group Data

There's another way to temporarily hide columns or rows and that's by using the grouping data option.

This allows you to group rows or columns so that you can easily hide them or show them once again by simply clicking on a plus or minus sign.

To do this, select a range of columns or a range of rows that you want to group together.

The columns or rows you group have to be adjacent. If you try to group non-adjacent columns or rows you'll get an error message. (Which is different from how it works with PivotTables.)

Here's my data. In this example I'm going to group address, product, unit, and unit cost so that I only see a customer name and total cost.

	A	B	C	D	E	F
1	Customer	Address	Product	Unit	Unit Cost	Total Cost
2	Jones	123 Sunny Lane	Widgets	10	$2.00	$20.00
3	Smith	456 Dreary Ct	Whatsits	5	$4.00	$20.00
4	Hernandez	321 Spruce St	Widgets	3	$2.00	$6.00

So I select Columns B, C, D, and E. I then go to the Outline section of the Data tab and click on Group.

Above my four columns that I wanted hidden as well as the next column there will now appear a line with a negative sign at the end. The columns are not yet hidden, but they are grouped at this point.

It will look like this:

If we were grouping rows, the line and the negative sign would appear along the left-hand side of the table.

To hide the columns (or rows if you grouped rows) you simply click on that negative sign. All columns or rows that are covered by the line will be hidden. It looks like this for our example:

The minus sign is now a plus sign and if you want to see the hidden columns once more you can simply click on that plus sign.

To ungroup a specific set of columns or rows, highlight them once more and then click on Ungroup from the Outline section of the Data tab.

To remove all grouping from a worksheet use Clear Outline in the dropdown menu under Ungroup in the Outline section of the Data tab.

Subtotal Data

In the same section as Group there is also an option called Subtotal that basically takes grouping your data one level further by also subtotaling it. I've used this in the past with a table that lists month, year, units sold, and amount earned for my books where I then wanted to have the yearly totals and be able to hide the monthly values at will.

Someone could just as easily use subtotals to get summary information by customer or product.

The way subtotal works is that at each change in your specified column value (such as year) it will subtotal the values in another column(s) in your data (such as amount earned).

It is not smart about this, though. If you don't sort your data first, you will have a problem because it will subtotal at each change in your column value meaning you could have multiple subtotals for the same value.

I'll show you an example in a moment, but first let's subtotal some data.

Highlight your selected data and in the Outline section of the Data tab choose Subtotal.

If you selected all cells in your worksheet, by clicking in the corner or using Ctrl + A, you may get a dialogue box that says that Excel can't determine what row to use for data labels. If you want it to use the first row, you can continue by selecting OK.

If you select just your data but not the header row you'll see a different dialogue box that asks if you meant to use the row directly above your data as your header row. Click Yes if that's the case.

Either way you will now see the Subtotal dialogue box where you can tell Excel which column to use for subtotals, which columns to add a subtotal to, and the function that you want Excel to use. (It's called subtotaling and the default is to sum the values, but the dropdown menu actually lets you take not just the sum but the count, average, max, min, or product of the values.)

Okay. So here's the dialogue box.

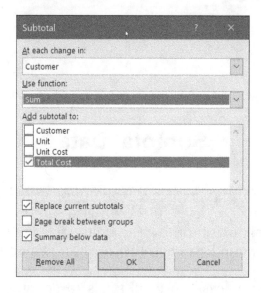

The first choice to make is at each change in what column value do you want to make a calculation. In this case we're going to do Customer.

The next choice is what calculation you want to make. Usually this will stay Sum but as I mentioned above you have some other choices.

The third choice is what to perform that calculation on. In this case I have unit, unit cost, and total cost. It wouldn't make sense to take a sum of unit cost (that would be something you could average though) so I'm going to check Unit and Total Cost.

Below that you have the option to replace current subtotals (usually something you should do), to add a page break between groups (up to you, I'd only do so with data sets where I need to print those results as standalone pages), and to add a summary below your data (as opposed to at the top). The summary will perform whatever calculation you chose on the entire data set.

So let's go ahead and do this with a sum of Unit and Unit Cost for Customer, replacing any current subtotals, and adding a summary below the data.

Here we go. The initial result is fully-expanded, meaning that you can see all of the detailed data as well as the subtotals that have been added in there. But because I intentionally made a mistake here, I'm going to minimize things so that you only see the subtotals.

1 2 3		A	B	C	D
	1	Customer	Unit	Unit Cost	Total Cost
+	3	Jones Total	10		$20.00
+	5	Smith Total	5		$20.00
+	9	Hernandez	33		$96.00
+	12	Jones Total	10		$40.00
+	15	Smith Total	15		$52.00
+	17	Jones Total	2		$4.00
+	19	Smith Total	21		$42.00
+	21	Hernandez	9		$27.00
-	22	Grand Tota	105		$301.00

Can you see what I did wrong?

Scan the list of Customer names for a second. See how there is a Jones subtotal but then four rows down there's another one? And two more rows after that? I didn't sort my data so at every change in the last name, Excel did its calculation. Not it's fault, mine.

So now let me go back, sort my data first and try this again. This is what I get initially.

1 2 3		A	B	C	D
	1	Customer	Unit	Unit Cost	Total Cost
	2	Hernandez	3	$2.00	$6.00
	3	Hernandez	7	$3.00	$21.00
	4	Hernandez	23	$3.00	$69.00
	5	Hernandez	9	$3.00	$27.00
-	6	Hernandez Tota	42		$123.00
	7	Jones	10	$2.00	$20.00
	8	Jones	1	$4.00	$4.00
	9	Jones	9	$4.00	$36.00
	10	Jones	2	$2.00	$4.00
-	11	Jones Total	22		$64.00
	12	Smith	5	$4.00	$20.00
	13	Smith	4	$2.00	$8.00
	14	Smith	11	$4.00	$44.00
	15	Smith	21	$2.00	$42.00
-	16	Smith Total	41		$114.00
-	17	Grand Total	105		$301.00

Now I have all of the results for each customer sorted by last name which means I have one subtotal per customer.

Those subtotal lines are each bolded while the detail data is not. At the very bottom, because I chose to place a summary below my data, I also have a Grand Total row that totals all of the individual entries.

I can click on that 2 on the left-hand side to hide all of the detail data and just see the subtotals. That's what I did on the last page where I showed you how I messed up.

When you do that, each subtotal will have a + sign next to it instead of a - sign. You can click on any individual plus sign to expand the details for just that one value. Or you can click on the 3 to expand all of the results at once.

Clicking on the 1 will give you just the Grand Total line.

(Sometimes you have to click on the 1, 2, or 3 a second time to get it to work. I think this likely comes down to what you were doing right before you clicked.)

To remove subtotals, go back to the Subtotal option in the Data tab, click on Subtotal to bring up the Subtotal dialogue box, and then click on Remove All in the bottom left corner.

I've found Ctrl + Z generally does not work well when dealing with subtotals so be careful that what you do is what you want because it won't be easy to fix if you get it wrong.

One more thing. If you want to keep your subtotals, but remove the groupings on the left-hand side, you can either click on Ungroup in the Outline section of the Data tab, which will bring up the Ungroup dialogue box, and then from there choose the rows option which will remove the highest level of grouping. (In this case the grand total grouping.)

Or you can click on the arrow under Ungroup to bring up the dropdown menu and then choose Clear Outline which will remove all levels of grouping but leave your bolded lines with the subtotals and grand total.

You can still choose to Remove All in the Subtotal dialogue box at that point to remove the subtotal lines.

Also, note that which number corresponds to which level of data will change as you ungroup your data but the principle remains the same. Clicking on the number up top collapses that level. Clicking on individual pluses and minuses expands or contracts individual groupings for a level.

Okay. Time to tackle a useful but challenging topic: PivotTables.

PivotTables

Before we get started, for the record I passionately hate how they write PivotTable as one word with capital letters in the middle. But that's how they do it, so that's how we'll try to do it. (I may slip up once or twice, but I'll try to catch myself. While we're on the subject I also passionately hate how their labels and menu options in their dialogue boxes don't use title case and so you'll often see that I do.)

Alright then. Now that that's out of my system.

If you learn one thing from this book let it be PivotTables. I literally chose to write the first two books in the original Excel Essentials series (*Excel for Beginners* and *Intermediate Excel*) in order to teach writers how to use Excel well enough for them to use PivotTables.

That's how useful these things are: I was willing to write thousands of words about the basics of Excel just to get people to the point where we are right now where I could teach them how to use PivotTables.

What They Do

So what are PivotTables? What do they do? Why are they so special?

A PivotTable takes rows and rows of data and lets you create a nice little summary table of that data based upon your chosen parameters.

Let me give you an example of how this can be useful.

Let's say you sell widgets, whatsits, and whatchamacallits. And every time you sell one of those items your distributor (the place you sell through) creates a line of data in an Excel worksheet that has the state where the sale occurred, the retail price, and the net amount due to you for that transaction, and you want to know what you've earned in each state so you can target advertising.

You could filter your data to see this or use subtotals even, but a far better option is to create a PivotTable of your data.

Let's do that. But first we need to cover some basic data principles.

Basic Data Principles

The data you use to build your table needs to be in the right format.

There should be one row at the top of your data table that contains the labels for each column. (I sometimes call this the header row.)

Everything needs to be in that one row. You cannot have multiple rows of column labels. So if you're going to have Year and Month, you can't put Year on Row A and then months on Row B, they need to be combined.

One header row.

Directly below the header row you put your data with one row per entry and nothing else in the midst of that data such as subtotals or grand totals.

Ideally your header row starts in Cell A1 followed by your data starting in Cell B1 and there is nothing else in the worksheet. But you can have data that starts elsewhere as long as once it starts it's header row followed by rows of data and nothing else.

The mistake a lot of people make is that they'll list information in one row and then below that row list a subset of information.

So maybe Row 5 is the customer information and then below that in Rows 6-10 is the transaction information and then Row 11 is a row for total values for that customer.

Don't do that. That is a report. That is something that is meant to be final and no longer subject to analysis. If you're still going to work with your data, leave it as raw and untouched as you can. Once you put in subtotals or break your data up into multiple lines, you can't sort it, filter it, use PivotTables, or create charts from it.

So don't do that. At least not in your source worksheet.

(As discussed more in *Data Principles for Beginners*, you should always have one place where you store your raw data.. You can then use that information to create your summary reports and analysis, or even "fix" the data. But always have that one document that is just the information and that is not changed or touched or messed with in any way so that you can go back to it if you make a mistake.)

(This helps especially if you sort your data wrong because that can pretty much break your data and you can't fix it. Keeping your source data pure lets you go back and start over.)

Also be sure to not have any blank rows or columns in your data set and to have only one type of data (date, currency, text) per column.

Blank rows aren't a deal-breaker, but Excel will treat them as valid sources of data so you'll end up with blank entries in your PivotTables.

Blank columns will generate an error message when you try to create the PivotTable because there is no valid field name for Excel to use for that column(s).

Various types of data in one column makes it almost impossible or at least very challenging to create any sort of analysis based on that data.

Okay. If you want to learn more about setting up your data in the best possibly way, check out *Data Principles for Beginners*, but we're going to move on now and create a PivotTable with one parameter using the following data table that shows state, retail price, and net due.

State	Retail Price	Net Due
AK	1.99	1.39
AK	2.49	1.74
AK	1.99	1.39
CA	3.99	2.79
CA	2.49	1.74
CA	2.49	1.74
CA	2.49	1.74
WA	1.99	1.39
WA	3.99	2.79
WA	2.49	1.74
WA	3.99	2.79

Building a Pivot Table

The PivotTable we want to build is going to calculate Net Due for each possible state. The initial steps for building a PivotTable are the same no matter how complex you're going to make that table.

First, highlight your data.

If it's the entire worksheet, you can just Select All by clicking in the top left corner or using Ctrl + A. If the data starts lower down in the worksheet or you just want to use a subset of your data then highlight the rows you want.

Be sure to highlight the header row as well as the data rows. This does not work if you do not have a header row. Furthermore, the header row must be next to the rows of data that you want to analyze.

Once you have your data selected, go to the Insert tab and in the Tables section on the left side choose PivotTable.

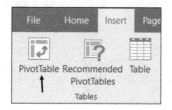

This will bring up the Create PivotTable dialogue box.

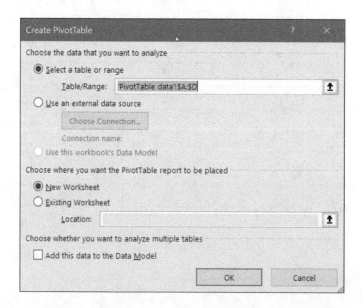

It should already have the data that you want to use selected and shown under Select a Table or Range.

(You could also link to an external data source if the data isn't in the worksheet, but I'm very hesitant to ever do this because if the external data source is moved, renamed, or unavailable that breaks the connection and you're left with a worthless worksheet until you fix that. For example, if you were working remote and couldn't access your servers, no analysis for you.)

The next section in the dialogue box has you choose where you want to put your PivotTable. I always choose to put my PivotTable into a new worksheet. If for some reason you had an existing worksheet where you wanted to put it, you could check that box and select that worksheet instead.

The checkbox for adding data to the Data Model is not something we're going to cover here so you can ignore it for now.

In summary, for a basic PivotTable you can almost always just click OK on this dialogue box without making any changes.

Once you click OK you should now see something like this:

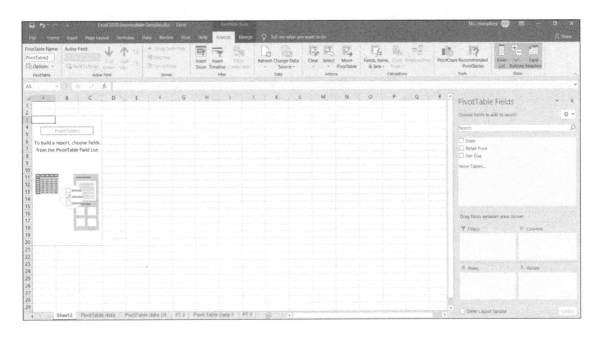

That's hard to see, so let's zoom in on the right-hand side for now.

The top section shows your available columns of data which can be used to specify the parameters used in the top row or the side column of your table, or as part of the calculated values in the center of the table, or as a filter for what subset of results appears in the table.

Our example here is going to be a very simple one that will use just state and then calculate net due for each state. We'll walk through more complex examples later.

The bottom section is where you assign each field to its role. You do this by clicking on the field in the top section and dragging it into position in the bottom section.

So I'm going to drag State into my Columns section and Net Due into my Values section. (You can also right-click on a field at the top and choose from the dropdown menu where you'd like to place that particular field. So I could have right-clicked on State and chosen Add to Column Labels.

Either way, the right-hand side should now look like this:

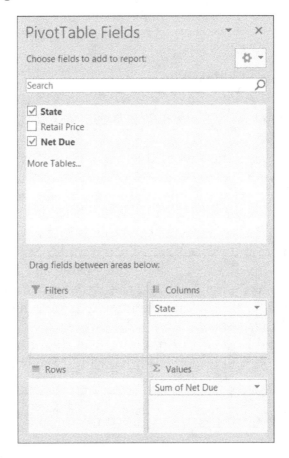

Up top you can see that the two fields I used have been checked. (That doesn't mean you can't use them again, but it does mean that they are currently in use somewhere in the table.)

Down at the bottom you can see that State is being used in the Columns section and Net Due is in the Values section. You can also see that Net Due is being summed so that the values shown are the sum of the net due of all entries for each specific state.

This is important to check, because often Excel will bring in a supposed numeric value and default to counting it instead of summing it.

So for any field you drag to the Values section, be sure that the correct function is being performed on that data.

We'll discuss later how to change it if the right function is not being performed in the Value Field Settings section. But for now, this is the PivotTable we get:

	A	B	C	D	E	F
1						
2						
3		Column Labels				
4		AK		CA	WA	(blank) Grand Total
5	Sum of Net Due		4.529	8.022	8.722	21.273

You'll see that Excel places the PivotTable a few rows down in the worksheet. (I think because of allowing room for a filter option up top, but it still doesn't really make sense to me to do so since PivotTables are meant to be dynamic and if I have more than one filter the table has to move down anyway.)

Because we had no Row parameter the table is just two lines. The first is our column labels,which are the various states listed under State in our source data.

The second is the sum of the net due values for each of those states.

That's what it looks like when we build this with State in the Columns section, but since we're dealing with only one parameter, I could have just as easily done so with State in the Rows section.

To move State to the Rows section, you just click and drag it from Columns to Rows. The PivotTable will update automatically. Now we get this:

	A	B
1		
2		
3	Row Labels	Sum of Net Due
4	AK	4.529
5	CA	8.022
6	WA	8.722
7	(blank)	
8	Grand Total	21.273

A table with two columns this time instead of two rows.

The states are now listed down the left-hand side and the sum of the net due for each of them is listed in the next column. Instead of a grand total on the right-hand side, it's now on the bottom.

Exact same results (AK 4.529, etc.) but just displayed differently.

Personally, for this limited data set I prefer this format to the first one, but if I were to add in product name on the other axis of this table then I would want my products in the rows section and my states back in the columns section.

Part of deciding where to put each field is knowing what your intent is when you build your PivotTable.

OK. So that was how to build a basic PivotTable. Select your data, insert PivotTable, drag and drop your fields where you want them, and you're done.

We'll cover more complex examples in a minute, but first let's talk about how to better format your results using the Value Field Settings option.

Value Field Settings

Look at the numbers displayed in the PivotTables we generated previously. In both tables you can see that the values are 4.529. 8.022, 8.722, and 21.273. We know that these are currency values we're looking at, but Excel doesn't know that so it just treated them like normal numbers.

To fix this, you could just highlight the visible cells and change the formatting to Currency or Accounting using the options in the Home tab. That will work. But PivotTables are dynamic and there's no guarantee that if you updated your data and then updated your table that the formatting would hold for the new data. It would depend on how exactly you had applied the formatting.

Change Formatting

There's a better way to change the formatting for the field you use in the Values section, and that is through the Value Field Settings.

To use this option, go to the Values section in the PivotTable Fields task pane, click on a field there (in this case Sum of Net Due) that you want to edit, and choose Value Field Settings from the dropdown menu.

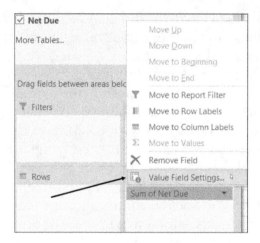

This brings up the Value Field Settings dialogue box where you can perform a number of different tasks, including changing the format of the calculated values in your PivotTable.

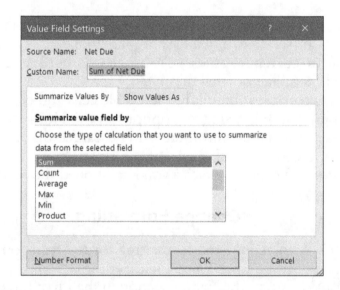

Let's do that now. First, we need to click on Number Format in the bottom left corner of the dialogue box. That will bring up the Number tab of the Format Cells dialogue box that we're all familiar with. (Or should be. It's covered in *Excel 2019 Beginner* if you're not.)

Click on the category of number format you want to use (in this case Currency), and then make any more detailed selection under that category (not applicable in this case). Click OK when you're done.

That will take you back to the Value Field Settings dialogue box where you will need to click OK one more time to close it out as well.

Your new formatting will be applied immediately. Like so:

Row Labels	Sum of Net Due
AK	$4.53
CA	$8.02
WA	$8.72
(blank)	
Grand Total	$21.27

Now all of the cells that are calculating the sum of net value have currency formatting and this will hold even if you refresh the data in the PivotTable.

Change Function

In addition to changing the format of the results in the middle of your PivotTables, you can also change the type of calculation Excel is going to perform on those values.

As I mentioned before, sometimes Excel wants to count numeric values instead of sum them. Since I almost always need it to sum, I almost always need to make this adjustment in the Value Field Settings.

To change the function Excel uses on the fields in your Values section, click on the field label that you need to modify, select Value Field Settings to open the Value Field Settings dialogue box, and then select the function you want from the list in the center of the main tab.

You can see (on the opposite page) what function is currently selected and what functions are available for selection.

Sum adds the values together, Count will count how many records meet the conditions, Average will average the values that meet them, Max will return the highest value, Min will return the lowest value, and Product will take the product of all of the values that meet those conditions.

You can scroll down to see more options which include Count Numbers, StdDev, StdDevp, and Var.

Show Values As

Before we move on, I want to point out one other thing you can do in the Value Field Settings dialogue box, and that's the options you have in the Show Values As tab on the main screen.

What we just looked at were the options you have under the Summarize Values By tab, which is the default, but right next to it is the Show Values As tab.

Click on that and you'll see a whole other set of options such as % of Grand Total, % of Column Total, % of Row Total, etc.

If you don't want to see absolute values but instead want to make relative calculations, this is where you can go to do so.

Here is the dialogue box. I've clicked on the dropdown menu that said No Calculation to show the first six options. You can use the scroll bar to see even more.

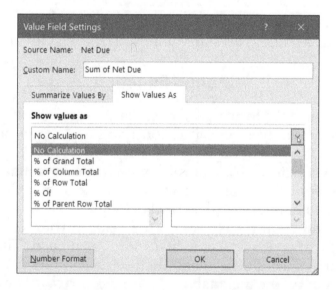

Remember how I said earlier that you can use a field more than once?

This is a perfect example of when you might want to do that. You can, for example, sum a value in one column and then right next to that place a calculation showing the percent of the total represented by that value.

Let's do that here. We'll have the sum of the net due in each state and then we'll put the % of the grand total in the column next to that.

Like so:

Row Labels	Sum of Net Due	Sum of Net Due2
AK	$4.53	21.29%
CA	$8.02	37.71%
WA	$8.72	41.00%
(blank)		0.00%
Grand Total	$21.27	100.00%

Obviously the column names need amended, but we have the actual values in the first column and then the percent of whole those represent in the second column. For example, AK is $4.53 and 21% of the total.

This looks good and is easy to interpret because we're only working with one row or column label. Adding in a column label to that table would start to look messy because you'd have two columns per column label.

So how did I do this? I simply dragged Net Due to the Values section a second time and then used Value Field Settings to change the calculation for that second instance of Net Due to % of Grand Total instead of Sum.

Alright. That's what you can do with the Value Field Settings dialogue box. Now let's talk about some simple edits you can make before moving on to more complex tables.

Refresh Your Data

If you change your original data that Excel is using to create your PivotTable, you can refresh your PivotTable so that it will show the updated results. To do this, right-click on the table and choose Refresh. Or you can click on the table and go to the Data section of the Analyze tab and choose Refresh from there.

Be careful when you refresh a PivotTable because, as I've mentioned before, they are dynamic. What this means is that the number of rows and columns in a PivotTable are not fixed. A PivotTable will shrink or grow to fit the data you give it and the parameters you set.

For example, if I changed the data table used above to include a fourth State value, my PivotTable would expand one row to show that data.

The best practice with PivotTables (in my opinion) is to work with them on a worksheet by themselves.

Do not do calculations or explanations or notes around an active PivotTable. It only takes one slip to erase your notes.

Also, say you wrote a note for AK which is currently on Row 4. But then the PivotTable updates and the AK data is now on Row 6. Your notes will not move with the data so will still be on Row 4 and now look like they apply to whatever state is on Row 4 after the data is refreshed.

This is why I often will generate a PivotTable and then click in the top left corner of my worksheet to Select All and use Paste Special-Values to paste the result back into that worksheet as data. It eliminates the PivotTable, but gives me a data table with the exact same information in it and no danger it will change.

Doing that works for me because I often use PivotTables as a one-off to summarize a large set of data. It would not work for someone who wants to refresh their analysis on a regular basis.

So, again, know why you're building your PivotTable and plan accordingly.

(There's also nothing to keep you from having an active PivotTable in one worksheet and copying and pasting special-values a version of that data to another worksheet. Just be sure if you do that to label either the tab or the first row of the second worksheet with the date you did so.

Changing the Order of Values in Rows or Columns

If you don't like the order that your entries are in, you can right-click on an entry and use the Move option to change the display order. Here I right-clicked on CA in our table:

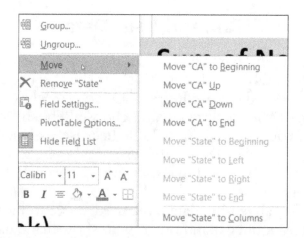

You can see that my options are to move it to the beginning of the list, to move it up, to move it down, or to move it to the end of the list.

(There's also another option at the bottom there that would move State from the Rows section to the Columns section, so that's another way to do that as well.)

If you have a lot of values and want to move them around it's a good idea to be strategic about doing so or else you'll end up moving some fields multiple times.

For example, if I move the field I want at the top to the top first and then have another field I want to move into the second-place position I'll either be stuck moving that second field up row by row (or over column by column because it works the same with columns) or I'll have to move that second row to the top and then move it down one.

I could save myself that effort by moving the second position field first.

By default your values in your row and column headers are going to be A to Z sorted but if you move things around and want to return to that state or want to sort in a different order, you can right-click on a value and choose Sort.

Display a Subset of Results in Your PivotTable

There are a couple of ways to tell Excel that you only want to see a subset of your data.

One is to use the Filters section in PivotTable Fields to place another field that can be used as your filter.

In this example we only have Retail Price left to work with, but that's fine, let's use it to narrow down the results in our PivotTable to just those for products sold with a Retail Price of $3.99.

First step is to add Retail Price to the Filters section of the PivotTable Fields.

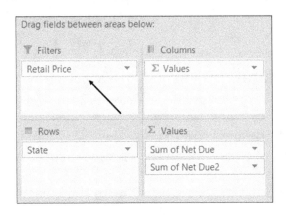

Next step is to go to the Filter dropdown menu that is now above the PivotTable and make our selection from the options there. It works just like normal Filtering in terms of checking/unchecking boxes.

Click OK and the PivotTable will update to only show results that correspond to that filter value. Like so:

	A	B	C
1	Retail Price	3.99	
2			
3	**Row Labels**	**Sum of Net Due**	**Sum of Net Due2**
4	WA	$5.59	66.67%
5	CA	$2.79	33.33%
6	**Grand Total**	**$8.38**	**100.00%**

You can see that next to Retail Price it now says 3.99 which is our filter value. (It would say All if there were no filter in place and Multiple if there was more than one filter choice selected.)

Also, note that we don't have AK as a row in the table anymore because there were no results for a Retail Price of 3.99 and AK. The table updated dynamically to remove that row since it wouldn't have values in it.

That's how you filter a table based on a value that isn't in the table itself.

If you want to display only a subset of the results in your table using the values in the rows or columns of the table itself, you can do that by clicking on the small gray arrow next to Row Label and/or Column Label.

So here we have that option for Row Labels.

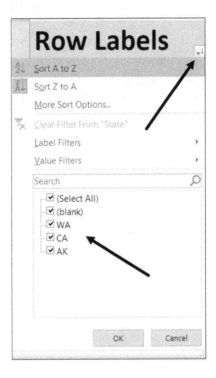

Filtering works just the same here as it would in a normal Excel worksheet. There should be checks in the boxes for the values you still want visible.

You can also filter by a set of parameters using the Label Filters or Value Filters options. If I have a long list of my titles, for example, I might filter by a word that's common to the titles I want to review like "Excel".

There's another way to hide data in a table that applies when you have more then one criteria in your row or column that we'll circle back to later.

Remove Subtotals or Grand Totals

For now we can cover how to remove grand totals from your data as well as subtotals (which we haven't yet encountered but will when we add in a second parameter field to a row or column.)

Click on a PivotTable and at the top of the screen you will see that there is a PivotTable Tools section that appears with two tabs that aren't normally there, Analyze and Design. (They appear after the Help tab.)

To remove (or edit) Grand Totals or Subtotals, go to the Design tab.

On the far left side in the Layout section you'll see dropdowns labeled Subtotals and Grand Totals. This is where you can remove subtotals or grand totals from your table or add them if they've been removed.

You can also change the options so that subtotals or grand totals only appear for columns or for rows.

I use this because I have some data that crosses years, so it covers 2015, 2016, etc. By default Excel adds subtotals to that data at every change in year. So I'll have twelve columns of monthly results and then a 2015 subtotal column, and then twelve more columns and then a 2016 subtotal, etc.

I often want to use that data with charts, so don't want my data broken up that way. I choose Do Not Show Subtotals from the dropdown to remove them.

Same goes for Grand Totals.

As another example, one set of data I work with also involves multiple currencies. It doesn't make sense to have a grand total of currency values when that means you're adding USD to AUD to GBP.

I alluded to it above, but removing grand totals works just the same. Click on the PivotTable, go to the Design tab, click on the arrow under Grand Totals in the Layout section, and choose "Off For Rows and Columns" to remove them completely.

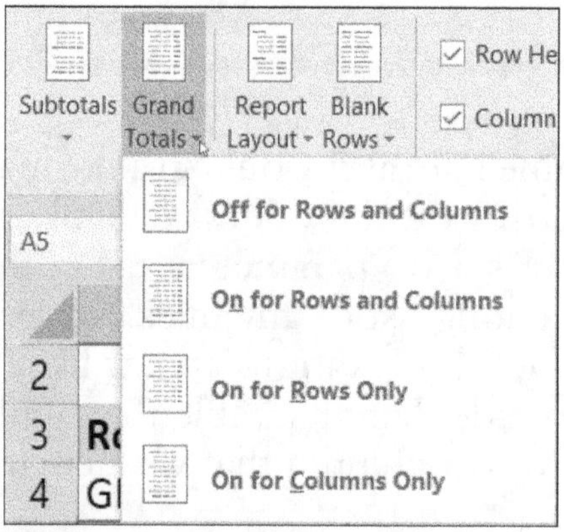

In the table on the next page, I've removed the Grand Total row from the table we've been working with. See how the data just ends and there's no final row anymore that provides the total value for each column? That was the grand total row and it's no longer there.

Row Labels	Sum of Net Due	Sum of Net Due2
(blank)		0.00%
WA	$8.72	41.00%
CA	$8.02	37.71%
AK	$4.53	21.29%

Okay. While we're in the Design tab, let's cover the rest of what's there.

Basic Formatting of a PivotTable

We'll start with PivotTable Styles.

PivotTable Styles

PivotTable Styles are shown on the right-hand side of the Design tab. I can see by default seven different styles. (If your screen is bigger or smaller that number may be different for you.) At the end of the visible styles there are up and down arrows that will let you see more available styles.

A quick count shows what looks like 85 different choices.

The default style that Excel uses in my version has a pale blue header row, no borders within the table, and bolded text for any summary rows.

To change that default is very easy. If you like the look of another option in the PivotTable Styles, just click on it. Holding your mouse over each style will change the table so you can see what that style will look like before actually selecting it. Here are two quick examples:

This first one just uses one color, no fill in any of the header or summary rows, and no bolding in the Grand Total row.

Retail Price	(All)	
Row Labels	Sum of Net Due	Sum of Net Due2
(blank)		0.00%
WA	$8.72	41.00%
CA	$8.02	37.71%
AK	$4.53	21.29%
Grand Total	$21.27	100.00%

This second one uses fill color in all of the cells, a darker fill color for the grand total and header rows, and white text in those rows.

Retail Price	(All)	
Row Labels	Sum of Net Due	Sum of Net Due2
(blank)		0.00%
WA	$8.72	41.00%
CA	$8.02	37.71%
AK	$4.53	21.29%
Grand Total	$21.27	100.00%

As you can see, a lot of variety to choose from and already pre-formatted to allow you to change your format within seconds.

It's also possible to use one of those PivotTable Styles and then further customize it using the formatting options in the Home tab, the mini formatting menu, or the Format Cells dialogue box.

PivotTable Style Options

To the left of the PivotTable Styles is a group of four checkboxes that are located in the PivotTable Style Options section.

☑ Row Headers	☐ Banded Rows
☑ Column Headers	☐ Banded Columns
PivotTable Style Options	

You can click onto the Row Headers and Column Headers options to remove or add fill from the row and column headers. So in the last example if I click on Column Headers that will remove the black band from the row that contains the text "Row Labels", "Sum of Net Due", and "Sum of Net Due 2".

With a PivotTable that is using the default format, Banded Rows and Banded Columns will apply gray shading on every other row or column, depending on the choice you make. This can be very useful to have on large data tables where it's difficult to distinguish between one row or column of data and the next.

Report Layout

Report Layout comes into play when you have a PivotTable that has multiple variables in the Rows section. It allows you to choose how your data will display within the table. We'll build this particular table later, but just to show you the different options, this is a table that has both Author Name and Title in the Rows section and is arranged so that data shows for each Author with details listed for each Title.

This is the rows layout when Show in Compact Form is selected:

Row Labels ▾	January
⊟ **Author A**	$67.46
Title A	$67.46
⊟ **Author B**	
Title B	
⊟ **Author C**	$148.27
Title C	$90.47
Title D	$46.50
Title E	$11.30

This is the layout when Show in Outline Form is selected. Note how Title is now in its own column:

Author Nam	Title	January
Author A		$67.46
	Title A	$67.46
Author B		
	Title B	
Author C		$148.27
	Title C	$90.47
	Title D	$46.50
	Title E	$11.30

This is Show in Tabular Form. The first value for Title is now sharing a line with the Author Name and the summary for each of the primary variables is listed below all of the entries instead of above on the line with the Author Name.

Author Nam	Title	January
Author A	Title A	$67.46
Author A Total		$67.46
Author B	Title B	
Author B Total		
Author C	Title C	$90.47
	Title D	$46.50
	Title E	$11.30
Author C Total		$148.27

These formats are good for a report, but not if you want to perform further data analysis.

For that, choose to Repeat All Item Labels, turn off Subtotals and Grand Totals, and use the Tabular Form to get something like this:

Author Nam	Title	January
Author A	Title A	$67.46
Author B	Title B	
Author C	Title C	$90.47
Author C	Title D	$46.50
Author C	Title E	$11.30

See how each individual row still lists the value for both Author and Name? That's what you need if you're going to take this table and use it as a data set elsewhere. (By copying and pasting with special values.)

Okay, then. Moving on.

Blank Rows

The final item in that Design tab that we haven't discussed yet is Blank Rows. With that dropdown you can either have Excel insert blank rows between each of your items or you can have it remove blank rows that have been inserted. This only works if you have more then one variable in the Rows section like in the table we were just looking at that has both Author and Title.

Changing Field Names

One other quick formatting option to cover and that's how you change a field name. I, for example, would not want to have a table where the second column was "Sum of Net Due 2". To change a column name, click into that cell and then type your new name into the formula bar and hit enter.

You can also double-click on the cell to open the Value Field Settings dialogue box and in the field called Custom Name you can type in the name you want to use.

(Or, if you were smarter than me, you would have done that already at the time you were creating that calculation, but I tend not to notice these things until I'm tidying up.)

PivotTable With One Row and One Column

Now let's move on to a more complex example where we have values across both the top of the table and along the side, and the calculations in the table are for when both values apply.

I'm going to add Product and Date of Sale columns to our data. This will give us a second category to work with as well as another filtering option should we need it.

Here's the new data:

◢	A	B	C	D	E
1	Date of Sale	Product	State	Retail Price	Net Due
2	1/3/2020	Item A	AK	1.99	1.39
3	3/1/2020	Item B	AK	2.49	1.74
4	4/15/2020	Item B	AK	1.99	1.39
5	6/4/2020	Item A	CA	3.99	2.79
6	4/7/2020	Item A	CA	2.49	1.74
7	9/10/2020	Item C	CA	2.49	1.74
8	11/11/2020	Item C	AZ	2.49	1.74
9	12/3/2020	Item A	WA	1.99	1.39
10	4/9/2020	Item B	WA	3.99	2.79
11	9/3/2020	Item B	WA	2.49	1.74
12	2/2/2020	Item A	WA	3.99	2.79

And here's our new selection options pane with State in the Columns section, Product in the Rows section, Net Due in the Values section, and Date of Sale in the Filter section.

This is what that looks like in the PivotTable itself:

	A	B	C	D	E	F	G
1	Date of Sale	(All)					
2							
3	Sum of Net Due	Column Labels					
4	Row Labels	AK		AZ	CA	WA	(blank) Grand Total
5	Item A		1.393		4.536	4.186	10.115
6	Item B		3.136			4.536	7.672
7	Item C			1.743	1.743		3.486
8	(blank)						
9	Grand Total		4.529	1.743	6.279	8.722	21.273

The values in the middle of the table are the sum of the Net Due for each combination of State and Product.

So Cell D5 which is 4.536 is the total net due for sales of Item A in CA. (The AK amounts are a little hard to read right now because the width of Column B is based on the text "Column Labels" and the values in the table are all right-aligned by default.)

Also, a quick note: if the PivotTable Fields task pane ever disappears on you, just click onto your PivotTable to bring it back. (If you're not actively working in the PivotTable that task pane as well as the extra PivotTable Tools tabs at the top go away.)

Pivot Table With Multiple Criteria In Rows and Columns

Now let's move on to a third, more complex example that has multiple criteria in both the rows and columns of the table. Here are the first few rows from the data we're going to use:

	A	B	C	E	F	G	H	I
1	Month	Year	Title	Author Name	Quantity	Royalty	Ad Cost	P or L
2	January	2015	Title A	Author A	0.00	$0.00		$0.00
3	January	2015	Title C	Author C	84.00	$108.82		$108.82
4	January	2015	Title D	Author C	23.00	$33.74		$33.74

And here is the first portion of the PivotTable created with that data:

	A	B	C	D	E	F
1						
2						
3	Sum of P or L	Column Labels ⌄				
4		⊟ 2015				
5	Row Labels ⌄	January	February	March	April	May
6	⊟ Author A	$0.00	$6.23	$11.76	$4.80	$6.79
7	Title A	$0.00	$6.23	$11.76	$4.80	$6.79
8	⊟ Author B		$0.52			
9	Title B		$0.52			
10	⊟ Author C	$142.56	$59.69	$26.81	$10.83	
11	Title C	$108.82	$28.07	$9.36	$5.41	
12	Title D	$33.74	$20.37	$9.43	$2.71	
13	Title E		$11.25	$8.02	$2.71	
14	⊟ (blank)					
15	(blank)					
16	Grand Total	$142.56	$66.44	$38.57	$15.63	$6.79

The columns section has year and then month. The rows section has Author and then Title. It's important if you're going to use multiple parameters that you get them in the right order in the PivotFields section or else your data can get very ugly very fast.

Here is what that looks like for this table:

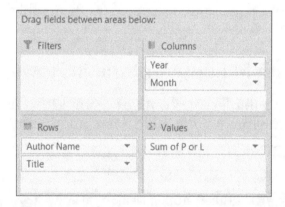

You can see that I have Year above Month and Author above Title. That sets the display order in the PivotTable so that all of the months for a specific year are listed first and then all of the months for the next year. Same with all of the titles for a specific author before the titles for the next author are listed.

If your data is displaying in the wrong order. Say, for example, I had Month above Year in that Columns section which would put all of January's results for every year first and then all of February's results for every year next, etc., it's a simple matter of clicking and dragging one of the fields into the correct order.

The table will update immediately with your changes so you can quickly see if you got it right.

One more note on this. Using multiple fields does not always work well. I almost always avoid using multiple fields in the Values section if I have more than one field in the Columns section. It just gets too busy to read easily.

Remove a Field

Another tip that we haven't talked about yet is what to do if you've placed a field into Filters, Columns, Rows, or Values and you decide you don't want it there.

One option is to click on the field name and choose Remove Field from the dropdown menu. Another is to uncheck the box next to the field name in the choose fields section. (That only works if you want to remove all uses of the field or if it was just used a single time.) You can also right-click on the field in the table itself and choose the Remove option from the dropdown there.

Hide Second-Level Data

Another thing you can do if you have multiple levels of data is hide the details from the second level of data so that you only see the summary values that pertain to the first level of data. You can do this on a case-by-case basis.

So in this data set we actually have data for 2015, 2016, 2017, 2018, 2019, and 2020.

2015 was not a very exciting year and it was a while ago. So maybe I don't care about seeing month-by-month data for that particular year.

I can click on the small negative sign next to 2015 and that will hide the monthly data for 2015 and just give me summary results. like so:

Sum of P or L	Column Labels		
	+2015	−2016	
Row Labels		January	February
−Author A	$51.09	$3.47	$2.98
Title A	$51.09	$3.47	$2.98
−Author B	$1.87		

Note that the minus sign is now a plus sign. To bring back the more detailed results, you just click on that + sign.

I could do the same on the left-hand side with Author so that I'm only seeing summary results at the Author level instead of the Title level.

To collapse all of the results at once instead of one-by-one, you can click into a cell in that row or column, right-click, and choose Collapse Entire Field.

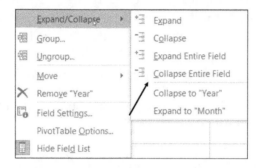

To expand it again, right-click and choose Expand Entire Field. Three's also an option to Expand or Collapse to a named level, "Year" or "Month", for example, which would come in useful if you had three levels of data in a row or column.

Grouping and Ungrouping

Another thing you can do in a PivotTable that I use somewhat often is group different selections.

For example, I have published audiobooks through two different distributors, ACX and Authors Republic. When I pull in my sales data it comes in under those two names. But sometimes when I'm generating summary reports I just want to look at overall audiobook numbers rather than specific numbers for each of those distributors.

There's no way for Excel to know that those two belong together without my somehow telling it that I want them grouped. (I could add a column to my data that puts them in an audiobook group, but since I haven't done that...)

To group two of the values in a column or row, highlight the labels of the rows or columns you want to group.

(They do not need to be next to one another. If they aren't you can use the Ctrl key as you select each one.)

Next, right-click and selected Group from the dropdown menu or go to the PivotTable Tools Analyze tab and choose Group Selection from there.

The entries you chose to group will now be next to one another and your data will have another level to it.

The group you created will be labeled Group 1, the rest of the entries at the new level will be labeled identically to their prior name.

Like so where I have chosen to Group Author A and Author C and they are now in Group 1 but Author B was left by itself so is now in a group labeled Author B:

Row Labels	
⊟ Group1	142.56
⊞ Author A	0
⊞ Author C	142.56
⊟ Author B	
⊞ Author B	
⊞ (blank)	
Grand Total	142.56

You can change the group name by clicking on the cell with the group name in it and then using the formula bar to type in the new name. Hit enter when you're done.

To ungroup values, click on a group name, right-click, and choose ungroup. This will remove all groupings at that level. You can also use the Ungroup option in the Analyze tab of the PivotTable Tools.

PivotTable Tools Analyze Tab

We've covered a lot so far and that's most of what I do in PivotTables, but there is a handy dandy Analyze tab under PivotTable Tools that's at least worth a quick look. Some of it we discussed already, like Refresh and Group/Ungroup, but let's walk through a few more of your options.

I'm going to do these in order of what I use rather than in order withing the tab so that if you start to get bored reading through this section you can just skip to the next section.

Fields, Items, & Sets

In addition to the calculations we already discussed, Excel allows you to add calculated fields to your table that combine more than one of the fields in your table to create a new value.

For example, let's say that I want to know my profit or loss per unit for my titles. I have a field that tells me units sold, Quantity, and I have a field that tells me total Profit and Loss, P or L. I can use the Calculated Field option under Fields, Items, & Sets to have Excel calculate P or L divided by Quantity for me with the data in the PivotTable.

Why do it this way instead of doing it in the source data table? Because in the source data we haven't aggregated our results. So I could calculate for every month what the profit or loss per unit was for a specific title and then take the average of those values, but I couldn't calculate the overall number since my data isn't aggregated until I do so through the PivotTable.

Let's walk through how to do that. Here's what we're going to start with. I've changed the column names, formatted the values, and filtered this to just 2015 data. (Note that when I changed the column name it also changed the name in the PivotTable Fields task pane so be aware that happens.)

Year	2015	
Row Labels	**Units**	**Profit**
Author A	27	$51.09
Title A	27	$51.09
Author B	2	$1.87
Title B	2	$1.87
Author C	405	$298.73
Title C	263	$162.84
Title D	86	$90.14
Title E	55	$45.75
Grand Total	434	$351.69

Click on the PivotTable and then go to the Analyze tab under PivotTable Tools.

In the Calculations section click on the dropdown for Fields, Items, & Sets and choose Calculated Field.

You'll then see the Inert Calculated Field dialogue box.

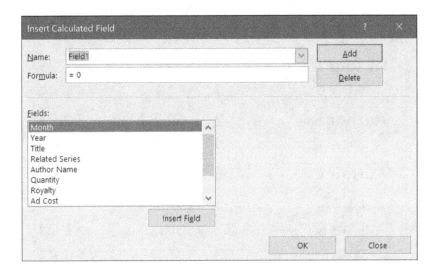

Under Name, type the name you want to use for the field.

Under Formula you need to type in a formula that will do your calculation. (We covered basic math operators in *Excel 2019 Beginner*. Use a plus sign for addition, minus sign for subtraction, asterisk for multiplication, and forward slash for division. If you want to do something more than that then look to *Excel 2019 Formulas and Functions* or use the Help function in Excel.)

You can click on the field names you need as you build your formula. They will be the original field names. So I clicked into that Formula box, left the = sign, deleted the 0, clicked on P or L, then typed a forward slash, then clicked on Quantity.

When you're done, click on Add. And then click on OK. Excel should add the new calculated field into your PivotTable. (If you don't click Add it may just add it to the list of available fields in the PivotTable Fields task pane.)

You can then format the new value like you would any other either in the PivotTable Fields task pane or the PivotTable cells themselves.

Because this was a summary table, Excel named the field in the table Sum of Profit Per Unit but what it's actually calculating is Profit divided by Units. So I'm going to ahead and rename it in my table but I have to tweak the name a bit because Excel won't let me use Profit Per Unit since that was the original name I used.

M.L. Humphrey

Here's what I end up with. A table that now has a third column Profit/Unit which is calculated based upon the values in two other cells in my table.

Year	2015		
Row Labels	**Units**	**Profit**	**Profit/Unit**
Author A	**27**	**$51.09**	**$1.89**
Title A	27	$51.09	$1.89
Author B	**2**	**$1.87**	**$0.94**
Title B	2	$1.87	$0.94
Author C	**405**	**$298.73**	**$0.74**
Title C	263	$162.84	$0.62
Title D	86	$90.14	$1.04
Title E	55	$45.75	$0.83
Grand Total	**434**	**$351.69**	**$0.81**

The nice thing about using calculated values is they adjust as you move the table around. I could have done this same calculation off to the side of the table for one row but it would've stayed in place if/when I updated the table and may not have lined up anymore to the correct row in the table.

Which reminds me that there is an issue if you do calculations outside of a PivotTable that use values in a PivotTable: The calculations do not move with the PivotTable. The cell references the calculation uses are basically the set of rules that build that specific value in the PivotTable.

It sounds confusing. Let me show you.

If I use the values in this PivotTable to divide the value in C5 (which is $51.09) by the value in B5 (which is 27 units), the formula Excel creates looks like this:

=GETPIVOTDATA("Profit",$A$4,"Author Name","Author A")/
GETPIVOTDATA("Units",$A$4,"Author Name","Author A")

That is very different from the formula it would create if this weren't a PivotTable. If this weren't a PivotTable it would be =C5/B5.

That difference means that even as the table is updated and values move around, this calculation will continue to use the values for profit and units for Author A.

The way the calculation is structured makes it impossible to quickly create and copy a formula that references cells in a Pivot Table. You have to create the calculation one row at a time. (Or use a calculated field in the table like we just did, or do what I often do which is build the table, copy and paste special to turn it back into only values and then do the extra calculation.)

Okay. On to the next one.

Change Data Source

Change Data Source can be found in the Data section of the Analyze tab. It allows you to change the data that is being used in your current PivotTable.

Even when I use the top left corner of a worksheet to tell Excel to Select All of my data to build a PivotTable what Excel actually does is finds the limits of my existing data and defines the data range to use that way.

So, for example, with the latest data set we were working with, Excel gave the data range as 'Pivot Table Data 3'!$A:$I.

That's saying that the data in use was coming from a worksheet named Pivot Table Data 3 and Columns A through I of that worksheet. But what happens if I add on more data into Column J? Or Column K?

Excel will not automatically pick up that new data. If I don't want to start over with a new PivotTable, I have to go in and change the data source instead.

To do so, go to the Analyze tab, click on Change Data Source and then Change Data Source again in the dropdown menu.

That will open a Change PivotTable Data Source dialogue box.

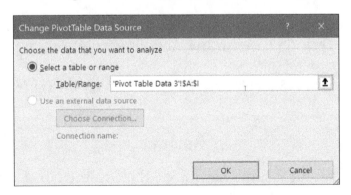

In this case, if I just wanted to change the range to include Column J, I could quickly click into that box and replace the I with a J and then click on OK. Once I did that my new field name would appear in the PivotTable Fields task pane

Another option is to use the backspace key to delete the current range, and then select your whole data range again.

Whatever you do, do not click into that space and try to use the arrow keys. If you do that, click cancel and try again. (When you use the arrow keys you're actually moving your cursor around within the data set and Excel is updating the data range to use but it's doing it one cell at a time. You could fix this by arrowing to the edge of your data set and then using the shift key as you select the rest of your data, but I find it easier to never go down that road in the first place.)

Refresh

We already discussed that you can use the Refresh option in the Data section of the Analyze tab to update the data in your table in case a change was made in the data set that Excel was pulling from.

I'm just going to make one more point here, which is that if you generate your PivotTable and find that there's an issue, for example, customer Albert Jones was entered as Albert Jones and Albert R. Jones, it's better to update the source data for your table than to try to manually fix it within the PivotTable. Manually fixing it fixes it just that one time. Updating it in the source data fixes it for life.

(Of course, in that kind of situation I would recommend having the raw data somewhere that you never ever touch and then the working data stored somewhere that you can fix. Just document what you've done.)

Clear

If you want to keep the PivotTable but start over fresh by removing all fields and settings, you can click on Clear in the Actions section of the Analyze tab, and then choose Clear All

To clear just the filters you've applied to the table, click on Clear and choose Clear Filters.

Select

The Select option in the Actions section of the Analyze tab allows you to Select the entire PivotTable, just the labels, or just the values. Click on Select to see the dropdown menu of your options.

Initially your only choice will be Entire PivotTable which will highlight all of the cells in the table, including any filters.

You can then choose Labels or Values from the dropdown and it will confine your selection to just the labels in the table or the values in the table. (There is also a Labels and Values option but that appears to be the same as Entire PivotTable.)

If you had a PivotTable on a worksheet with a bunch of other information and just wanted to copy that PivotTable, this option would let you do that.

Move PivotTable

The Move PivotTable option in the Actions section of the Analyze tab allows you to move your entire PivotTable to a new worksheet or another location in the current worksheet. This is useful when you have other data in the worksheet and want to just move the PivotTable.

(When I was playing around with all of this I couldn't insert rows because of a PivotTable in an existing worksheet and used Move PivotTable to put that table elsewhere.)

Insert Slicer

Insert Slicer basically works like a filter except that the criteria you can choose from are visible on the screen in a separate dialogue box.

To insert a Slicer go to the Analyze tab under PivotTable Tools and choose Insert Slicer from the Filter section. That will bring up a list of your available fields, click on one and a slicer will appear on the screen that lists all of the values for that field.

Here I've created a Slicer for Title and then selected just Title B. You can see that the PivotTable updated to show that.

To select more than one field you can use the shift or control keys or you can click on the multi-select option at the top. It's the list with the checkmarks next to each line. After you select that, you can click on all the fields you want without needing to use Ctrl or shift. If you use multi-select, click on it again to turn it off.

To clear your selection, click on the funnel image in the top right corner of the slicer box or use Alt + C. (You may have to click on it more than once depending on where you were before you tried to click on it.)

You can also have more than one slicer open at once.

When you have a slicer open and are clicked onto it, there will be a Slicer Tools Options tab available that lets you format the slicer and determine its position on the page.

Slicers can be useful if you want to filter your data by more than one value and want to see what values you've chosen since in that case the standard Filter option would just show Multiple.

It can also come in handy if you are giving access to the PivotTable to other users and you want them to be able to click on the available choices without having to use a Filter dropdown.

To remove a slicer, click on it and then hit the delete key.

Insert Timeline

Insert Timeline works with date fields and lets you narrow down your results by month, quarter, year, or day.

This is very handy for data where you have just the date (8/9/15) but want to see the data by month or year without having to add new fields to your original data source. (And certainly beats my old method of filtering by date and then checking/unchecking boxes.)

Here is a timeline from our second data set which included Date of Sale:

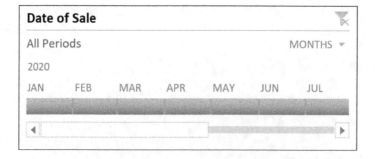

You can either click on those individual months to see the data for a specific month or that dropdown on the right can be changed to show years, quarters, or days instead.

I have at times found Excel didn't want to acknowledge a field as a valid date field, but when it does, using the timeline is very helpful

* * *

Alright.

Hopefully that was a good, solid beginning with respect to pivot tables. If you want to go further with them, your best bet is the Microsoft help options.

Charts – Discussion of Types

Charts are a great way to visualize your data. They take a big pile of numbers and turn them into a pretty picture. And, like they say, a picture is worth a thousand words.

I'm pretty good at recognizing patterns if you let me skim an entire data set, but a chart can show what I feel is true (such as that a large percent of sales are coming from one source) with just a few clicks and a big block of color.

Data Format

First things first, your data needs to be arranged properly to create a chart.

Specifically, for most of the charts we're going to discuss, you need one set of labels across the top and one set down the side with values listed in the cells where those two intersect. Do not include subtotals if you can avoid it (you'll have to select around them if you do) and same with grand totals (you'll have to leave them out when you choose your cells). Also, don't include anything in the top left corner of the table where the row labels and column labels intersect.

Here are two examples which would work equally well for this data set.

DATA TABLE OPTION 1						
	201701	201702	201703	201704	201705	201706
Amazon	$100.00	$107.00	$114.49	$122.50	$131.08	$140.26
Createspace	$37.00	$39.59	$42.36	$45.33	$48.50	$51.89
ACX	$23.50	$25.15	$26.91	$28.79	$30.80	$32.96
Con Sales	$10.00			$25.00		$8.00

DATA TABLE OPTION 2				
	Amazon	Createspace	ACX	Con Sales
201701	$100.00	$37.00	$23.50	$10.00
201702	$107.00	$39.59	$25.15	
201703	$114.49	$42.36	$26.91	
201704	$122.50	$45.33	$28.79	$25.00
201705	$131.08	$48.50	$30.80	
201706	$140.26	$51.89	$32.96	$8.00

This is fictitious sales data for each month for various sales platforms. In the first example, the sales channels are listed down the side and the months are listed along the top with the intersection of those two showing the dollar value of sales for that sales channel for that period.

In the second example, each month is listed down the side and each of the sales channels is listed across the top.

How you format your data can impact how your data appears in your charts, especially if you add in a data table which we'll discuss later, so I highly recommend formatting the data in your source table. For example, when looking at my revenue numbers, I don't need to see the cents portion of the value so I usually format my currency entries to remove that.

Alright.

Let's walk through the basics of creating a chart and then we'll discuss the different chart options and what they look like.

Create a Chart

To create a chart from your data, highlight the cells that contain your labels and your values. Remember, do not include any subtotal rows or grand total rows.

If your data is not connected, so you can't just select a single range of values, you can use the Ctrl key to select non-continuous rows or columns.

To do this, select your first range, hold down the Ctrl key, and select your second range. Continue on doing so until all of your data is selected.

Just be sure that each of the selected ranges has the same number of rows or columns so that if they were put together they would form a table with an even number of rows and columns

(The reason this matters is for data integrity, because there's no way to know in your chart whether you're missing results for a particular combination of criteria because it doesn't exist or because you simply didn't select the proper cells. Both will look the exact same in your chart.)

Once you have your data selected, go to the Charts section of the Insert tab and click on the dropdown menu for the chart type you want, and then choose your chart from there. The chart will appear in a new window on top of your worksheet.

Clicking on Recommended Charts in that same section will bring up the Insert Chart dialogue box.

Clicking over to All Charts will show you every available chart type Excel has to offer, listed by category.

If you've selected a set of data that Excel understands (i.e., connected rows and columns) then when you click on Recommended Charts the Recommended Charts tab in the Insert Chart dialogue box will show a handful of charts that Excel thinks match your data. Like this example for our data table on the last page.

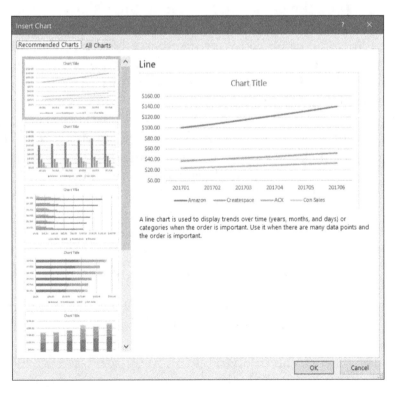

This can be a convenient starting point if you're not sure how you want to display your data. (We will walk through the most common types of charts in a moment after we finish discussing how to create a chart.)

If you're not sure what chart you want, in the Charts section of the Insert tab if you hold your mouse over each chart selection the chart will appear in a separate window so you can easily tell whether it's what you want before you make your selection. But you need to actually click on your selection for it to stay.

Which Chart To Choose

The general rule when choosing a chart is that for time series data like the examples above that include multiple variables (your sales channels) across multiple time periods (each month), the best choices are column charts, bar charts, and line charts.

For data where you have multiple variables but no time component (like total sales for the year), a better choice is a pie or doughnut chart.

Scatter charts are good for random data points where you're looking at the intersection of two or three variables to see if there's any sort of relationship between them.

Histograms allow you to bucket your results so that you can look at how many results you have in a specific range of values. This can often let you see a normal distribution of results, for example, where the majority of the values fall in the center with outliers in either direction.

Excel does offer additional chart types like treemaps, sunbursts, bubble charts and radar charts, but we're not going to cover them in this guide. If you need a chart like that you'll know how it works in general and hopefully our walkthrough of the most common chart types here will let you figure out how to create what you need.

Okay then. Time to discuss Column Charts, Bar Charts, Line Charts, Pie and Doughnut Charts, Scatter Charts, and Histograms in more detail.

Column and Bar Charts

Excel has switched things up a bit for Excel 2019 and now column charts and bar charts are combined under one dropdown in the Charts section of the Insert tab.

(Previously they were treated separately. In the Insert Charts dialogue box they still are. But since they're basically the same thing with the exception that one is horizontal and one is vertical, it kind of makes sense to combine them.)

To create a column or bar chart highlight your data, go to the Charts section of the Insert tab, and click on the dropdown arrow for the top left chart option.

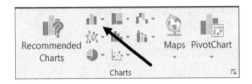

You will then see a dropdown menu with a series of choices. The first two sections are for column charts, the second two sections are for bar charts.

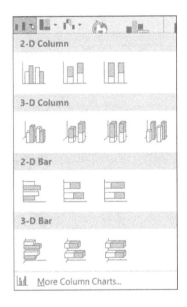

We're going to ignore the 3-D options. They're basically the exact same as the 2-D options just with that three dimensionality (which honestly, truly is probably not needed outside of consulting presentations or annual reports.)

The final 3-D option is a more advanced chart type that creates a three-variable graph, and we're not going to cover that in this guide. (Consider it an Advanced Excel Topic.)

With column and bar charts Excel gives you three choices of chart type. You can choose from clustered, stacked, and 100% stacked.

The clustered option puts the results for each variable (sales platform in the below example) side-by-side for each observation (month in the below example).

You can easily see the height difference between different results, but it can quickly become too busy if you're dealing with a large number of variables.

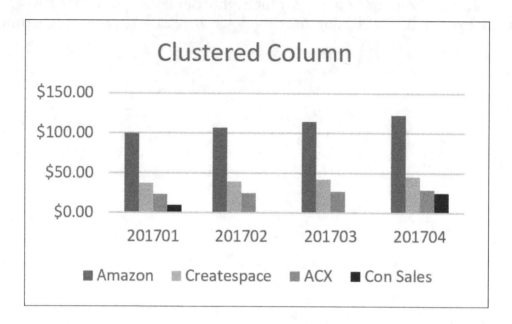

The bar chart version is basically the same thing except the bars are horizontal instead of vertical. The observations move from bottom to top instead of from right to left like in the column chart.

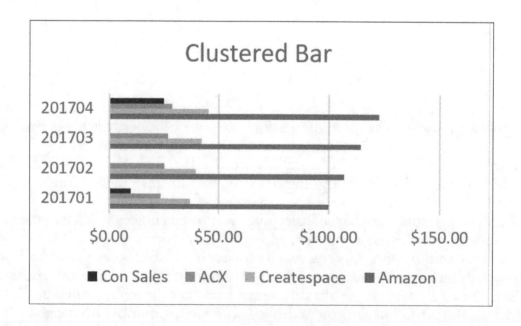

When you have a large number of variables, like I do with my sales channels, then the stacked option is a better choice.

Like with the clustered option, the stacked option has bars of different sizes for each variable based on their value relative to the other values in the chart, but this time the bars are stacked one atop the other instead of shown side-by-side.

So you end up with only one column or bar per time period but you can still identify which one is the largest value based upon the portion of the column or bar it takes up. Like in this Stacked Column chart where Amazon clearly dominates:

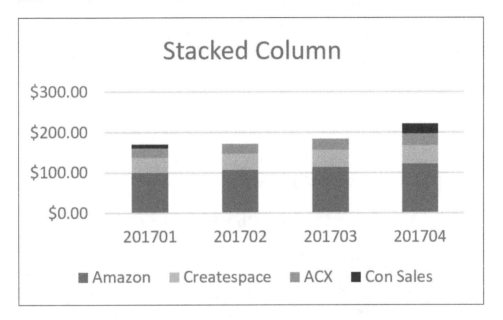

The stacked option is good for showing the overall change from time period to time period.

The 100% stacked option presents all of the information in one column just like the stacked option does. But instead of basing each section's height on its value, it shows the percentage share of the whole which means every single column or bar is the exact same height (which represents 100%).

While you lose any measurement of value (a column chart with values of 2:5:5 will look the exact same as one with values of 20:50:50 or 200:500:500), you can better see changes in percentage share for each variable. (A variable that goes from 10% share to 50% share will be obvious.)

This is an example of the same data as above but in a 100% Stacked Column chart.

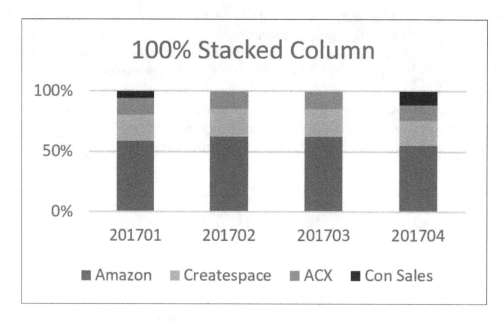

The stacked and 100% stacked bar charts are basically the same as the column chart equivalents except the bars are horizontal instead of vertical.

Line Charts

Line charts are the first chart type shown in the second row of choices. In Excel 2019 they have been combined with area charts, which we're not going to cover.

We're also not covering the 3-D options. And I'm actually only going to cover two of the six 2-D options.

(The other four are meant to do what the stacked columns graphs do and show relative values. I have seen them used by epidemiologists this year to explain data, but I think they're generally counterintuitive unless set up properly with shading under each line.)

So for our purposes all we want are Line and Line with Markers which are the first and the fourth choices.

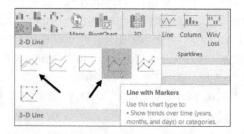

The difference between the line chart and line chart with markers is basically whether there is a point on the line for each observation or not.

Here they are for our data set where we've chosen to chart amount earned per period for four time periods for our four sales channels.

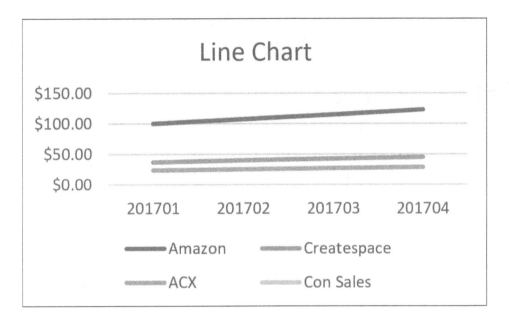

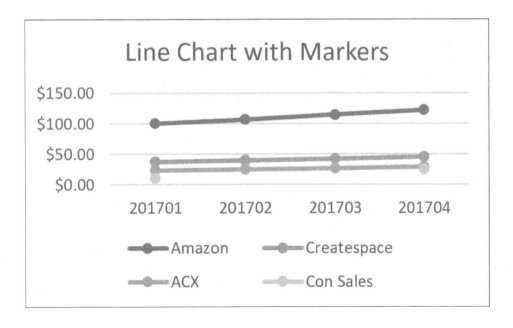

Alright, so that covered the three primary options when dealing with time-series data. But what about data that is all for one time period. For example, sales in a given month or in a given year. That's when the next chart types can be used.

Pie and Doughnut Charts

Pie and doughnut charts are best used when you have one set of observations and want to see the share of the total for each value.

The pie and doughnut chart option is at the bottom on the left-hand side of the chart options. In the dropdown you'll see one 3-D choice as well, but we're just going to use the 2-D ones.

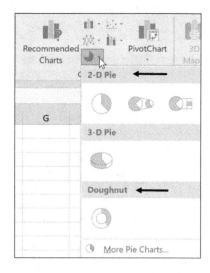

For the pie charts, you can choose between a standard pie chart, a pie of pie chart, or a bar of pie chart. The doughnut chart just has the one option which is the equivalent of the basic pie chart.

If you're only focused on who or what accounts for the biggest share, then use the standard pie chart or the doughnut chart. Each one will assign a section based on relative value for that category. (So share of sales for the period for each sales channel, for example, where the circle is equal to 100%.)

If you want to be able to clearly see the results for all of your segments, even the smallest ones, then the pie of pie chart or the bar of pie chart are potentially better choices. (Although I'm not a fan of either one, to be honest.)

Now let's look at examples. I've used the 201701 data to build each of these.

Here are the basic pie and doughnut chart:

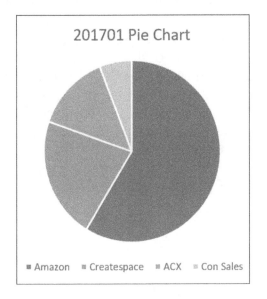

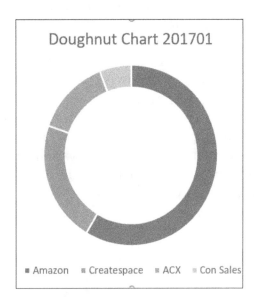

Each chart took the values for a channel (Amazon, CreateSpace, ACX, Con Sales) and assigned it a slice of the pie or circle based upon its relative share ($100, $37, $23.50, and $10) of the whole.

The only difference between the two is that a doughnut chart is hollow in the center.

Now on to the pie of pie charts and the bar of pie chart. Here is an example of a pie of pie chart:

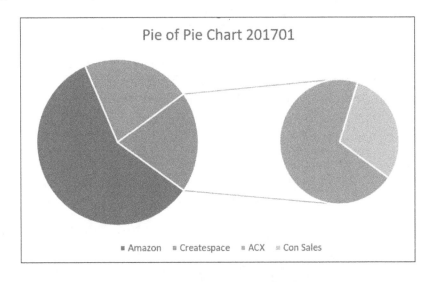

The pie of pie chart creates one main pie chart in which it combines the smaller results to form one segment. Those smaller results are then broken out into another pie chart of their own.

So in the chart above we have ACX and Con Sales that are represented in the main pie chart as one "slice" alongside the other two slices for Amazon and CreateSpace. Those two channels, ACX and Con Sales, are then broken out in their own pie chart on the right-hand side where the size of the slices is base don their value relative to one another. So even though they only represent about 20% of the total between them and Con Sales are only 1/10 of Amazon sales that's not obvious from the way this data is displayed.

The bar of pie chart does the same except it breaks out the smaller results into a stacked bar chart like so:

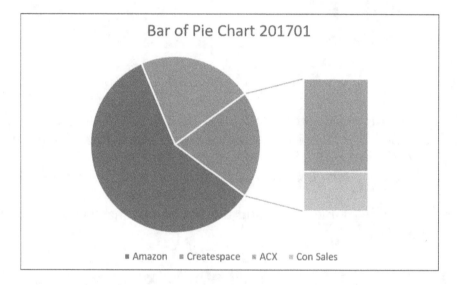

In order to avoid confusion I think the bar of pie chart is probably the better choice of the two since it more clearly distinguishes that it's a subset of data, but honestly I wouldn't use either one if I could avoid it.

(The best charts can be read without explanation and I'm not sure that would be true for either the pie of pie chart or the bar of pie chart for your average user.)

Scatter Charts

Scatter charts (or scatter plots) are the second option on the bottom row of the chart types.

Scatter charts plot the value of variable A given a value for variable B. For example, if I were trying to figure out if gravity is a constant, I might plot how long it takes for a ball to reach the ground when I drop it from varying heights. So I'd plot time vs. distance. From that I could eventually see that the results form a pattern which does indicate a constant. (Thanks high school physics teacher for making physics fun.)

There are five scatter plot options.

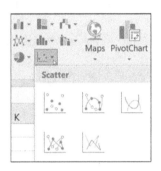

The first one is a classic scatter plot. It takes variable A and plots it against variable B, creating a standalone data point for each observation. It doesn't care what order your entries are in, because there's no attempt to connect those entries to form a pattern.

Here we have some sample height and time values that we've plotted using that first Scatter option. There is a clear pattern to the data that will be much more obvious if we change the chart type to connect those points.

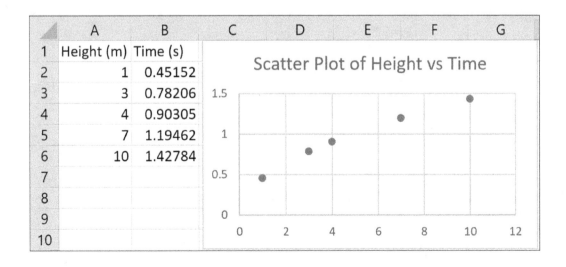

That's where the other four scatter plot options comes into play. They all include lines drawn through the plotted points.

The two smooth line options try to draw the best curved line between points. The straight line options just connect point 1 to point 2 to point 3 using straight lines between each point.

The charts with markers show each of the data points on the line, the charts without markers do not.

Now. One quirk of Excel is that it draws the line from the first set of coordinates in the data table to the next set of coordinates.

This introduces another factor into the table since the order of your data impacts the appearance of your chart.

If the order in which you recorded your observations does not matter, like in this example where it doesn't matter if I drop a ball from 1 meter or 10 meters first, then you should sort your data before plotting it.

In the chart above, because there were no lines to connect the dots whether the data was sorted or not didn't matter. But here's that same data in random order and with a smooth line connecting the data points.

This one has markers so you can still see the curve in the underlying data, but if I were to take those out it would just look like a giant scribble on the page.

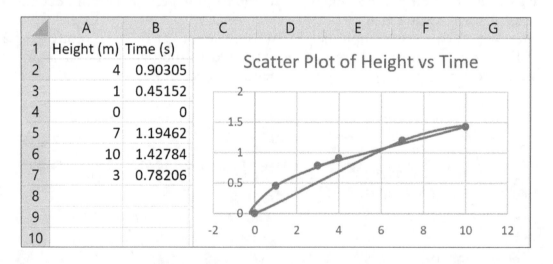

Here is that same data now sorted by height. (I could have as easily sorted by time.) I've used the same plot type of smooth line with markers so you can see the difference.

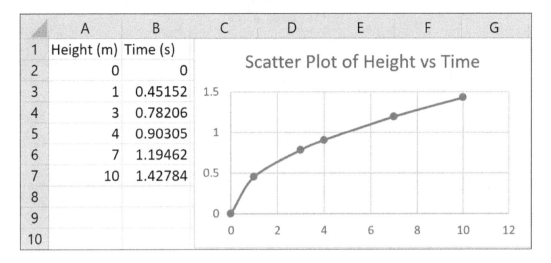

Okay. That was an example with just two data points in it. But you can map multiple sets of data in a basic scatter plot by adding another column of data. The first column will serve as your control value and then the next two columns are the values you're plotting against the control values.

For example, let's say you have sales numbers for two car sales representatives for the first four months of the year and want to compare them to one another.

Here is our data as well as a scatter line plot with straight lines and no markers.

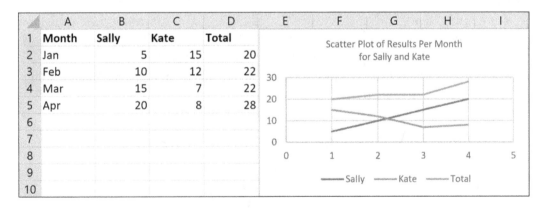

The lines let you clearly see the trend for each of the three categories. Sally is doing better each month, Kate has been doing worse. For the total between them there was a slight increase in the last month measured.

You can technically do a plot like this without plot lines. Each data point will be color-coded, but I don't recommend doing so. It's not near as easy to interpret as the versions with lines connecting related observations.

Histograms

On to one I didn't cover in the original *Intermediate Excel* because it's relatively new but that I think is useful enough that we can cover it here. And that's histograms.

In Excel 2019 the histogram option is located under the center chart choice, Insert Statistic Chart. It is the top choice under that dropdown.

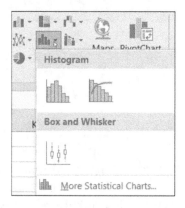

A histogram is perfect for seeing the general distribution of your data results. Rather than plot individual points what it does is buckets your values together into ranges called bins.

So, for example, instead of treating 31, 32, and 33 as separate values a histogram might have a bin for any value between 30 and 39. This can let you more easily see where your values cluster together without getting lost in the minutiae.

Here's our example. I've made up a series of high temperatures for January for a random location similar to Colorado.

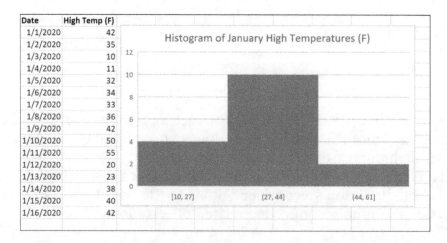

You can see that the range of values has been put in three bins by Excel and that the majority of the values fall into the center bin which contains all values between 27 and 44. The height of each bin is based upon how many values fall into the given range.

(We'll talk next about editing charts. In the chart formatting task pane for a histogram you can set the bin width and/or the number of bins.)

Okay?

Now that you understand the basic chart types, let's talk about how to edit your charts to get them to look exactly like what you want.

Charts - Editing

Chances are, once you've created a chart you'll want to edit it. With the sample charts I showed you in the last chapter I edited the name of each one, resized them, and moved them. But you can do much more than that and we're going to walk through a lot of those options now starting with the Chart Tools Design tab.

Chart Tools Design Tab

The Chart Tools Design tab is only available when you're clicked onto a chart. Once you do so the Chart Tools Design and Format tabs will appear to the right of the Help tab.

We're going to discuss the Design tab and the options on the right-hand side first because these are the ones you can use to fix a chart that doesn't seem to be working the way you expected it would.

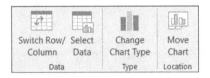

Those options are Switch Row/Column, Select Data, Change Chart Type, and Move Chart.

Switch Row/Column

Once you've created your chart you may find that the data you wanted along the bottom is along the side and the data you wanted along the side is along the bottom. Or even that the data you thought should be in the chart as the results isn't in the chart but is instead along one of the axes.

The first way I try to fix this is by click on Switch Row/Column data. Often that does it. (If that doesn't work then you'll need to consider whether you've selected the correct data and whether the chart type you're using is the right one.)

Select Data

If you realize that the data in your chart isn't what you wanted, you can either delete the chart and start over, which is sometimes the easiest choice if you've done nothing to customize the chart yet.

Or you can go to Select Data and change the data you've selected.

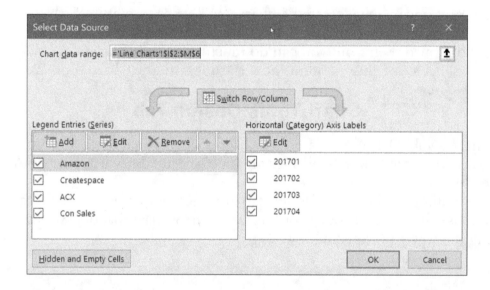

When you click on Select Data this will bring up the Select Data Source dialogue box. You can also see on the screen in the background the selected range of cells that are being used in your chart.

The chart data range at the top shows the selected cells that are being used in the chart. You can manually edit this by clicking into the box with the cell range or edit it by clicking on your worksheet and selecting a new range of cells there.

(I usually use another method for this, which is to click on my chart until I see my selected range of data highlighted and then to click and drag on the square that appears at the edge of the selected range until my new data is also selected.

On my screen those squares are purple, red, or blue and I usually want the purple one that is at the bottom of my left-hand labels. I click and drag down to add more rows of data to the range or drag up to remove rows from the range of data selected.)

If the problem is that you included a category you didn't want to include, like Grand Total, you can also just uncheck that category in the bottom section. For example, under Legend Entries for this table I could uncheck any of the sales channels to remove it from the chart or under Horizontal Axis Labels I could uncheck any of the date values to remove that date range from the chart.

To permanently remove one of the Legend Entries, select it and choose Remove. That will automatically update your data range above as well.

To add a series, you can also click on Add, give the series a name or click on the cell that contains that name already, and then in the series values field select the data to include from your worksheet.

To edit a series under Legend Entries, select the series you want to edit, click on Edit, and then change the selected cells or the name to what you want.

To change the order of the series elements, click on one of the elements and use the up and down arrows.

Change Chart Type

Sometimes you realize that the chart type you chose is the wrong one. Maybe you chose a stacked columns chart and realize that the 100% stacked columns chart is the better option. One way to change to the new chart is to click on Change Chart Type in the Chart Tools Design tab.

That will bring up the Change Chart Type dialogue box with the All Charts tab showing. If you're not sure what you want, you can see suggestions on the Recommended Charts tab that we talked about before. Or you can just select the chart you want from the All Charts tab.

(Another option is to go to the Insert tab and choose a new chart type from there. That will work, too.)

Move Chart

I will confess I never use this. But if you want to move a chart to a new worksheet you can click on that chart and then click on Move Chart and it will give you the option to move the chart to a new worksheet or an existing worksheet in the current workbook.

I usually just select the chart, copy or cut, go to the new location, and paste it.

(We'll talk in a few pages about how to move a chart around within a worksheet, but for now let's finish up with the Design tab.)

The left-hand side of the Design tab (below) is more about the appearance of the chart. I'm going to work from right to left because the left-most option will take an entire page or two to explain.

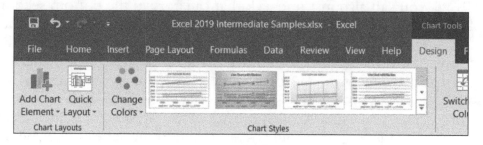

Chart Styles

Excel 2019 provides a number of pre-defined Chart Styles you can choose from.

The number of choices varies depending on the type of chart, but there are usually a variety with different colors and chart elements included or excluded.

In the screen shot above, you can see four examples for a line chart. On the left-hand side of those four options is a scroll bar that will allow you to see even more options.

If you want to see what a style will look like before you choose it, just hold your mouse over it and your chart will update to show the style. Once you find a style you like, click on it and Excel will apply that style to your chart.

I'd say that for me none of the chart styles are ever exactly what I want, but if one is close it can sometimes be easier to select it and then customize from there, especially if you're not quite sure what Chart Element that style is using that gives the chart the appearance you like.

Change Colors

I actually used this for a few of the chart screenshots in the last chapter because the default colors that Excel uses for charts are blue, orange, gray, and yellow and that doesn't always allow for the best contrast when looking at an image in black and white.

We'll talk later about how to change the colors for each item individually to exactly the color you want, but if what you're looking for is a quick and easy option for other color schemes, then Change Colors is the easiest way to get that.

First, click on Change Colors to see the dropdown menu of options. I count seventeen choices. The first few use a variety of colors, the rest use shades of one specific color.

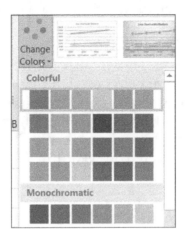

As with Chart Styles you can hover your mouse over each option to see what it will look like. When you find one you like, click on it and Excel will apply it to your chart.

Quick Layout

The Quick Layout dropdown provides a variety of layout options to choose from. The exact number will again depend on the chart type you've chosen.

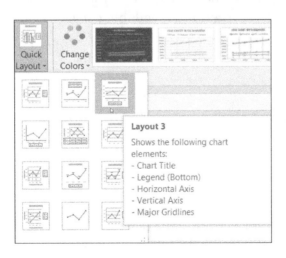

The layouts include various configurations of data labels, axes labels, legends, and grid lines. (One option for scatter charts even includes an r-squared calculation.)

To use a Quick Layout, click on the dropdown and choose the one you want.

Just like with the other quick formatting options, you can hover over each one to see what it will look like before you make your choice. When you do that, as you can see in the above image, it will also list out for you what the different formatting elements are that are being used in that Quick Layout.

If you use a Quick Layout after you choose a Chart Style the color scheme and background colors will stay the same as the Chart Style, but the layout will update. If you choose a Quick Layout and then a Chart Style, the Chart Style will override your Quick Layout, so if you want to combine the two start with your Chart Style.

Add Chart Element

This is the one I use the most. Because I almost always want a data table under my chart so that I can combine the visual chart with the actual results. But there are a lot of other options available here, too.

This is where you go to have more granular control over your axes, titles, data labels, etc.

The options available vary by chart type. If an option isn't available it will be grayed out. For example, Data Table, Lines, and Up/Down Bars are not available for scatter plots.

To see your choices, click on the Add Chart Element arrow. This will bring up a dropdown menu. You can then hold your mouse over each option in the list to see a secondary dropdown menu of available choices.

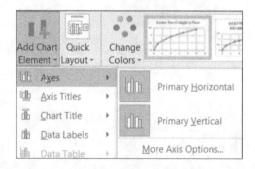

As above, holding your mouse over an option will show that choice on your chart, but you have to click on it to keep it.

If you click on the More Options choice at the bottom of one of those dropdown menus, that will bring up the chart formatting task pane on the right-hand side of the screen which will give you even more control over your charts.

We'll talk about the task pane in a bit. First, let's walk through the options in the Add Chart Element dropdown.

Axes

Axes allows you to add (or remove) the data point labels on each axis.

For example in this chart I clicked on Primary Vertical to remove the vertical axis values which were there by default.

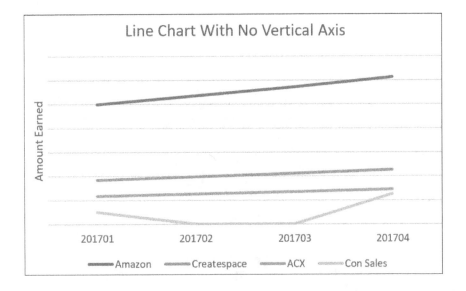

You can no longer see the $ values represented by each line on the chart. You just know that Amazon is much higher than the other lines but not by how much. This could be $5 compared to $1 or $5,000 compared to $1,000.

Axis Titles

Axis Titles allows you to add (or remove) a title for each axis.

In the image above I clicked on Primary Vertical to add a label to the vertical access. I then clicked into the box that was added and changed it to "Amount Earned". The chart above does not have a horizontal axis title.

Chart Title

Chart Title allows you to either (a) remove the chart title entirely, (b) place it at the top of the chart, or (c) place it in a centered overlay position.

All of the examples you've seen so far have the title above the chart.

Data Labels

You can use Data Labels to label each of the data points in your chart.

I find this particularly useful with pie charts and for those will usually choose the Outside End option or the Best Fit option, like below.

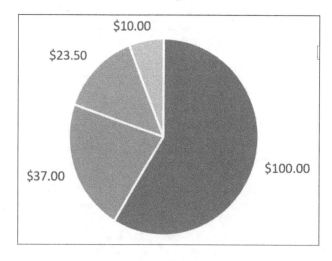

I do sometimes have to click on the labels and drag them to a better location. If you drag them far enough a line will appear connecting the label to its slice.

The default is to show the value, like above, but you can go into the task pane and make that into a percent share instead.

Data Table

Data Table allows you to add or remove a table below your chart that shows the data that was used to create it.

If you're going to do this, you should also at the same time consider removing the legend from the table since you can use the Data Table With Legend Keys option to combine the data table with a legend.

Below is an example of what this looks like with a 100% stacked column chart.

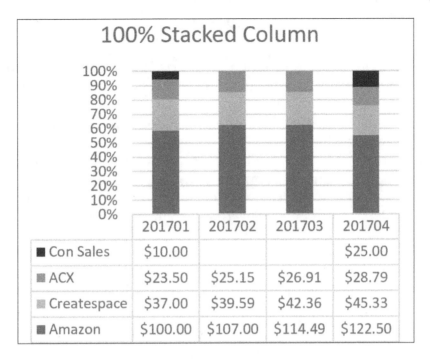

	201701	201702	201703	201704
■ Con Sales	$10.00			$25.00
■ ACX	$23.50	$25.15	$26.91	$28.79
■ Createspace	$37.00	$39.59	$42.36	$45.33
■ Amazon	$100.00	$107.00	$114.49	$122.50

When you add a data table you will likely have to resize the chart and make it taller to get it to look good. Otherwise it tends to get smooshed up into nothing.

In this example I have added a data table with legend keys, removed the legend that was there, and increased the overall height of the chart.

Error Bars

You can add bars that show the standard error, standard deviation, or percentage error in your data. (Usually you would use these if you had a data set that was predicting values and you wanted to show your potential error range. I wouldn't recommend using these on a chart unless you're dealing with data of that type and know what you're doing.)

Gridlines

The gridlines option allows you to add (or remove) horizontal or vertical lines to your chart. These can make it easier to identify the approximate value of a specific point in the chart. There are Primary Major Horizontal gridlines on the chart above.

Legend

The column, bar, line, pie, and doughnut charts that Excel creates come with a legend which is the listing of the categories in the chart and their corresponding color.

(For the charts we looked at earlier, those little boxes with Amazon, CreateSpace, etc. at the bottom were the legend.)

You can remove the legend using this dropdown like I did above, or you can change its position to right, left, top, or bottom.

If you choose top and bottom, the legend elements will be in a row. If you choose right or left, they'll be displayed in a column.

Lines

Lines allows you to add high-low lines or drop lines to a line chart.

Trendline

You can use Trendline to add a line onto your data to see if it fits a pattern like a linear or exponential relationship. Depending on the data set, you may be limited in your choice of lines you can add. Also, beware of using something like a linear trendline on exponential data. Excel will do it, but it's not the best fit for that sort of data.

Up/Down Bars

You can use this to add Up/Down bars to a line graph if you need them.

* * *

Now that you have all of the elements in place, time to discuss how to change the aesthetics of the chart. Things like size, position, and colors. Some of this you can do directly on the chart in the worksheet and some of it requires using the Chart Tools Format tab.

We'll start with a discussion of what you can do in the Chart Tools Format Tab.

Chart Tools Format Tab

Chart Size

You can go to the Size section on the right-hand side of the Format tab under Chart Tools and specify a width and height for your chart.

Be careful because it doesn't automatically adjust both dimensions. So if it matters that you keep your values proportional, calculate that before you make your change.

I usually use the Size option when I want multiple charts to be the exact same size. Otherwise, I actually change my chart size on the chart itself.

In Excel 2019, if you click onto a chart you've created you'll see white circles appear at each of the corners as well as in the middle of each side. Hover your mouse over each of them and you'll see that the cursor turns into a two sided arrow. If you don't see the two-sided arrow, click on one of the circles and hold your mouse over it again and it should work the second time.

Once you see the two-sided arrow, left-click and drag and you can increase or decrease the size of your chart. Click and drag from the corners to change both horizontal and vertical size at the same time.

With either method, all of the elements within the chart will resize themselves automatically to fit the new size.

Shape Styles

The easiest way to change the color of your chart elements like the bars in a bar chart or pie slices in a pie chart is to use Change Colors.

But if those colors aren't sufficient, you can use the Shape Styles section in the Format tab to change the color of each separate element in the chart one-by-one.

To do so, left-click on the element with the color you want to change. In a bar or column chart all sections that correspond to that category should be selected when you do that. If they aren't try double-clicking.

Also, be careful with pie charts because Excel likes to select all of the slices in the pie, not just that one. If that happens, click on the slice you want one more time and it should select just that slice.

Once you've chosen the element to change, you can click on one of the Shape Styles options which change the fill, outline, and text color. Or you can use the Shape Fill or the Shape Outline dropdown arrows to select a fill or outline color.

Use Shape Fill for bar, column, and pie graphs and Shape Outline for 2-D line graphs.

(If you ever create a 3-D line graph be careful, because if you use Shape Outline you'll only be changing the color on the edges of the line, not the entire line. For those you need to use both Shape Fill and Shape Outline.)

If you use one of the Shape Styles that will automatically be applied to your selected chart element as soon as you click on it. You can hover over each option to see what it will look like before you make your choice.

With Shape Fill or Shape Outline what you will see in the dropdown is a selection of colors as well as the ability to use a custom color with More Color.

With Shape Fill you can also use a picture, gradient, or texture. (Just don't go overboard on that, please. My little corporate soul cringes at the idea of how that could be abused to create truly hideous charts.)

With Shape Outline you can change the weight and type of line used. So you could have a dashed line instead of a solid line, for example.

If you don't like the result, remember to use Ctrl + Z to undo and try again.

There's another option in that section called Shape Effects that allows you to add things like beveling and shadows to the elements in your chart, but I'd encourage you to remember that the central purpose of a chart is to convey information to others and that sometimes adding a lot of bells and whistles gets in the way of that. But you do you.

WordArt Styles

For text in your chart you can apply fancy formatting to the text using the Word Art Styles options. Just select the text you want to format and then choose the WordArt Style you want.

You can also change the text color of text using the dropdown menu next to that which is called Text Fill. (The Home tab formatting options work as well but here you can also apply a picture, gradient, or texture instead of just a solid color.)

In the dropdown after that you can add lines of various widths or patterns around your letters. And in the dropdown after that you can add shadow, glow, reflection, etc. to your letters.

Please use sparingly. I know it's not my business but as someone who has been forced to sit through one too many garish presentations, I have to try.

Edits To Make Within A Chart

As mentioned above, there are some edits you can make directly in the chart. We already talked about changing the chart size that way. Now let's discuss a few other options you have.

Move a Chart

If you want to move a chart within your worksheet, left-click on an empty space within the chart, hold and drag. (You may have to click on the chart once and then click again and hold and drag.)

Don't click on an element within the chart, like the title, because that will just move that element around instead of the whole chart. If you do that, like I sometimes do, just Ctrl + Z to put the element back where it was and try again.

If you want to move a chart to another worksheet or even another file (including a Word file or PowerPoint presentation, for example), you can click onto an empty space within the chart and use Ctrl + C to copy it or Ctrl + X to cut it, and then go to the new destination and use Ctrl + V to paste it there.

Move Elements Within a Chart

You can manually move elements within a chart by left-clicking on the element and then clicking and dragging it to where you want it.

You should see a four-sided arrow when you are able to do this. For fields that can be edited or moved like the various title fields, this may require you to put the mouse along the edge of the field before you can click and drag to move.

Rename a Chart

To change the name of a newly-created chart, left-click on where it says Chart Title to select the title. You should see the title is now surrounded by a box with blue circles in each corner. Click into that box and highlight the existing text, delete it, and then add your own text.

If you're just editing an existing chart name you basically do the same. Click on it to see the box, click into the box, make your edits.

Rename a Data Field as Displayed in the Legend

To change the data labels used in the legend, your best bet is to do so in the data table that's the source of the data in the chart. As soon as you do that, the chart legend will update as well. I mention this here because it can be tempting to assume you can do those changes within the chart and you really can't.

M.L. Humphrey

Change Font Properties

If you want to change the font, font color, font size, or font style (italic, bold, underline), another option is to just click on the text element in the chart and then go to the Home tab and change the font options there just like you would with ordinary text in any cell.

Chart Formatting Task Pane

I've alluded to it a few times before, but you may have noticed as you work in your charts that sometimes on the right-hand side an extra box of options appears. This is what I refer to as the chart formatting task pane. There are actually a number of them that appear depending on the chart type and what you clicked on to make it appear.

For example, I'm looking at one labeled Format Plot Area right now. It has that name at the top but right under that is a dropdown menu where I can go to other task panes for that type of chart. Within each of these task panes there are then a few categories of changes that you can make and under each category there are subcategories to choose from that then let you make a series of choices about your chart layout.

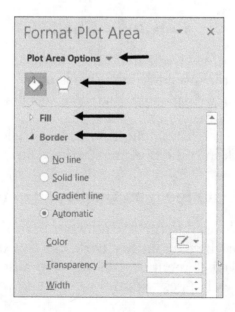

As mentioned before, you can open a task pane by choosing the more options choice for an element under Add Chart Element. Or you can double-click on your chart.

The options you'll be given vary depending on the type of chart and where you've clicked within that chart. You can do things like edit the fill style for chart elements, change the chart border, specify the size of the chart, choose how the text within the chart displays, etc. Basically, all of the things we've already discussed how to do elsewhere. But there are other options that you can only perform in the task pane as far as I know.

For a pie chart this is where I go to change the values shown on the data labels to percentages. (You have to have data labels added already and then it's Label Options, Label Options, and then click on Percentage and unclick Value under that second Label Options section.)

I also come here to "explode" my pie so that there is some space between the pie slices. (Pie explosion is in Series Options, Series Options, and then Series Options again. Move the slider under Pie Explosion to move the slices in the pie apart.)

For a histogram this is where I'd go to change the number of bins or the size of the bins. (Which is under Horizontal Axis, Axis Options, and then Axis Options again. Click on the buttons for what you want to change and the grayed-out values will become editable.)

Basically if there's something you want to do with a chart and you can't figure out where to do it, poke around in the chart formatting task pane.

* * *

Alright. That was charts. Lots and lots to cover, but now we're done and can move on to some much simpler topics.

Remove Duplicate Values

Sometimes I find myself with a data set that has values listed more than once, but all I really care about is the unique values. For example, you might have a listing of client transactions and want to extract from that a list of your client names. You don't need John Smith listed three times and going through and manually deleting those duplicate entries is painful.

Excel makes it very easy to remove duplicate entries using the Remove Duplicates option which is in the Data Tools section of the Data tab.

To get started, highlight the column(s) of data you're working with, go to the Data Tools section of the Data tab, and click on Remove Duplicates.

You'll then see the Remove Duplicates dialogue box which lets you choose which columns to remove duplicates from and also lets you indicate whether or not your data has headers.

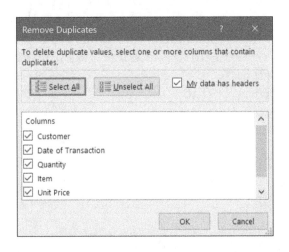

If you say that your data has headers, the first row of data will be excluded from the analysis.

Once you've made your selections, click OK.

You will then see a dialogue box from Excel telling you how many duplicates were found and removed and how many unique values remain.

With a single column selected, Remove Duplicates will return for you one instance of every unique entry in that column listed in continuous rows and all other data in that column will be deleted.

If you choose to remove duplicates from more than one column of data, Excel will consider the values in all of the selected columns when determining if a duplicate exists.

So if you remove duplicates from Columns A and B, Column A could have the same value listed more than once as long as it's paired with unique values in Column B.

Excel is looking for unique combinations of values between the two columns in that case.

It will then return values in the selected columns that are unique combinations of those values and delete extra rows.

If your selected a data range that had more columns than the ones you used to remove duplicates that means Excel may delete other data that wasn't unique. So if Column C had two values for one combination of Columns A and B, Excel only keeps one of them (and doesn't tell you it did that.)

This is a good point in time to repeat one of the key rules to data analysis: Keep your source data untouched. Always work with a copy. You never know when something you do will introduce an error and you won't realize it right away. You need that clean source data to go back to when that happens.

My recommendation on this is that you either use all of the columns in the range to remove duplicates or that you separate the column(s) you care about into a separate data set before you remove duplicates. Do not remove duplicates only using a subset of columns in a data range. It is not pretty. You will lose data that you don't know you lost.

Okay. On to Converting Text to Columns.

Convert Text to Columns

Converting text to columns allows you to take information that's all in one cell and split it out across multiple columns.

The most basic use of this is when you have something like comma-delimited data where all of the data is listed as one long entry with commas separating each piece of information, This happens with .csv files for example, although in modern versions of Excel, Excel does this for you automatically when it opens the file.

I also will use this as a trick to separate data if I just want one component of it or want to separate it into component parts.

For example, I was recently given a listing of employees where the entire employee name for each employee was in one cell with first name followed by last name. So "Bob Smith," "Alfred Jones," "Katie Clark," etc.

Because there was some variation in people's first names (Jim instead of James or a guy whose legal first name was Albert but who went by Dave), I wanted to change that list to one I could sort by last name.

Text to columns allowed me to easily do that by taking those name entries and splitting each one into one column for first name and one column for last name. I was then able to recombine the entries as Last Name, First Name.

Let's walk through how I did that first part:

Before you start make sure that there isn't any data in the columns to the right of the data you want to convert to columns because Excel will overwrite any existing data you have in those other columns when it separates out your values.

If you do have data in the columns to the right of the column you're converting, just insert columns to make space for the conversion. I'd recommend inserting a few more columns than you think you'll need.

(All it takes is one Alfred David Jones, Jr. in your list to create havoc.)

Next, highlight the cells with the data you want to convert, go to the Data tab, and in the Data Tools section click on Text to Columns.

This will bring up the Convert Text to Columns Wizard dialogue box which walks you through the conversion process.

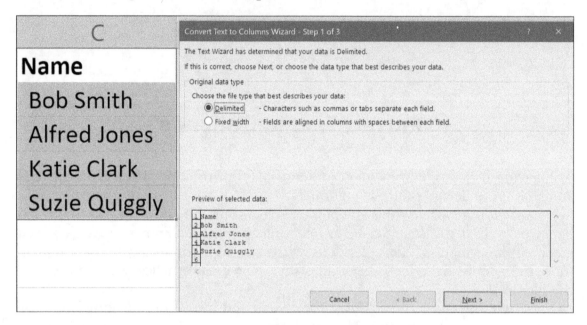

You have two options on the first screen: Delimited or Fixed Width.

Fixed Width lets you split your data into columns based upon number of characters/spaces without any consideration for what the actual content is.

Fixed Width conversion is useful when you have standardized entries that are all built the same way and you need to separate out a portion of those entries. For example, with a customer ID where the first three letters are a location identifier, you could use the fixed width option to separate the location portion of the identifier.

It's also nice because it doesn't require there to be a space or a comma or some other character like delimited does.

Delimited allows you to separate results of different lengths based upon the presence of a specified character or characters like a comma, a space, or a tab.

Once you've selected between Fixed Width and Delimited, click on Next.

This will take you to the second screen where you can set the break locations for Fixed Width or specify the delimiter(s) for Delimited. For both, the second screen has a preview section at the bottom that gives you an idea of what your results will look like.

For Fixed Width the lines you insert on the bottom will show where the data breaks. Breaks can be of any size. To insert a break line just click on the preview at the bottom. To delete it, double-click on the line you created. To move it, click on the line, hold that click and drag it to where you want it. As you drag it will look like a hatched line. When you release your click it will appear in the new location.

For Delimited you need to select at least one Delimiter. Below is the second screen for the Delimited option:

The top section has the available delimiters. These are where your breaks will occur, at each occurrence of the delimiter.

You can choose one or more of the listed options by clicking the checkboxes. You can also list a custom delimiter by using the Other box.

As you do so, the data preview section at the bottom will update to show how your data will be separated. Above I've chosen Space for my delimiter and you can see that there is a line showing between the first and last names where there's a space in my original data.

Any delimiters that you specify will be deleted from the final data. In this example, that means there will be no spaces left in either of the two columns that are going to be created.

On the third and final screen you can specify how each of your new columns should be formatted. If they don't need special formatting just click Finish on the second screen and you're done.

If they do need special formatting then click Next and select each column in the preview section of the third screen to specify your desired formatting (General, Text, Date, or do not import). Once that's done, click Finish.

You should now see that your entries have been split across multiple columns. In our example, "Bob Smith" in Column A becomes "Bob" in Column A and "Smith" in Column B. The space between the words is gone since that was our delimiter.

That scenario was pretty easy but not every scenario you'll encounter will be as simple.

For example, if the names in that list had been written as "Smith, Bob" instead, then I would've had to choose both commas and spaces as my delimiters. Otherwise, if I'd just chosen the comma as the delimiter it would have kept that space between the two words and I would've ended up with both a space and the word Bob in Column B. (If that ever happens to you, a quick fix is to use the TRIM function to trim the excess spaces around words.)

Some data is even more challenging to work with than that and requires multiple steps to convert.

For example, if you have "Smith, Bob, electrical engineer, Colorado" as your text string, you can't just specify space and comma as your delimiters. That would separate electrical engineer into two columns and you'd have significant issues if there were other work titles in your data that were shorter, like auditor, or longer, like senior vice president, because your data would no longer line up.

All Excel knows is what you tell it. If you tell it that spaces and commas are delimiters, that's what it does. It doesn't understand that that third entry is a title listing and that those words need to be kept together.

(In that scenario I'd separate using a comma and then TRIM the text to remove the excess spaces.)

As you can see from the above examples, it's important to always check your data after you convert it.

Limit Allowed Inputs Into A Cell

One of the biggest challenges with analyzing older data sets is that a lot of them didn't use standardized values. For example, one of the data sets I worked with started with paper forms that people completed by hand and that data was then input into a database exactly as it was written. Which meant that for a field like country you ended up with USA, U.S., Unites States, America, and all sorts of creative spellings of those words.

When that happens, it becomes an incredible challenge to do any sort of analysis on that data set. You can't just say, count all entries where country is United States, because you'll miss all those other entries. So then you have to create a list of all the possible variations that mean the same thing or you have to go through and standardize the data.

(Which I have seen backfire as well. That same data set had two separate questions that were merged into one in later forms. When someone went back to standardize the data they overwrote the old answers and made half of them incorrect. Never ever mess with the original data. Always do those sorts of things elsewhere so you can fix your errors when you discover them.)

Anyway. This issue with creative answers is why if you're building any sort of tracking or input form you should try to limit the allowed values to the extent possible.

Things like State and Country are obvious examples. But in the financial services industry you might also limit financial objective or income or net worth to pre-defined values or numeric ranges.

Or, if you want exact numbers, at least limit the input field so that only numbers can be provided. If you don't, you'll end with someone somewhere who puts something like, "Refuse to Disclose" in a net worth field.

So ask yourself, with the data you're dealing with, what can you standardize? Once you know that, if you're using Excel to track this kind of information, you can impose limits on those cells. You do this with Data Validation which can be found on the Data tab under Data Tools. Clicking on that option brings up the Data Validation dialogue box which gives you a variety of validation choices.

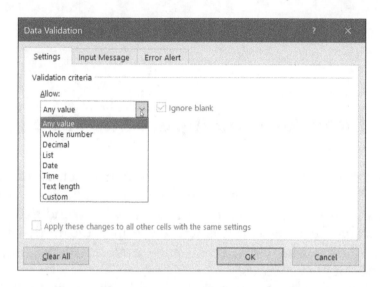

The default is Any Value which lets you enter anything you want into that cell or range of cells.

The Whole Number option limits inputs to whole numbers (so no decimals) within a range of values you specify.

Decimal lets you input a decimal value such as 12.50.

List only allows users to input values that are on a referenced list. This is the one you would use for State, for example, and then elsewhere within the workbook you'd likely have that list on a hidden and locked worksheet. When you have a list in place it also works as a dropdown menu of options to choose from.

Date only allows the user to input a date within a specified range.

Time works the same for time.

Text length allows a user to input any text they want but limits the number of characters allowed. This is where you'd have a text box that allows up to 250 characters of explanation or comment, for example. It could also be used if you have a value that people are supposed to enter that is an exact length.

Custom lets you create custom input criteria. For example, phone number with a set format.

To apply Data Validation to a range of cells, select those cells and then click on Data Validation and then Data Validation again. Choose your validation criteria from the dropdown menu and then enter your additional parameters based upon your choice. Excel does require that you enter parameters.

If you don't care what the range is, you can enter something like a minimum of -1,000,000 and a maximum of 1,000,000 for Whole Number, for example.

But it's a good idea to consider the information you're going to collect and try to use reasonable constraints around what you know about your data. So for Income I might limit the values allowed to a minimum of zero and a maximum of 10 million under the assumption that people don't generally have a negative income and my particular firm isn't dealing with high net worth individuals.

(This is another example though of how a list can be a better choice sometimes. Because with income if I used a list of value ranges my last value in that list could be $10 million + and then I'd cover all possible answers.)

Keep Ignore Blank checked unless you are requiring that the cell have a value in them. It won't give you problems until you input a value in the cell, but once you do if Ignore Blank is unchecked you won't be able to leave that cell without there being a value in it that fits the parameters.

The Input Message Tab lets you tell the user what you want in that cell or give them other directions or information. By default the message will appear when a user clicks onto a cell with data validation if this is in place.

The message will appear with the Title portion in bold and the rest of the text unbolded. Like so:

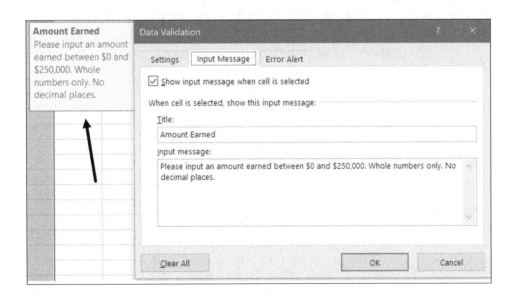

The Error Alert tab lets you generate an error alert when a user inputs the wrong value. You can choose the type of symbol to display (an ex, an exclamation mark, or a small i for information) and then you can enter a title for your error message and accompanying text.

I usually do something like "Invalid Value. Please enter a value that is a whole number between $0 and $250,000."

Click OK once you've made all of your choices.

To remove data validation, highlight the same set of cells, pull up the Data Validation dialogue box once more, and choose Clear All in the bottom left corner. If you're not sure what range of cells have Data Validation, select more than you think do and when you try to open Data Validation you'll see an error dialogue box telling you that you've selected a range with more than one type of validation and would you like to erase the current setting and continue. Clicking OK will clear the data validation from all of those cells.

(Obviously, don't do that with a range where you still wanted to keep the validation in some of the cells.)

One caution about using data validation. Be sure before you limit the inputs into a cell that you've thought through all the possible options. There is nothing more annoying than trying to input valid information and getting an error message and having no way to work around it.

I worked on a large project where we were trying to come up with these sorts of lists and when you really dig in, it isn't always as straight-forward as it seems. There are standardized lists out there for country, U.S. state, and currency code, for example, but sometimes the decision of which one to use is political. For example, do you list Burma or Myanmar? Where do you list Puerto Rico? How about including currencies that no longer exist?

All I'm saying is think it through before you roll it out to your users, test it with them once you do, and then be open to making changes as needed. Unless there's a good reason not to, I like to include an Other option with a free-text field when I'm rolling out a new list. I then monitor to see what gets entered in that field so I can either update the list with an entry I missed, provide education to those misusing the Other field, or accept that there are sometimes one-off situations that will require that Other option to always exist.

Hide or Unhide a Worksheet

To hide an entire worksheet so that other users don't see it when they open the workbook (for example, if you have dropdown lists and you want to use one worksheet for storing them), right-click on the worksheet name and select Hide.

To unhide a hidden worksheet, right-click on the name of any worksheet that's visible, choose Unhide, and then select which of the hidden worksheets you want to unhide from the Unhide dialogue box.

If you combine hiding a worksheet with protecting the workbook, no one will be able to access that hidden worksheet unless they have the password and can unprotect the workbook first.

Lock Cells or Worksheets

Since we just talked about setting up a worksheet for others to use, we should also cover how to lock a range of cells so that users are only editing the portions of the worksheet they're meant to.

For example, I had a worksheet I created once for work where users input values into the first five or six columns and then those values were used in formulas that made up the rest of the worksheet. Because I didn't want anyone to change the formulas, I locked the cells that contained those formulas.

Depending on how you go about it, you can either just lock a cell for editing or you can completely lock the cell so that a user can't even see what's in it.

Again, think about your users and their needs when doing this because it is easy to mess these things up and lock the wrong thing, not lock something that needed locked, or hide information that users actually need to see.

As another example, my company used to have us use some locked worksheets and I seem to recall one where I couldn't see the formula which meant I couldn't figure out how they needed me to enter the value they were asking for. I had to go through trial and error to figure it out. I was not happy with them by the end of that.

Anyway.

To lock a range of cells, first select the cells you want to lock, right-click, and choose Format Cells. In the Format Cells dialogue box, go to the Protection tab and click the Locked box. Then click on OK. In my worksheet the cells were already listed as protected by default, but always good to go through the process anyway. This is also means you may have to unlock cells instead to make things work correctly.

(If you also don't want users to be able to see the formulas used within those locked cells, also click the checkbox for Hidden.)

The cells are not locked at this point. You now need to add protection to the worksheet. To do that, go to the Cells section of the Home tab and click on Format. You should see an option to Protect Sheet. Select it and you'll see the Protect Sheet dialogue box.

You can input a password to lock the worksheet. Be sure you remember it if you do. If you don't input a password then anyone will be able to unprotect the sheet just by going back to the Cells section of the Home tab and choosing Unprotect Sheet from the Format dropdown.

In the Protect Sheet dialogue box there are a number of options for what you can allow users to do even when a worksheet is protected. It's a little backwards since you're choosing what you're willing to allow instead of what you're not willing to allow, but it is what it is.

The default is to allow people to select cells in the worksheet. Unless they shouldn't be copying the information for any reason, this is fine to keep.

I can also see an argument for allowing people to format columns in case they enter a value that's too big for the current column width, which I've had happen with locked worksheets in the past. (It's very annoying to enter a number, see ### instead, and not be able to widen the column.)

What to allow from the rest of that list is a judgment call. I try to lock down as much as I can without interfering with functionality, so I'd probably lock too much and then wait for complaints and fix it then. It very much depends on the environment you work in. Is it better to allow users to do most everything and then find out that they do crazy things like delete the most important column in the worksheet? Or is it better to lock it down too tight and have to fix it when someone complains, which may damage your department's reputation and could, if you have the wrong kind of boss, lead to your boss yelling at you?

That's why beta testing is so important. Make your best choice and then give it to a bunch of users to test for you before you give it to everyone. See what they complain about and adjust from there. (That's the ideal scenario.)

Once you've protected a sheet, you'll see that the options that you didn't allow are no longer available in the menus and dropdowns for that range of cells.

To remove protection from a worksheet just go back to the Format dropdown, select Unprotect Sheet, and provide your password.

You can also add or remove protection on a worksheet or for an entire Excel file (workbook) on the Review tab in the Protect section using Protect Sheet or Protect Workbook.

A Few Tips and Tricks

We're about to wrap up here but there are just a few little thoughts I had as I was going through this that I haven't covered yet but wanted to point out.

Auto Fill Options

In *Excel 2019 Beginner* I covered the basics of copying values in a cell using Copy. But I want to explore another copy option here that I use often.

Every month I transfer the sales reports I receive from each of my sales channels into an Access database. Some of those reports list the date of a transaction. Some list a date range. But what I want is a column with the current month and a column with the current year, so I always add those two columns to my Excel file before I import my data to Access.

One option for doing this is to type in the month and the year I'm working with in the first row of my data and then select those entries, use Ctrl + C, highlight the rest of the entries for those two columns in my data set, and use Ctrl + V to paste the values and then hit enter or Esc. Done.

But sometimes I'm dealing with hundreds or thousands of rows of data and Shift + Ctrl + arrow keys don't properly select the range of cells where I want to copy those values and manually selecting them with the mouse is annoying.

That's where the double-click in the corner trick comes in handy. This is where you double-click in the bottom right corner of the selected cells and Excel copies the results down the rest of the rows for you.

Your cursor should look like a little black plus sign when you're in the right place to do this.

When you use AutoFill like this, Excel will try to find a pattern in your data and will copy down that pattern. So my initial entry for October 2020 turns into November 2021 on the next row and then December 2022 and so on. It's finding a pattern for my month and my year values, which is not what I want.

Fortunately, at the bottom of the entries where it copied down there is an Auto Fill Options box that appears.

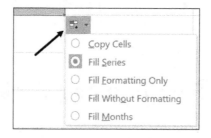

It's tiny and because of how Excel works I can't get a good picture of it, but there's a shaded cell in the top corner with unshaded cells to the side and below and a little plus sign on the right side.

Click on it and you will see a dropdown menu like the one pictured above.

As you can see, the default choice is Fill Series, but click on the button for Copy Cells and all of the values you copied down will now be identical to the first entry.

Fill Months will keep the year column untouched but change the month column. Fill Formatting Only will copy your formatting but nothing else.

Keep in mind that the AutoFill option only fills down as far as your existing data, so this only works when there are existing values in the next column over so that Excel knows how far to go.

Cell Error Messages

There are times when Excel will flag a value in a cell with an error message.

One of the times this happens is when working with formulas and when the formula in one cell is not like the formula in other nearby cells or when it doesn't do what Excel expects like uses values that are not next to the cell and skips the ones that are.

But another type of error message I wanted to talk about here is the error message you may see related to the format of the values in a cell. The most common one of these is "Number Stored as Text".

You will know there's an issue that Excel has flagged when you look at your data and see a green mark in the top left corner of a cell. Usually if it's the number stored as text error you will see this little mark for every single cell in that column. Below is an example of this from one of my vendor reports.

F	G
Consumption Value	Royalty Rate
0.003900	0.250000
0.003900	0.250000

Both of these columns have values that have been flagged by Excel. You can see the four little marks in the corners above the values for both Columns F and G.

To figure out what issue Excel has, click on one of the Cells and you'll see a little alert icon appear on the top left side outside of the cell. Click on that and a dropdown menu will appear.

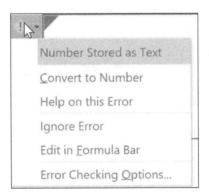

| Number Stored as Text |
| Convert to Number |
| Help on this Error |
| Ignore Error |
| Edit in Formula Bar |
| Error Checking Options... |

The first row in that dropdown menu tells you what the issue is. In this case Number Stored as Text. If you don't care about that, you can click on Ignore Error and the green mark will go away. If you want Excel to convert the value to a number, click on Convert to Number.

To convert all of your cells at once, highlight them all first, then click on the alert icon, and then make your choice about to handle it.

Pinned Workbooks

Another trick I've found useful is pinning a workbook (file) that I use often so that it's always right there and available when I need to open it.

To pin a file you need to have recently opened it so that it's listed in your Recent files section. Once that's true, open Excel or go to the File tab for an open file, find the file you want to pin in the Recent list, and then click on the little thumbtack pin image at the end of its name.

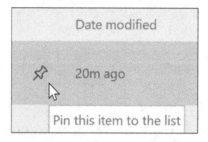

Once you do this, that file will always be available under the Pinned section so that you can easily find it no matter how many files you've opened since it was last used.

To unpin a file, just click on the pin image again.

Quick Access Toolbar

By default the Quick Access Toolbar at the top left of the screen for Excel 2019 includes the icons for save, undo, and redo. But you can add to this list if there are other tasks you complete in Excel on a regular basis that you want to have always available to you.

Just click on that little arrow at the end of the options and then click on the options you want available on the toolbar. More Commands at the bottom of the list will open the Excel Options dialogue box which contains the full list of options you can place there.

The Quick Access Toolbar is available for any Excel file you have open.

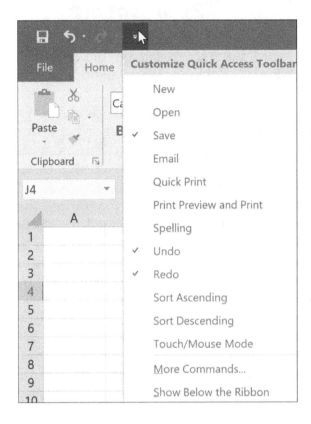

Spellcheck

This is less likely to be needed in Excel instead of Word, but can still be useful especially if you're working with a lot of text.

To check the spelling in your document click on the Spelling option in the Proofing section of the Review tab.

It's going to default to just checking from the cell(s) you have highlighted forward but will then ask if you want to also start checking from the beginning of the worksheet. Usually you'll want to say yes to that.

If it finds a spelling error the Spelling dialogue box will appear and will show you the text that Excel believes is misspelled as well as suggestions for fixing it.

Your choices are to ignore the error once, ignore it always, add that word to Excel's spelling dictionary so it doesn't flag it again, change the word once to the highlighted selection, or change the word everywhere it occurs to the highlighted selection.

Excel Options

I'm not going to go into this one in detail, but under the File tab there is an Options choice at the very bottom. Clicking on that will bring up the Excel Options dialogue box.

This is where you can go to control things like AutoCorrect.

I, for example, usually turn off the AutoCorrect option that turns a (c) into a copyright sign because of my regulatory background where I'm much more likely to be citing a rule violation involving subsection c than I am to be writing the copyright symbol. (That's under Proofing.)

You can also change your AutoRecovery settings under the Save section.

Basically, if there's something Excel does all the time that annoys you, this is most likely the place to fix it. Just be careful doing so because other users who use your version of Excel may expect it to work differently and/or you will expect new versions or other user's versions of Excel to do things for you that they don't do by default.

Zoom

If you want to increase the size of the cells you see in Excel so that the text is easier to read, you can Zoom In. If you want to decrease the size of the cells so that more are visible on the page, you can Zoom Out.

The easiest way to do this for me is in the bottom right corner. You'll see a little slider with a minus on one end, a plus on the other, a darker vertical bar somewhere in between those and a percentage shown off to the right-hand side. You can click anywhere in the space between the minus sign and the plus sign and that will increase or decrease the level of zoom in your worksheet. Left of the vertical bar to zoom out, right of the vertical bar to zoom in.

One thing that is weird about Excel is that only the cells will adjust. So dialogue boxes, dropdown menus, tab options, etc. all stay the same size and the only way to see those as bigger than they are is to zoom your monitor display through Windows (or equivalent) which can make things blurry if you zoom too far.

Another place to go for the Zoom option is the Zoom section of the View tab. You can click on the 100% option to Zoom back to 100% or click on the magnifying glass to bring up the Zoom dialogue box which has preset choices as well as a custom zoom option. Zoom to Selection will zoom in or out to fit the selected cells. If it's just one cell selected it zooms in to a space that's about four cells wide.

Help Options

Alright. What's left is basically formulas and functions which are covered in detail in the next book, more advanced topics like macros and forecasts and data models, which we're not going to cover, and a few one offs like comments that most users are not going to need so we're not going to cover either.

What I've tried to do between this guide and *Excel 2019 Beginner* is cover 98% of what the average reader will need in Excel. And, hopefully, give you a strong enough understanding of Excel that you can find the rest of what you need yourself.

If I did my job right there were times when you read this book where you were like, "Yeah, yeah, go here, do this, just like the last ten times. Got it." Because Excel is arranged in a fairly logical manner. Once you learn the logic it follows it's pretty easy to guess where things will be or how they'll work or if they can be done.

For example, I didn't cover every chart type in Excel, but after walking through the handful we did cover I'm pretty confident you could use one of the other types if you needed it.

But what if you didn't see something in Excel and don't know what it is?

That's where the help functions come in. And they're very good for the most part. A book like this helps because it provides a path to follow, but there's nothing I talk about in any of these books that you couldn't find on your own using Microsoft's help options.

So let's talk about them.

First, most of the options on the Excel toolbar have a description of what they do. All you have to do is hold your cursor over the option and it usually provides a one or two sentence summary as well as a name for the option. It will often also tell you if there's a Ctrl shortcut.

For example, Cut on the Home tab in the Clipboard section says "Cut (Ctrl + X)" and then has a description "Remove the selection and put it on the clipboard so you can paste it somewhere else."

At that point you have a basic understanding of what that particular image lets you do and you know what it's called.

If that isn't enough, some of the more complex options in Excel also have "Tell me more" at the bottom of that description which you can click on to bring up a Help task pane specific to that task. Format Painter on the Home tab is a good example.

That's the best way to pull up help for a specific topic. But to do that you have to already know where the task is.

Your other option within Excel is to click on the Help tab. (Used to be a question mark off in the corner in prior versions of Excel and now it's a tab.) From there click on Help again. That will bring up the Help task pane as well but this time it's the generic start screen.

From that point you can search for your topic or click on the various options such as Get Started, Collaborate, Formulas & Functions, etc.

F1 will also open that generic Help task pane for you.

In Excel 2019 there is now also a Show Training option under the Help tab which gives you access to Excel's help videos and text which used to be mostly hosted on the website.

Some of these are very good and often there is a visual demonstration to walk you through what you need to learn.

If your question is more along the lines of "is this possible" as opposed to "how does this specific thing work exactly.", you can also do an internet search to see if anyone has covered how to do what you want to do before. Usually they have.

So, for example, I had a user ask if it was possible to build a cell that had a slanted line in it and allowed you to input values on either side of that line. Turns out there were a number of blogs that had written ideas on how to do that.

The Community link in the Help tab will also take you to the Microsoft forums where you can ask your question or others have asked theirs.

I tend to advise against asking your own question in tech forums because they tend to attract a certain type of personality more interested in telling people they didn't ask a question properly than in giving an answer. But that's me.

Also, you can always email me (mlhumphreywriter@gmail.com). If I know or can find the answer quickly, I will definitely help out or point you in the right direction. Knowing what wasn't clear enough or wasn't covered but was needed helps me improve the books for the next edition.

And if it turns out you need really detailed help, like someone to do the work of building your worksheet for you, I do have a consulting rate. Although I'm not sure anyone outside of a large corporate environment would want to pay it.

Conclusion

Alright. That's it. That's intermediate Excel. If you want to learn more about formulas and functions, then the next book in the series *Excel 2019 Formulas and Functions* will definitely do that for you. If you want to move on to macros or SQL, I'm afraid you'll have to find someone else to cover those topics.

But I do hope at this point that you feel pretty confident that you can use Excel for day-to-day purposes and to do some more complex data analysis.

Don't be scared to experiment. Half of what I've learned in Excel was because I decided it should be possible to do something and went looking for how to do it.

You can almost always undo it if it goes wrong. Ctrl + Z is your friend.

Also, save a safe version of your file if you're experimenting or building a worksheet with a lot of moving parts.

I do this all the time when initially building a worksheet. I'll figure out Column A's calculation and save a draft of the file. Then I'll take a copy of the file and work on Column B's calculation. And so on and so on until the whole thing is built. That lets me not lose everything if on Column E's calculation I suddenly realize I messed something up that can't be fixed.

By using the YYYYMMDD date format in the file name and version numbers if needed you can easily sort your files by name and find the most recent version. (So 20201101 Sales Revenue Calculation, 20201102 Sales Revenue Calculation v1, 20201102 Sales Revenue Calculation v2, etc.)

Take risks. Try new things. Don't beat yourself up if you get it wrong the first time. This is a learning process and I've sometimes learned the best lessons from my failures.

Alright, then. Best of luck. Reach out if you get stuck.

Excel 2019 Formulas
& Functions

EXCEL ESSENTIALS 2019 BOOK 3

M.L. HUMPHREY

CONTENTS

CONTENTS (CONT.)

CONTENTS (CONT.)

CONTENTS (CONT.)

CONTENTS (CONT.)

Introduction

Mastering formulas and functions in Excel will help you take what you can do with Excel to an entirely new level because many of the functions available in Excel (and we'll define what that means in the next chapter) allow you to shortcut tasks that would otherwise be very tedious or time-consuming.

For example, say you want to take units sold in Column A and price per unit in Column B and you want to determine the total earned across a hundred rows of data. If you did that manually, you'd have to type in =A1*B1 in Column C, copy that down all hundred rows, and then find a way to add all those values together, which, without the SUM function would require writing a formula that said =C1+C2+C3 all the way to +C100.

That's pretty time-consuming.

But there's a function that would do that for you called SUMPRODUCT. With SUMPRODUCT you can just write =SUMPRODUCT(A1:A100,B1:B100) and you're done.

So functions are valuable to learn because they save you a lot of time. And not just with numbers. I love the TRIM function which lets me remove excess spaces from around text entries, an issue that I've encountered more than once over the years, especially when breaking apart grouped data.

Now, are *you* going to need SUMPRODUCT? Maybe not. Maybe you never need TRIM either. Maybe you need some other functions within Excel that I barely ever use. There are certainly a wide variety of them.

That's why I saved formulas and functions for the last book in this series. Because formulas and functions are incredibly useful, but until you have some grounding in Excel you're not going to leverage them the way you could. You won't know what you can and can't do otherwise and how they fit into the bigger picture.

In this book I cover approximately sixty functions in detail and touch upon about a hundred of them.

I've chosen functions most likely to be useful to a wide range of users but even then most users will probably only use two dozen functions on a regular basis, if that. So I can guarantee you right now that this book will cover at least one function you will never use and probably don't care about.

(The problem is, I don't know going in which ones you in particular need so we're going to cover some you don't in order to cover enough that you feel comfortable with all functions by the time we're done.)

Another thing to know before we start is that I am not doing this alphabetically.

I am going to start with ten of the most useful and/or representative functions (in my opinion), then cover the base functions and logical functions you need to effectively work with the various IF functions, and after that cover the actual IF functions. Then we'll move on to a sampling of functions under various categories such as Lookup Functions, Statistical Functions, Math Functions, Text Functions, and Date & Time Functions.

There is an index in the back that lists all of the functions mentioned in this book in alphabetical order if you're looking for one function in particular. The main sixty or so functions are listed in the table of contents up front.

(If you're reading in ebook you should be able to use the search function.)

While not every function will be useful to every reader of this book, at least be sure to read the introductory chapters and the chapters at the end that are generic to all formulas and functions and I do encourage you to read through up to the point where I mention that you can start skipping around.

As with the other books in this series, this book is written specifically for Excel 2019. If you're using an earlier version of Excel, *50 Useful Excel Functions* and *50 More Excel Functions,* which are part of the Excel Essentials series, my original series on Excel, were written to be more generic and are more comprehensive when read together. Functions that get a passing mention here get their own chapter in those books.

For the most part it won't matter which book you read, but this book does cover a few newer functions like IFS and TEXTJOIN that were not covered in those prior books.

Okay then, let's get started.

How Formulas and Functions Work

For purposes of this book, we're going to define a formula in Excel as anything that is started with an equals sign and asks Excel to perform a calculation or task.

(Technically, as discussed in *Excel 2019 Beginner* you can start a formula with a plus or a minus sign as well, but I'm just going to ignore that because unless you're coming from a specific background where you learned to do things that way, you shouldn't do that. Also, Excel transforms those formulas into ones that use an equals sign anyway.)

I'm going to define a function as a command that is used within a formula to give instructions to Excel to perform a pre-defined task or set of tasks.

A function is basically agreed-upon shorthand.

So a formula in Excel could be as basic as:

$$=A1$$

It starts with an equals sign and is telling Excel that this particular cell where we've written our formula should have the exact same value as Cell A1. The "task" Excel completes here is pulling in that value.

But usually a formula will be more complex than that.

Look at the example I gave you above with SUMPRODUCT. (A function so I write it in capitals. All functions in this book will be written with capital letters.)

$$=SUMPRODUCT(A1:A100,B1:B100)$$

Still a formula, because we started with the equals sign and are asking Excel to perform a task. But in this case we've used the function SUMPRODUCT as shorthand to tell Excel that for every row in that range it should take the value from Column A and multiply it by the value in Column B and then should sum the resulting values and return the total.

Formulas can actually combine a large number of functions and calculations. For example the following formula combines two functions, TRIM and CONCAT, as well as four cell references, and four fixed values that indicate spaces:

$$=TRIM(CONCAT(A2," ",B2," ",C2," ",D2))$$

This is still a fairly simple formula. It can get much more complex. But as long as you can build the formula in the right way, Excel will perform all of the tasks you assign it.

The basic rules of building a formula are start with an equals sign and if you needed to use an opening paren make sure that it's paired with a closing paren.

All *functions* require the use of parens. You write the function name, the next thing you include is that opening paren, then you tell Excel the information it needs to perform that function (which varies by function), and then you end with a closing paren.

As you can see above with CONCAT, a function does not have to start a formula. It can and often will, but that is not a requirement.

For example, this is a perfectly legitimate formula that uses a function but starts with a cell reference instead:

$$=A1+SUM(B1:B5)$$

After you enter your formula in your cell, hit enter. (Or leave the cell by arrowing, using the tab key, or clicking away.)

The cell will then display the result of the formula. The formula will remain visible via the formula bar.

To see the formula that was used in a cell (if any), you can click on the cell and look to the formula bar.

Like so where I've clicked on Cell C1 which contains the formula =A1+B1:

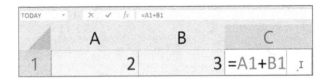

You can also double-click into the cell itself (Cell C1 here) and the cell will display the formula and also highlight any cells used in the formula. Like so:

It's a little hard to see in print, but Cells A1 and B1 are highlighted in colors that match the color shown for their cell references in the formula in Cell C1. This makes it easy to see which cell is being used in which part of a formula, which becomes especially helpful when dealing with very complex formulas.

If you double-click on a cell to see the formula in the cell, exit the cell using Esc, Enter, tab or by clicking away. Do not arrow away because Excel may try to select a new range of cells to use in the formula instead of leaving the cell.

When you exit a cell with a formula, the cell will return to showing the calculated value.

With either method, the formula bar will always contain the formula for the cell you have selected.

Okay. Next we're going to take a quick detour into basic math calculations that don't require any functions at all, but are just simple formulas.

Basic Math Calculations

Alright. Now let's take a quick detour with formulas before we go further with functions and walk through some basic math calculations that you can do without using a single function.

If I want to add two numerical values together in Excel, I could just go to any cell and type the formula into a cell using the plus sign (+) to indicate addition.

So here I'm adding 2 to 3:

$$=2+3$$

If those values were already showing in other cells, let's say Cells A1 and B1, I could write the formula to reference those cells instead:

$$=A1+B1$$

(If you aren't familiar with cell notation in Excel, see Appendix A.)

If I use cell notation, like in the second example there, then any change I make to the values in Cells A1 or B1 will also change the result of my formula because my formula is no longer performing a fixed calculation, like 2+3, but is instead performing a conditional calculation based on what's in Cells A1 and B1.

To subtract one number from another you use the minus (-) sign. To multiply two numbers you use the asterisk (*) sign. To divide two numbers you use the forward slash (/). So:

$$=3-2 \text{ would subtract 2 from 3}$$

=3*2 would multiply 3 times 2

=3/2 would divide 3 by 2

As I mentioned above, your formulas can either use cell references or numbers. So:

=A1-B1 would subtract the value in Cell B1 from the value in Cell A1

=A1*B1 would multiply the value in Cell A1 by the value in Cell B1

=A1/B1 would divide the value in Cell A1 by the value in Cell B1

Those are the most common non-function operators in Excel, but you can also use others such as the caret (^) symbol to indicate taking a value to a power. So:

=2^2 would be 2 times 2

=4^.5 would take the square root of 4

=3^3 would be 3 times 3 times 3

=27^(1/3) would take the cube root of 27

In that last example, by putting 1/3 in parens I told Excel to make that calculation first before take the root of 27.

If you're going to combine calculation steps within one cell, you need to be careful that you properly place your parens so that calculations are performed in the correct order.

There is a help document on this titled "Calculation operators and precedence in Excel" which you can find through the Help tab by searching for "order of precedence".

That help document lists the order in which calculations are done by Excel and also lists a number of operators (such as > for greater than) that are useful to know when working with formulas and functions in Excel. We'll cover those later as they come up in relation to certain functions like the IF function, but they're basically the same as you ran into in math class except you write >= and <= in Excel because there is no combined symbol for greater than or equal to or for less than or equal to.

If you're building a really complex formula it's always a good idea to test it as you go to make sure that all of the components are working properly and that the end result is the expected result. So I will build each component separately before combining them all in one cell.

But do check to see if there's a function that already does what you want. Especially when dealing with common calculations, there just might be. For example, there is a function for calculating net present value.

Also, before we move on to functions, remember the saying "garbage in, garbage out". Excel is not a person. It can't read your mind and know what you meant, all it can do is take what you give it and return the result. So always, always gut check any result you get from Excel. Does that actually make sense?

I will often double-check a complex formula by creating the same calculation two different ways to see if the result is the same.

For example, with the net present value function, when first working with it, I'll also do that calculation old school in Excel using basic math like we just discussed to see if I get the same result both ways. Once I'm comfortable that I'm giving Excel the right inputs, then I can stop doing that.

Also, if you give Excel the wrong kind of inputs or fail to give Excel the inputs it needs, you will get an error message. We discuss the types of error messages at the end, but in the meantime if you do get an error message I'd suggest that you check that the data in your formula is formatted as the right data type, confirm that you have matching opening and closing parens, and verify (for a function) that you provided all of the required inputs. That's usually where things go wrong.

Alright. Next we'll talk about where to find functions in Excel.

Where To Find Functions

In this book we're going to cover approximately one hundred Excel functions, sixty in detail, that I thought were most useful for the largest number of people. But there are far, far more functions than that in Excel, and chances are at some point you'll need one I didn't cover here.

To find the functions available in Excel, you can go to the Formulas tab. There is a section called Function Library that lists various categories of functions. Mine shows Recently Used, Financial, Logical, Text, Date & Time, Lookup & Reference, Math & Trig, and then there's a dropdown for More Functions that shows the categories Statistical, Engineering, Cube, Information, Compatibility, and Web.

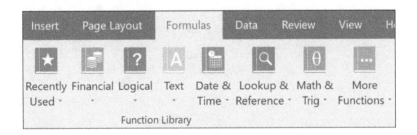

Click on the dropdown arrow next to any of the categories and you'll see a listing of functions that fall under that heading.

Now, unless you know what you're looking for, this listing probably won't help you much because the functions are named things like ACCRINT and IFNA.

You can hold your cursor over each of the names and Excel will provide a brief description of the function for you, but for some of the lists that's a lot of functions to look through.

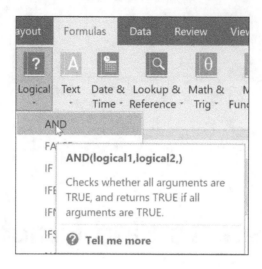

Each description also includes a Tell Me More at the end of the description. If you click on that option, the Excel Help task pane will appear. You can then click on the category for the function (in this case Logical) and then choose the function from the list you see there.

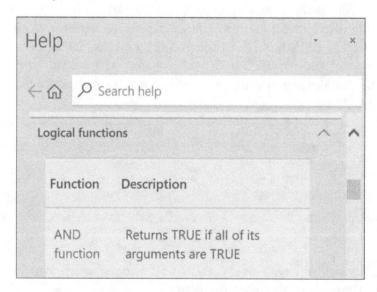

This will bring up an additional set of information specific to that function that will generally include the definition for that function as well as examples and further discussion of how the function works and any limitations it might have. The complexity of the help varies by function.

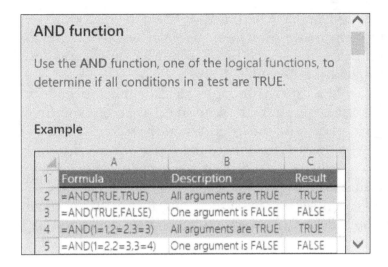

That will give you information on a function, but I do it differently because I'm usually looking to use a function.

Instead, what I do is click into my cell and then use the Insert Function option available on the far left-hand side of the Formulas tab.

Clicking on Insert Function will bring up the Insert Function dialogue box.

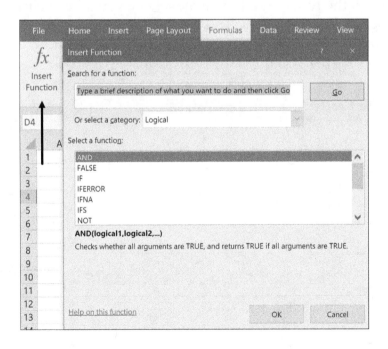

In the top section under where it says "Search for a function" you can type what you're looking to do and then click on Go. (Be sure that the category dropdown right below the search box is set to All unless you know for sure what category your function falls under.)

Excel will provide a list of functions that it thinks meet your search criteria. (Sometimes this list is very far off, so don't just accept the first choice blindly.) You can left-click on each of the listed functions to see a brief description of the function directly below the box where the functions are listed.

You will also see in the description for each function a list of the required inputs for that function as well.

For AND you can see in the screenshot above that it requires at least two logical inputs but allows for more and that it is described as a function that "Checks whether all arguments are TRUE, and returns TRUE if all arguments are TRUE."

For every function we cover in this book I will list that description that you see right there at the very top of the section.

If you need more information on a function, you can click on the "Help on this function" link in the bottom left corner of the dialogue box which will bring up a website specific to that function.

Otherwise, you can just click on the function you want and choose OK.

This will insert the function into whichever cell you'd been clicked into before you chose Insert Function. You will also see a Function Arguments dialogue box that lists the inputs your function needs and provides a location for you to input those values so that Excel can build your formula for you.

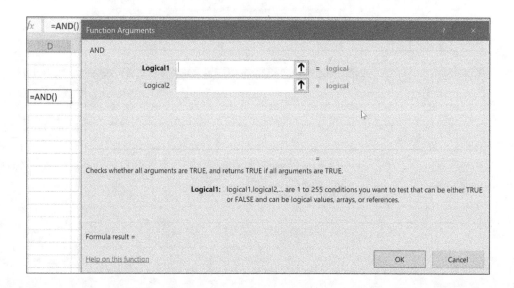

You can use the dialogue box if it helps or close it out by clicking on OK and then OK on the error dialogue box and then typing in the values directly into the formula bar or cell that you want to use which will now contain the function minus its required inputs. So =AND() as an example.

If you use the dialogue box, you can either input numeric values in those boxes or use cell references by clicking on the cells in your worksheet or typing the cell references in.

At the bottom of the list of inputs Excel will show you a sample value based upon the inputs you've chosen. The sample also appears in the bottom left corner of the dialogue box.

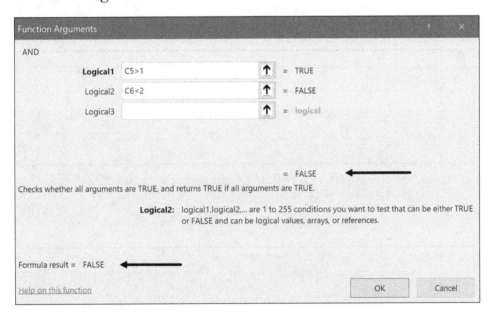

Even with the help of the Function Arguments dialogue box, sometimes you still need to know what a function is doing in order to get a result that makes any sort of sense. In this case, to get the AND function to really work I had to put more than just cell references into the input boxes. I had to give it criteria to apply to those values.

(We'll talk about this more when we discuss the AND function, but what's happening up there is that I'm asking Excel to tell me if both the value in Cell C5 is greater than 1 and the value in Cell C6 is less than 2. Because both of those are not true, the answer it's giving is FALSE.)

If you use the dialogue box, when you're done, click OK and the calculated value will appear in your cell.

You can always go back to the cell and edit the formula either through the formula bar or by double-clicking on the cell.

* * *

If you already know the function you want to use but aren't sure about the required inputs, you can start typing the function into your formula in a cell in your worksheet. As you type the function name Excel will suggest functions in a list below the cell and for the selected function name will show a definition for that function like it's doing below for the AND function.

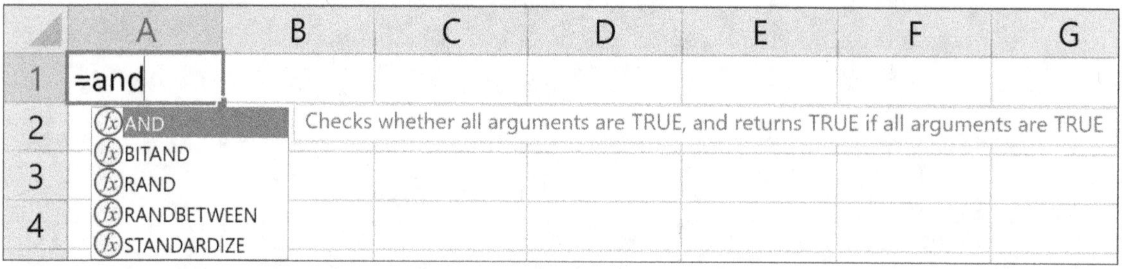

After you type the opening paren for the function you want, Excel will then show the required inputs for that function and their required order.

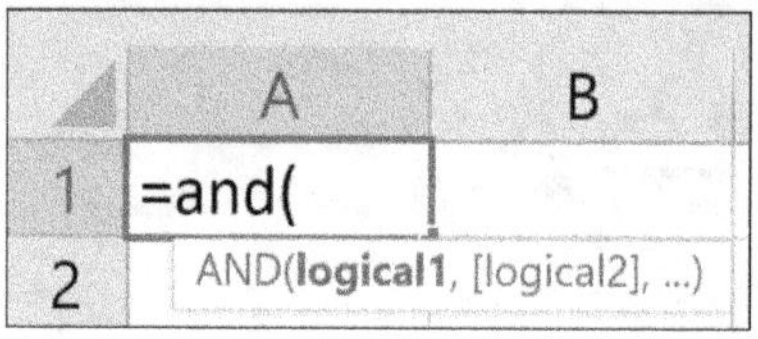

If you click on the function name in that small pop-up box after you've typed the opening paren, Excel will open the Excel Help task pane specific to that function.

* * *

If none of that works to help you find the function you need, then an Internet search is probably your best option.

A quick search for something like "How do I get Excel to identify the day of the week from a date?" will usually get you the answer you need. You can then use one of the above options to learn more.

Best Practices

Now let's discuss a few best practices when it comes to using formulas and functions.

Make Your Assumptions Visible

You can easily build a formula where all of the information to make the calculation is contained within that one cell.

So if I want to add the values 10, 20, and 30 together I can do that in one cell using =10+20+30 and all anyone will see in the worksheet is the result of that calculation, 60.

You may be tempted to do this because it's clean. All that people see is what you want them to, the result of your calculation.

And maybe you don't expect to have to adjust those values so you don't see an issue in having your formula built that way.

I would encourage you not to do this. In my experience, a best practice in terms of building formulas is to have any fixed values or assumptions visible in the worksheet. The reason to do this is so that someone looking at the sheet can see what assumptions fed the calculation.

Here's an example:

Let's say you're calculating how much you'll make if you sell your house. You figure you'll have to spend $2,500 to clean the place up a bit, pay a commission of 5%, and that the house is worth $500,000.

Now, if you sat down to discuss this with your spouse you could just show them the results of that calculation (the value on the left below) or you could show them the results of the calculation and the assumptions you made (the value on the right).

	B	C	D	E
1	**Option 1**			**Option 2**
2			**Home Price**	$500,000.00
3	$472,500.00		**Commission**	5%
4			**Fix Up Cost**	$2,500.00
5				
6			**Net**	$472,500.00

Depending on your spouse, they still might want to see the formula, but at least here they can see the assumed sales price, commission, and fix-up cost and say, "That doesn't seem right. Houses in the area like ours have been selling for $400,000 not $500,000 and the neighbors up the street worked with a great broker who only charges 4% commission."

Without showing them your assumptions, they aren't given a chance to provide their input.

Also, even if it's just for you, if you bury your assumptions in your calculation field they're easy to forget about. That can be dangerous if they're wrong or circumstances change.

Use Paste Special - Values

The other thing I do that you may or may not want to do depending on why you're using Excel is that I frequently use Paste Special – Values when I'm done with performing a set of calculations.

Do not do this if the calculations you performed need to be updated on an ongoing basis.

But I do a lot of calculations where I want to keep the results for reference but will not be recalculating any values, and I want to lock those values down so that I don't lose them or inadvertently recalculate them by changing a value in an input cell or deleting data that fed those calculations.

(Deleting data I used in a calculation to tidy things up and turning my calculation fields into error messages is something I do far too often.)

The simple way to do this is to select the cells, use Ctrl + C to copy, and then right-click and under Paste Special choose the Values option (the one with the 123 on the clipboard). This will replace any calculated cells in that range with just the values of the calculation.

You basically just copy your formulas and paste the results from the formulas right on top.

After you do that, instead of a formula, for example, =A1+B1, you'll have a cell that just contains the result of having added Cells A1 and B1 together. That means if you then delete the values in Cells A1 and B1 it won't change the cell with the result in it.

Don't Mess With Your Raw Data

I mentioned this in the other books, but am going to mention it again here because it is so, so important.

To the extent possible, you should always store your raw data in one location and do all of your calculations and manipulations on that data elsewhere.

(Ideally you would also record all of the steps you followed to take that raw data and turn it into your final product, but it's not as easy to do in something like Excel as it is in a program like R where you are basically writing a script of steps to follow.)

If you don't keep your raw data untouched all it takes is one bad sort or one bad function and your data can be irreparably changed in a way you can't fix after the fact. Usually you can undo if you notice it immediately, but chances are you won't.

If, on the other hand, you keep your raw data separate, there is nothing you can't come back from. You might have to redo a lot of work, but you won't be left with a data set that's useless.

I also save versions of my worksheets when I'm working on something particularly complicated. That way I can go back to a stage where everything was working without having to start over from scratch. Just be sure to label your files clearly so that you know which is the most recent version. (File V1, File V2, etc.)

Test Your Formulas

I think I already touched on this one earlier, but let's cover it again.

If I'm going to apply a formula to a large range of data I will usually test that formula on a much smaller sample of my data where I can visually evaluate the results.

M.L. Humphrey

So if I'm writing a formula to sum customer transactions for customers from Alaska who bought Widgets (using SUMIFS), I'll run that formula against just ten rows of data to make sure that it's doing what I think it should before I apply it to ten thousand rows of data.

As much as possible you should always either check you formulas on a subset of data or "gut check" your results. Don't just accept the value Excel gives you without questioning whether it actually makes sense. (Because garbage in, garbage out. Excel's ability to perform calculations is limited by your ability to write those calculations properly, and we all make mistakes. One missing $ sign or one > instead of >= and the result you get will not be the result you wanted.)

Be especially wary when it comes to edge cases. Those are the situations where you want the results that are equal to or greater than 25, say. In that situation the edge case would be when the value is 25, 24.99, or 25.01. You want to check that those all give the result you expected.

(I personally have a bad habit of wanting 25 or greater and writing the formula as greater than 25 and having to go back and fix it when I realize my mistake)

So, test, test, test. And then check, check, check.

Consider Your Audience

I've said this before and I'll say it again and I will keep saying it forever. When creating anything in Excel, keep your audience in mind. I once created a beautiful workbook that did lots of complex calculations for a consulting client. It was a masterpiece. Only problem was, they didn't have the version of Excel I did and I'd used a function (SUMIFS) that didn't exist in their version of Excel. So that thing of beauty I created? Worthless. I had to go back and re-create the same calculations without using SUMIFS. It was a painful but valuable lesson.

Less likely to happen these days with Microsoft 365, but still something that could happen. So if you're going to share Excel files with people outside your organization be very careful what functions you use to create whatever you're going to share. Make sure they're backwards compatible as much as you possibly can. I think we're about at the end of needing to save files as .xls files, but there's still the issue of number of rows in each version of Excel, functions used, filtering used, etc. that can really trip you up if you're not careful.

Copying Formulas

Before we move into discussing specific functions, I want to cover how to copy formulas and how to keep cell references fixed. I covered this before in *Excel 2019 Beginner*, but it's well worth discussing again because the way in which formulas copy in Excel is key to what makes them so powerful.

That's because you can write a formula once, copy it, and paste it to thousands of cells, and Excel will automatically adjust that formula to its new location

It's fantastic.

But the default for copying formulas is that every single cell reference in the formula adjusts for the new location of the formula.

So if the original formula was in the first cell of the third column (otherwise known as Cell C1) and was written to add the value in the first cell of the first column to the value in the first cell of the second column (otherwise known as =A1+B1) then when you copy that formula over to the second row of the sixth column (Cell F2) everything in the formula will adjust by three columns and one row as well (so that you now have =D2+E2).

Great when that's exactly what you want. Horrible if you're working with any fixed values.

There's something I often like to build for my own analysis that's called a two-variable analysis grid that takes two inputs and calculates the potential combinations of the two.

For example, given a variety of hours worked per week and money earned per hour worked, what are the possible amounts you could earn?

Or, given various sales prices for a home and various commission rates, what could you earn from selling your home? What about if you included a fix-up cost in that calculation?

To do these calculations properly requires telling Excel to keep certain portions of the cell reference in your formula fixed.

You do this by using a $ sign.

So let's just build this right now so you can see it at work using the mortgage example above. That will let us demonstrate all three ways to use the $ sign to fix or partially fix cell references.

Here's our set-up. We haven't done the calculations yet, but I've put in the numbers we're going to use. We want to see what the different outcomes are if the house sells for between $400,000 and $500,000 and when we have to pay a sales commission of 3% to 6%. This only works with two variables the way I have it set up so we're assuming that fix-up costs are set at $2,500.

	A	B	C	D	E	F	G
1	Fix-Up Cost	$2,500.00					
2					House Sale Price		
3			$400,000	$425,000	$450,000	$475,000	$500,000
4	Commission to Realtor	3%					
5		4%					
6		5%					
7		6%					

First, we write the formula for Cell C4 using the values in Cells B1, C3, and B4.

$$=(C3*(1-B4))-B1$$

That's saying take our sale price on the home (C3) and reduce it by the commission amount (B4).

(The way to reduce it by the commission amount is to use 100% minus the commission, in this case 3%, to get our net amount to us of 97%.)

And then with the money we earn from the sale, pay for our fix-up costs (B1).

You could re-write that formula for each and every cell, but who wants to?

Instead, we're going to copy the formula to all the other cells. But first we have to tell Excel to keep certain parts of the formula fixed.

For fix-up costs, B1, we want that to not change at all. It will always be the value in Cell B1. We write that using $ signs in front of both the column and row portion of the cell reference, so $B$1 means never change the B or the 1 as the formula is copied.

The house sale price is trickier. Because when we copy our formula to Columns D, E, F, and G we do want the column reference to change, but not the row reference. To accomplish that we replace the C3 with C$3. That keeps taking the values from Row 3 but lets the column change.

With the commission value as we copy to rows 5, 6, and 7 we want the columns to stay fixed, but the row numbers to change. To accomplish that we replace the B4 with $B4. That keeps the value in Column B but lets the row change.

Our new formula becomes:

$$=(C\$3*(1-\$B4))-\$B\$1$$

And when we copy it to the rest of the cells in that table, all of the calculations work correctly for that combination of values.

	A	B	C	D	E	F	G
1	**Fix-Up Cost**	**$2,500.00**					
2					**House Sale Price**		
3			**$400,000**	**$425,000**	**$450,000**	**$475,000**	**$500,000**
4			**3%** $385,500	$409,750	$434,000	$458,250	$482,500
5			**4%** $381,500	$405,500	$429,500	$453,500	$477,500
6	Commission to	Realtor	**5%** $377,500	$401,250	$425,000	$448,750	$472,500
7			**6%** $373,500	$397,000	$420,500	$444,000	$467,500

I can double-click into Cell G7 and see that the formula in that cell is:

$$=(G\$3*(1-\$B7))-\$B\$1$$

And that the correct cells are being referenced for that particular calculation. We're still referencing Cell B1 but now we reference Cells G3 and B7.

A two-variable analysis grid is incredibly useful and will come in handy in any number of analysis scenarios. (Units sales and price is another one that comes to mind.) And to build one with ease relies completely on this particular trick.

Another time when I find that I need to be careful about cell references when I'm copying a formula is when I'm dealing with cell ranges.

Sometimes I'll want to look at a value as a percent of the total and I'll use a formula that references the specific range of values instead of the entire column, maybe because I have a grand total row at the bottom that would interfere with just using the entire column. So I'll use an equation like:

$$=A1/SUM(A1:A25)$$

The problem comes when I copy that to Cell A2 and and not only does my A1 in the beginning of the formula adjust to become A2, which I want, but my A1:A25 in the second part of the formula becomes A2:A26, which I don't.

So a scenario like that requires writing the formula like so:

$$=A1/SUM(\$A\$1:\$A\$25)$$

That lets the A1 in the first part of the formula change, but keeps the referenced cell range in the second part of the formula fixed.

(In this specific scenario I can check that my calculation is working by taking the total of all of my calculations which should add up to 1 or 100%.)

Also, if you just need to move a formula to a new location but don't want any of the cell references to adjust then remember to cut and move the formula instead of copying it.

You can either click on the cell and use Ctrl + X if you don't need to leave the formula in its original location.

Or, if you do want to keep the formula in its original location as well but don't want it to change, click on the cell, go to the formula bar, highlight the formula there, copy it, hit Esc, go to the new cell, and then paste using Ctrl + V or Paste in the Home tab. (Enter doesn't work for this one.)

OK. That's it for the preliminaries. Time to start talking about specific functions. We'll start with ten of the most useful functions first, which I've chosen to give you a good idea of what's possible in Excel as well as based upon how often I've used them or will use them going forward (since a couple were only introduced recently.)

Top 10 Functions

Alright, we're going to start with ten key functions that I've chosen either because I use them all the time and think others will as well (SUM is probably the most commonly-used function if I had to guess), or because I think they're useful and representative of the power and variety of functions within Excel.

A few of these are either new or close to new but if you're only going to be working in Excel 2019 and don't need backwards compatibility they are incredibly powerful and worth learning. For example, I would have in the past put IF on this list but in Excel 2019 I'm putting IFS which is a newer function that has the potential to largely take the place of the IF function.

Same with TEXTJOIN. In the past I would have used CONCAT (which used to be CONCATENATE) to do what TEXTJOIN now does and does with far less effort involved.

Okay, let's get started with SUM.

The SUM Function

Notation: SUM(number1, [number2],...)

Excel Definition: Adds all the numbers in a range of cells.

The SUM function is probably the most basic function in Excel and I'd suspect the most widely used. What the SUM function does is add numbers together. These can be numbers that you type directly into the function (not recommended as discussed above under best practices) or they can be values that are stored in other cells. Cells do not need to be touching for their values to be added together, although it's much easier to write your SUM function if they are.

To use the function you use SUM and must include at least one number (or cell range) within the parens.

Some examples of formulas that use the SUM function are:

=SUM(2,3,4)

This adds the numbers 2, 3, and 4 together. So it's the same as using =2+3+4 as your formula.

=SUM(A1,A2,A3)

This formula does the exact same thing as the first formula except it's using cell references to add the values in Cells A1, A2, and A3 together. You could also type =A1+A2+A3 in a cell and get the same result.

=SUM(A1:A3)

This is where the SUM function becomes necessary. It's a cleaner way to write the second example since we've replaced A1, A2, A3 with A1:A3 which is saying "Cells A1 *through* A3." Because of the cell notation it requires use of the SUM function to work. For three cells it's not that big of a difference, but what about:

$$=SUM(A1:A100)$$

Now you can see where the SUM function comes in very, very handy because with one small function we can sum all the values in Cells A1 through A100.

Here's an example that uses two different ranges of cells:

$$=SUM(A1:A3,B2:B6)$$

This one is saying to add all the values in the range from Cell A1 to Cell A3 (so Cells A1, A2, and A3) as well as all the values in the range from Cell B2 to Cell B6 (so Cells B2, B3, B4, B5, and B6). Because of the use of the cell ranges, this one also requires use of the SUM function. The alternative would be to write =A1+A2+A3+B2+B3+B4+B5+B6 which no one wants to do.

$$=SUM(A:A)$$

This example is saying to sum all of the values in Column A.

$$=SUM(5:5)$$

And this one is summing all of the values in Row 5.

* * *

Neither of those last two can be easily replaced with a formula that uses the plus sign. They demonstrate just how powerful such a simple function can be.

So, pretty simple, right?

Start with an equals sign, SUM, opening paren, whatever you want to add together using cell notation, closing paren. Done.

And as I mentioned above, you can also combine functions in a larger formula. So, for example, if I had a value in Cell A1 and I wanted to subtract all of the values in Column C, I could write that as:

$$=A1-SUM(C:C)$$

Or if I wanted to subtract the values in Column C from A1 but then also add the values in Column E, I could do that as well:

$$=A1-SUM(C:C)+SUM(E:E)$$

Note that when a function doesn't start a formula that you don't need to put the equals sign in front of it.

Alright.

Next up is ROUND.

The ROUND Function

Notation: ROUND(number, num_digits)

Excel Definition: Rounds a number to a specified number of digits.

ROUND is a simple but potentially useful function. It takes a value and rounds that value to a specified number of digits.

(You can use the formatting options in Excel to give the appearance of having rounded a number. So Number or Currency or Accounting will all format a number to show two decimal places, but using the ROUND function actually transforms the number so that it now only has that number of decimal places.)

The inputs into the ROUND function are the value you want to round and then the number of digits to round that number to.

If you use 0 for the number of digits the number will be rounded to the nearest integer. So

$$=ROUND(111.2345,0)$$

rounds the number 111.2345 zero digits and will return 111 as the value.

If you use a positive number, such as 2, for num_digits the number will be rounded to that many decimal places. So

$$=ROUND(111.2345,2)$$

rounds 111.2345 to two decimal places and will return 111.23 as the value.

If you use a negative number for num_digits, such as -2, the number will be rounded to that number of 10's, 100's, 1000's places, etc. So

$$=ROUND(111.2345,-2)$$

will round 111.2345 negative 2 digits and return a result of 100.

ROUND does not force a specific number of decimal places on a number, however.

For example, if I use

$$=ROUND(1.23,4)$$

which means to round the number 1.23 to the fourth decimal place, ROUND will return a value of 1.23 not 1.2300. (You would need to use TEXT to enforce that type of formatting or you would need to format your cells that way using one of the number formatting options.)

The way Excel decides whether to round up or round down is by looking at the digit one past the one you're going to keep. If that digit is a 0 through a 4, Excel will round down. (Thus keeping the rest of the number unchanged.) If that digit is a 5 through a 9, Excel will round up and the final digit that you're keeping will go up by one.

This is easier to understand if we look at some examples:

$$=ROUND(1.234,2)$$

says to change the number 1.234 to a number with just two decimal places. So the question is does that become 1.23 or 1.24? The answer is 1.23 because the digit one past the 3, which is the last digit we're keeping, is a 4. Since that value is in the lower range, 0 through 4, we round down.

$$=ROUND(1.235,2)$$

says the same thing and we have the same two choices, 1.23 or 1.24. But now our last digit after the one we're keeping is a 5 so we round up and our final value becomes 1.24.

Where it gets interesting, for me, is when you have multiple numbers that you're not keeping. So

$$=ROUND(1.2347,2)$$

says to convert 1.2347 to a number with two decimal places as well. If you started at the end and rounded each number at a time you would go from 1.2347 to 1.235 to 1.24. But that's not how Excel works. (And not how rounding in general works either. I looked it up.)

As I explained above, Excel takes the 1.23 that we want to keep and ONLY looks at the next digit in the number. In this case that's a 4 so Excel would round down and return a value of 1.23.

So there you have it. That's how ROUND works.

If you want to force the direction in which your value is rounded, you can use ROUNDUP or ROUNDDOWN. If you don't want to round at all but just want to cut the number off at a specific point, you can use the TRUNC function. The INT function will round a number down to the nearest whole number (integer).

Okay. Now let's move on to RANDBETWEEN.

The **RANDBETWEEN** Function

Notation: RANDBETWEEN(bottom, top)

Excel Definition: Returns a random number between the numbers you specify.

Sometimes when working with data you need to have a random start. For example, if I want to sample a series of transactions and be able to extrapolate my results to that entire population of transactions, I need to start at a random point and then take every nth transaction from that point forward until I've worked my way through the entire sample back to my starting point.

You can use a function like RAND or RANDBETWEEN to choose that random value. The RAND function can be used to randomly generate a value between 0 and 1, but I chose to cover RANDBETWEEN here because it allows you to specify a range of values to use for your random number generation, and the number it returns is always a whole number which makes it the more useful function for taking samples or choosing from a numbered population.

So say I have a set of 532 transactions I need to sample and want to know which transaction to randomly start with. I can write:

=RANDBETWEEN(1,532)

When I hit enter, Excel will show me a random whole number between 1 and 532. I can then use this number to identify my starting transaction.

Be careful though. Because every time you press F9, make a new calculation in your worksheet, or reopen your worksheet it will calculate a new random value. And once it does that there's no way to go back to your prior value. Ctrl + Z will not work. That number is gone and it's not coming back.

So if you use RANDBETWEEN and you need to record the random number Excel generates, which you likely will, use copy and paste special – values to store the value as a number. Or you could build a process that acts on that value as soon as it's generated.

Another option to lock in your result is to click on the cell with your formula in it, highlight the RANDBETWEEN() portion of the formula, hit F9, and then hit Enter. That will lock in the calculation as of that moment in time. (This trick works with any portion of a formula as long as you can select the entire function name, the opening paren, the argument, and the closing paren.)

Be forewarned though that paste special-values and the F9 + Enter trick both leave you with a fixed value and get rid of the function entirely.

Now on to the CONVERT function.

The CONVERT Function

Notation: CONVERT(number, from_unit, to_unit)

Excel Definition: Converts a number from one measurement system to another.

CONVERT is an incredibly useful function that will allow you to easily convert from one measurement to another.

(Let me note here that if the conversion you need is just a one-off you can easily use an internet browser to do this. Just type in "20 degree Celsius to Fahrenheit" in the search bar and hit enter, for example, and the top result or one of the top results will be the answer. But if you have a range of values you need to convert or you need to keep doing this conversion on a regular basis, then this function is the way to do it)

In the help text for the function there is a very long list of options for what you can convert spread across the following categories: weight and mass, distance, time, pressure, force, energy, power, magnetism, temperature, volume (or liquid measure), area, information (bits to bytes), and speed. In addition there is a list of prefixes and binary prefixes that can be prepended to any of the metrics to change the magnitude of the value.

The function itself is very easy to use. The hardest part of using it is knowing what abbreviation to use for your from_unit and to_unit options. You can find all of the available abbreviations in the Help text dialogue box for the function or you can just start entering your function and look at the options provided when you reach each input field.

For example, when you reach the from_unit option you'll see a dropdown menu of the available measurements and you can just scroll down and double-click on the one you need. Same with when you reach the to_unit portion of the function. If you do it this way, the to_unit portion will only display the available options that are in the same category as the from_unit option, saving you the potential of having an error due to type mismatch between your from units and to units.

Let's walk through a few straight-forward examples:

I have a number of friends who live overseas and are always talking about how hot it is there, because it's 40 degrees out. Now, being from Colorado you tell me that it's 40 degrees out I'm bundling up before I head outside. This is because my friends are talking about Celsius temperatures and I'm talking about Fahrenheit temperatures.

So to find what 40 degrees Celsius is in Fahrenheit temperature, you could use:

=CONVERT(40,"C","F")

(That's 104 degrees Fahrenheit and, yes, I'd agree that's pretty darned hot.)

It's as simple as that. The first part of the function is the value you need to convert, the next part is its current units, and the final part is the unit of measurement you need to convert to.

Note that the abbreviation for the measurement has to be in quotes and is case-sensitive.

What about if you know an event is occurring in 1,200 days but aren't sure how many years from now that will be?

You can just use:

=CONVERT(1200,"day","yr")

Result? 3.285

Those are just two very simple uses for CONVERT. I'll note here that it's listed as an Engineering function and you can see that it might be useful in a context like that if you scroll through the list of available conversion options as well as the list of prefixes that are available.

Make sure your units to and from are in the same category or you'll get a #N/A error. Same with if you try to use a measurement abbreviation that doesn't exist. This includes if you input the value using the wrong case. So "day" is a valid unit value, but "Day" is not.

Let me add here, too, that even though it's not on the list of available options you can use "km" for kilometers. Also, "mi" is the miles option you want if you're just trying to convert a good old standard mile to a different distance measurement. (The Help text refers to "mi" as a statute mile.)

Also, in the Help dialogue box they show how to handle squared units by doubling the CONVERT function. So to convert 100 square feet into square meters they say to use:

$$=CONVERT(CONVERT(100,"ft","m"),"ft","m")$$

By nesting the two CONVERT functions that way it appears to work to convert a squared unit to a squared unit.

(I tested it with squared inches to squared feet and it worked on that as well, I'm just using hedging language here because I haven't personally thought through *why* that works the way it does. I'm sure someone more mathematically inclined than I am could write up a little mathematical proof to show me why that works that way, but suffice it to say it does.)

The TEXTJOIN Function

Notation: TEXTJOIN(delimiter, ignore_empty, text1, [text2],…)

Excel Definition: Concatenates a list or range of text strings using a delimiter.

This function is new in Excel 2019. Previously I would have used CONCATENATE or CONCAT to accomplish the same task, but with a lot more angst and effort.

What TEXTJOIN does is takes text entries in multiple cells or in a list that you provide and combines them into one cell. If you specify a delimiter it will use that delimiter between each of the values that you want combined. You can also tell Excel to ignore any cell that is empty or to include it anyway.

Beautiful.

So how would you use this? Why put it here?

One of the things I've had to do in the past is take entries such as first name, middle name, last name, suffix, and combine them to form one single entry. So instead of Mary, Jo, Jones I want to create an entry that reads Mary Jo Jones.

TEXTJOIN makes this very easy to do. In this scenario we want a space as our delimiter which we can represent using " " where the space is in the quotes. And because some people won't have middle names we want to tell Excel to ignore empty cells, which means we use a 1 for TRUE. (Or you can just use TRUE.)

So let's do this. Here's my sample data:

	A	B	C	D
1	**First**	**Middle**	**Last**	**Suffix**
2	Mary	Jo	Jones	
3	Mark		Allen	Jr
4	Elizabeth		Zhan	

In Cell E2 I can add a TEXTJOIN function that reads:

$$=\text{TEXTJOIN}(" ",1,A2:D2)$$

And then copy that down for Rows 3 and 4. The A2:D2 is my range of values that I want Excel to combine. When I copy that down that will change for each row.
Here are the results:

	A	B	C	D	E
1	**First**	**Middle**	**Last**	**Suffix**	**TEXTJOIN**
2	Mary	Jo	Jones		Mary Jo Jones
3	Mark		Allen	Jr	Mark Allen Jr
4	Elizabeth		Zhan		Elizabeth Zhan

Easy enough.
There is a limit on the function but it's pretty high. You can't have more than 32,767 characters or else you'll get a #VALUE! error message.
The delimiter I gave it above was a blank space, but if you wanted to do a list of values separated by a comma you would use ", " instead which puts a comma as well as a space for the delimiter.
If you do use something like a comma and space for the delimiter and choose not to ignore blanks you can end up with something fairly unattractive where you have , , , if there are missing values.
The help text for this function shows an interesting way to provide a cell range instead of a single delimiter to handle a situation where you need multiple delimiters. In their example they use three commas and then a semi-colon as their delimiters by referencing a cell range that contains those marks.
It works in their sample because all of the data had the same number of inputs. There was a city, state, zip code, and country in every line of data and there were not blanks.
But applying it to our scenario above to try to add a comma before the suffix, I got weird results. This is because I have entries where the number of values in the end result are the same, but the third value is a suffix for one line (Mark Allen, Jr) and a last name for another (Mary Jo Jones). When you use a cell range to specify the delimiter what you're doing is telling Excel that the first delimiter is in the first cell of the range, the second delimiter is in the second cell of the range, etc.

So if I take the middle name value for Mary Jo Jones out of my data above, I can get this to work. Like so:

	A	B	C	D	E
			f_x	=TEXTJOIN($A$12:$B$12,1,A7:D7)	

	A	B	C	D	E
6	First	Middle	Last	Suffix	TEXTJOIN
7	Mary		Jones		Mary Jones
8	Mark		Allen	Jr	Mark Allen, Jr
9	Elizabeth		Zhan		Elizabeth Zhan
10					
11	First Delimiter	Second Delimiter			
12		,			

What I've done is in Cell A12 I've added a space. And in Cell B12 I've added a comma and a space. I've then changed the formula to:

$$=TEXTJOIN(\$A\$12:\$B\$12,1,A7:D7)$$

I use the $ signs so that I can copy that formula to the other rows and not lose the fixed reference to my delimiters that are in Cells A12 and B12. Only Cell E8 needs a second delimiter so it's the only one that uses the comma. This only works because I said TRUE (1) for ignoring empty cells. If I'd used FALSE (0) instead, I'd have

Mary , Jones

Mark , Allen Jr

Elizabeth , Zhan

Which brings up an interesting quirk in using a range of delimiters. And that's that if you have more delimiters needed than you provided in the list, Excel will go back to the beginning and start using the delimiters over again. For example, I applied these two delimiters I set up to a range of cells with the values 1 2 3 4 5 6 7 8 and the result was 1 2, 3 4, 5 6, 7 8 because it used the space, then the comma with a space and then started over at the start again with the space followed by the comma with a space.

(Maybe that's only interesting to me. But this is a new-to-me function so I like to kick the tires a bit when I find a function I haven't used before.)

One more thought here. If you do end up using this function and have a situation where you have the potential for double spaces to appear (so maybe you said FALSE to ignoring empty cells and used a space as your delimiter, you can put the TRIM function, which we'll talk about next, around the entire function to remove those double spaces as you generate your results.

Something like this:

=TRIM(TEXTJOIN($A$12:$B$12,0,A8:D8))

The TRIM Function

Notation: TRIM(text)

Excel Definition: Removes all spaces from a text string except for single spaces between words.

The TRIM function can come in very handy if you're trying to clean up text entries that are messy like the ones we just discussed had the potential to be.

If I used TEXTJOIN to merge a list of names that had first name followed by a space followed by middle name followed by a space followed by last name and I didn't suppress blank entries I would very likely end up with a list of entries with extra spaces in it.

Because for every entry that didn't have a middle name there would be an unwanted space.

So I might have "Albert Jones" as one of my entries. There's an extra space there between Albert and Jones because there was no middle name.

To remove those extra spaces, you can use the TRIM function. If that entry was in Cell B2, I'd just write

$$=TRIM(B2)$$

Done. My new entry would be "Albert Jones".

I could also do that in the entry itself as I mentioned above by putting the TEXTJOIN function inside the TRIM function.

$$=TRIM(TEXTJOIN(\ldots))$$

where the ... represents the values for the TEXTJOIN function.

Just make sure that you have enough closing parens when you do something like that. One for each of the functions you used.

TRIM also works with text pasted directly into the function as long as you use quotation marks around the text. For example,

$$=TRIM("Albert\ Jones\ ")$$

would return Albert Jones without the extra spaces.

Also, remember that when you use TRIM it's still a formula. To get just the text entry and not keep the formula you need to copy your data and then paste special – values when you're done. (That goes for TEXTJOIN above as well.)

You probably won't need to use TRIM often, but it's very useful when you do need it. Also, if you're pulling information off a website and have issues, see the TRIM Excel Help text for more guidance on how it can help with that.

The TODAY Function

Notation: TODAY( )

Excel Definition: Returns the current date formatted as a date.

I wanted to include a date function in the top ten functions and the TODAY function is very simple and basic but useful at the same time.

If you need today's date formatted as a date, you just enter

$$=TODAY( )$$

into a cell or a formula and that's what you'll get. You need the empty parens after TODAY for it to work. (The space between the parens is not needed.)

Now, you might be asking yourself why you'd bother doing something like this. I mean, can't you just type in today's date? Yes, you can.

But the reason to use TODAY is because you are creating a worksheet that uses the current date, whatever that is, in a calculation. So let's say you want to track which of your customer invoices are past thirty days. In other words, who should've paid you by now.

You can have a cell in your worksheet that uses TODAY so that you never have to re-enter today's date when making your calculations. That cell will update each time you open your worksheet, and then you can combine that with a calculation that looks at date billed to calculate how many days past due someone is on their payment. That, too, will automatically update each time you open your worksheet.

It is possible to place TODAY directly in a calculation formula if you want. (But remember the best practice is to have all of your assumptions visible. If you bury TODAY in a formula and someone doesn't realize it they may believe the values are static when in fact they will change each day as that value updates.)

So Option 1 is to put =TODAY( ) into Cell A1, have the date of the invoice in Cell C3, and then have the formula =A1-C3 to calculate the difference.

(Be sure that you format the cell with the calculation in it as a number because otherwise it will default to a date format that will look like a date sometime around 1900. We'll discuss how Excel handles dates later when we talk about more date functions, but the basic gist is that every date in Excel is actually stored as a number.)

Option 2 is to put =TODAY( )-C3 into a cell where C3 is the date the customer was invoiced.

Both work.

If you wanted to put both dates directly in your calculation formula, you'd likely have to use the DATE function for the other date, which we'll discuss later in the Date & Time Functions section.

If the time of day matters you can use the NOW function instead since TODAY is set to include a time of midnight.

Okay. Now on to one of the most powerful functions that Excel has, in my opinion, the IFS function.

The IFS Function

Notation: IFS(logical_test1, value_if_true1,...)

Excel Definition: Checks whether one or more conditions are met and returns a value corresponding to the first TRUE condition.

This is another function that was new with Excel 2019 and as far as I can tell can completely replace the IF function. But if you need backwards compatibility then you'll need to work with the IF function instead (which will be discussed briefly later).

The IF function was always one of my favorite functions, if such a thing can exist, so I'm certain that I will also love IFS.

IFS at its most basic lets you write a formula that says, "If X happens return Y, otherwise return Z." That's pretty simple. Powerful but simple.

But the reason I always loved the IF function was because I could nest them. So I could say, "If X happens, return Y. If X doesn't happen, but G does, then return H. And if neither X nor G happens, then return Z."

And I could keep going and going and going with that until I had twenty possible outcomes. I won't deny that it was very tricky to build a nested IF function. That's where my warnings about matching up your opening and closing parens come from, because if you don't it all turns to mush with nested IF functions.

But the beauty of IFS is that it is designed to make it easier to build a nested IF function. No more keeping track of a million closing parens.

Let's walk through some examples.

First we'll build a simple function to give free shipping to any customer who spends at least $25. Any customer who spends less than $25 will pay 5% in shipping costs.

To calculate our shipping cost, we write that as

$$=IFS(A1>=25,0,TRUE,A1*0.05)$$

Let's break that down.

The first part, the IF part of our first condition, is A1>=25. We're saying that if the customer's purchase in Cell A1 is greater than (>) OR equal to (=) 25 then we want the first outcome.

We then place that first outcome after the comma. In this case that's 0.

Which makes the THEN part of our first outcome 0. If the customer's purchase is equal to or greater than 25, then don't charge for shipping.

That leaves us with the third part, our ELSE portion of the decision tree.

Because this is the IFS function and we could list out ten of these conditions before we get to the end we have to put TRUE to tell Excel this is the closing condition, otherwise Excel won't know we're at the end.

So the next entry is TRUE and then there's a comma and then we have our calculation of the shipping cost when the transaction is for less than $25.

And that's

$$A1*0.05$$

Notice that for the calculation A1*.05 we don't have to use quotation marks. (Unlike some other functions where you do.)

Also note here that we are calculating the *shipping charge*, not the customer's transaction cost. If we wanted the total customer cost we would use A1*1.05 for that last section and A1 for the earlier value.

Okay. That was a basic IFS function. One condition, two possible outcomes.

The complexity level ratchets up when you start to nest conditions. Let's look at the basic format of an IFS function again.

It's IF-THEN-ELSE, right? IF x, THEN y, ELSE z.

Or IF-THEN-OTHERWISE. IF x, THEN y, OTHERWISE z.

When you start to add conditions using the IFS function it becomes a situation where you're saying, "If this, then that, but if it's not this but instead this other thing, then…but if it's not that other thing either but it is this thing over here, then…" and so on and so on and so on.

You can write an IFS function with 127 different conditions in it. (Although Excel and I both would not recommend doing so because the order in which you add your conditions is crucial and that would be really hard to get right.)

Confused yet? It sounds horribly complicated doesn't it?

Let's walk through an example which should help this come clear.

We're going to build an IFS function that calculates a customer discount that escalates as customers spend more and more money.

If a customer spends at least $25 they get $5 off. If they spend $75 they get $10 off. If they spend $100 they get $15 off. And if they spend $250 they get $25 off.

For me the easiest way to do this is to build a table of the values and discounts and work from there. Here it is with our discount table up top and our test values down below.

	A	B	C
1	**Order Amount**	**Discount Amount**	
2	$25.00	$5.00	
3	$75.00	$10.00	
4	$100.00	$15.00	
5	$250.00	$25.00	
6			
7	**Customer Spend**	**Rebate**	**Formula in Column B**
8	$10.25		
9	$27.50		
10	$74.95		
11	$100.00		
12	$225.00		
13	$250.00		

We have the cut-off order amounts in Cells A2 through A5 and the discounts the customer will receive at each level in Cells B2 through B5.

Below that starting in Cell A8 are the values we're going to use to test our discount formula.

Let's start building our function. Our first condition is that if they spend under $25 they receive no discount.

We write that as

$$=IFS(A8<A2,0$$

The next condition is that if they spend less than $75 (the value in Cell A3) but at least $25 (which we've already determined is true with the first part of the function) they will get $5 off (the value in Cell B2).

Let's add that to our formula:

=IFS(A8<A2,0,A8<A3,B2

(Note that because of the way I built my table the order amount and the discount amount are pulling from different rows in this example.)

From this point onward we just keep adding each layer of discount until we've added all but the last one:

=IFS(A8<A2,0,A8<A3,B2,**A8<A4,B3,A8<A5,B4,**

At which point we add our final closing condition which is going to be TRUE,B5 and we close it out with a closing paren.

Adding in $ signs to fix our table reference so that we can copy this formula down to the rest of the cells we end up with:

=IFS(A8<$A$2,0,A8<$A$3,$B$2,A8<$A$4,$B$3,A8<$A$5,$B$4, TRUE,$B$5)

That looks like a complex mess, but it's actually simpler than the same formula using an IF function because with an IF function we would have had to insert an IF between every change in condition and made sure that all our closing parens were in the right place. Here we just have one function to do the same thing.

Here are our results and the formula for each row.

7	Customer Spend	Rebate	Formula in Column B
8	$10.25	$0.00	=IFS(A8<$A$2,0,A8<$A$3,$B$2,A8<$A$4,$B$3,A8<$A$5,$B$4,TRUE,$B$5)
9	$27.50	$5.00	=IFS(A9<$A$2,0,A9<$A$3,$B$2,A9<$A$4,$B$3,A9<$A$5,$B$4,TRUE,$B$5)
10	$74.95	$5.00	=IFS(A10<$A$2,0,A10<$A$3,$B$2,A10<$A$4,$B$3,A10<$A$5,$B$4,TRUE,$B$5)
11	$100.00	$15.00	=IFS(A11<$A$2,0,A11<$A$3,$B$2,A11<$A$4,$B$3,A11<$A$5,$B$4,TRUE,$B$5)
12	$225.00	$15.00	=IFS(A12<$A$2,0,A12<$A$3,$B$2,A12<$A$4,$B$3,A12<$A$5,$B$4,TRUE,$B$5)
13	$250.00	$25.00	=IFS(A13<$A$2,0,A13<$A$3,$B$2,A13<$A$4,$B$3,A13<$A$5,$B$4,TRUE,$B$5)

I only had to write the formula once because after I'd finished in Cell B8 and the $ signs were in place, I could just copy and paste down to the other cells.

Note that the A8 references in the above formula did not get $ signs because that's the cell reference that needs to change with each row. But all the others did because they needed to be fixed references.

Also, always remember with an IFS function to check the edge cases. In this instance that's values of $25, $75, $100, and $250, to make sure that they are falling into the correct category.

The way I just showed you is one way to write that function to get the result we needed, but I could have just as easily written it using greater than and equals to instead.

Let's do that now for just the first two conditions, a discount of $5 at $25 and a discount of $10 at $75. In this case we have to start with the highest discount first to get it to work.

So our first condition is if the customer spend (in Cell A8) is greater than or equal to our highest order level ($75 in Cell A3) then they will get our highest discount ($10 in Cell B3):

$$=IFS(A8>=A3,B3$$

If that's not true, then if the spend is greater than our next level spend cutoff (in this case $25 in Cell A2) then they will get our next level discount (in this case $5 in Cell B2):

$$=IFS(A8>=A3,B3,A8>=A2,B2,$$

And if that's not true either then we're out of discounts and we close it off with TRUE and a discount of zero.

$$=IFS(A8>=A3,B3,A8>=A2,B2,TRUE,0)$$

Note how in this version the customer spend and discount amount were pulled from the same row for each discount level.

Okay.

Don't get upset if you write one of these wrong the first time, I usually do. I did on this last one. Because it was easier for me to mentally build from the lowest level up like we did the first time rather than start on the highest level and work my way down like we had to on this one.

I just keep faith that this is all logic, pure and simple, and that if something isn't working the way it should it's because I haven't mapped out the steps properly and I just need to keep trying until I figure out where I went wrong.

If you really, really get stuck, pull out a piece of paper and starting drawing one of those branching decision trees. You know, "we started here, branch one is this, it got us here, branch two is this, it gets us there," etc. until you've drawn out the whole thing.

For example, with the function we just wrote: We started with any purchase amount. If that amount was greater than or equal to $75 that's our first branch and it took us to a discount of $10. But if it wasn't $75 or more then we take the other branch Okay. Now what? What happens down that branch? If it's equal to or more than $25 then we go down a branch that takes us to a discount of $5. But if that branch isn't true, where does that take us? To a discount of zero.

It's a little bit of mental gymnastics. Some take to it better than others. But if you can master it, I personally think the IFS function and its related functions (COUNTIFS, SUMIFS, etc.) are some of the most useful functions in Excel.

Okay. On to something simpler. The AND function.

The AND Function

Notation: AND(logical1, [logical2],…)

Excel Definition: Checks whether all arguments are TRUE, and returns TRUE if all arguments are TRUE.

I wanted to include one logic function in this top ten list and the AND function is the one I probably use the most.

At its core, the AND function is very basic. You use it to determine whether more than one condition has been met. So, is that value greater than 10 AND less than 20? Is that customer from Alaska AND has he bought Widgets?

It doesn't have to be just two criteria either. You can use more than two with an AND function. (Although the help text for the function doesn't say exactly how many you can use.)

In my numeric example above, you would write that as

$$=AND(A1>10,A1<20)$$

If the value in Cell A1 was greater than 10 and less than 20 Excel would return a value of TRUE. Otherwise it would return a value of FALSE.

In the second example I gave, you could write that as

$$=AND(A1="Alaska",B1="Widget")$$

where Cell A1 contained the State and Cell B1 contained the Product.

Again, if both criteria were met, Excel would return a value of TRUE.

In addition to working with numbers, like the first example above, and text references, like the second example above, AND works with cell references. So:

$$=AND(A1>D1,A1<D2)$$

looks to see if the value in Cell A1 is greater than the value in Cell D1 and also less than the value in Cell D2.

I rarely if ever use AND on a standalone basis. You could, like I showed in the examples above, but what I've used it for instead was if I had an IF function where I needed two criteria met.

For example, if I wanted all customers who bought Widgets and live in Alaska to qualify for 50% off their purchase amount where the purchase amount is in Cell C1, I could write an equation to calculate total cost as:

$$=IFS(AND(A1="Alaska",B1="Widget"),C1*0.5,TRUE,C1)$$

Or, using the IF function which is simpler to write in this case:

$$=IF(AND(A1="Alaska",B1="Widget"),C1*0.5,C1)$$

Either of those options would take 50% off the purchase amount if both conditions were met. In this case, the IFS function is the more complex one because it needs that TRUE in there to complete the function. But you could create a nested function where you walk through multiple discounts, Alaska & Widgets, California & Whatchamacallits, etc. and then the IFS function would be the easier one to work with.

Okay. Let's close out our top ten with a function that many of my friends swear by and that I've come around on but am still not a hundred percent in love with, VLOOKUP.

The VLOOKUP Function

Notation: VLOOKUP(lookup_value, table_array, col_index_num, [range_lookup])

Excel Definition: Looks for a value in the leftmost column of a table, and then returns a value in the same row from a column you specify. By default, the table must be sorted in an ascending order.

As I just mentioned, I have friends who think that VLOOKUP is the best function in Excel. These are people whose jobs involve computers and databases and analysis, so they should know what they're talking about.

For me personally, it feels like every time I've wanted to use VLOOKUP it's caused me more problems than it's been worth. But that's because I'm always trying to use it after the fact. So my columns aren't in the right order or I forget that my data has to be sorted and it annoys me.

When I set out up front to use VLOOKUP and specifically build my table to work with it, I actually like it. If you've done that it's easier than building a series of nested IF functions. (Or working with IFS.)

So. To effectively use VLOOKUP you need a data table that has two things: one, values that can be looked up that are sorted in ascending order and, two, values in a column to the right of the first values that can be returned when a match is found.

A perfect use for VLOOKUP is something like the discount example above.

VLOOKUP can take each value, compare it to the purchase cutoffs in that discount table, and return a discount amount.

If you have a value that falls between two of the values in your reference table, for example, $10 is going to fall between $0 and $25, and you haven't told Excel to limit your results to exact matches, it will return the result that corresponds to the lower value. So, the one that corresponds to $0 in this example.

(This is why the sort on your table is so important when using VLOOKUP.)

So let's go ahead and pull the same values using VLOOKUP that we did using IFS.

The one adjustment we need to make to the table from above is we need to add a zero order amount row so that Excel has a value to pull for any input we give it that's below our first discount threshold of $25.

We can then quickly and easily write our VLOOKUP function. Here it is in the table and then we'll walk through what we're looking at:

	A	B	C
1	**Order Amount**	**Discount Amount**	
2	$0.00	$0.00	
3	$25.00	$5.00	
4	$75.00	$10.00	
5	$100.00	$15.00	
6	$250.00	$25.00	
7			
8	**Customer Spend**	**Rebate**	**Formula in Column B**
9	$10.00	$0.00	=VLOOKUP(A9,$A$1:$B$6,2)
10	$27.50	$5.00	=VLOOKUP(A10,$A$1:$B$6,2)
11	$74.95	$5.00	=VLOOKUP(A11,$A$1:$B$6,2)
12	$100.00	$15.00	=VLOOKUP(A12,$A$1:$B$6,2)
13	$225.00	$15.00	=VLOOKUP(A13,$A$1:$B$6,2)
14	$250.00	$25.00	=VLOOKUP(A14,$A$1:$B$6,2)

The first input for VLOOKUP is the value from your data that you want to look up. So in the first row of our table that's going to be Cell A9.

$$=VLOOKUP(A9,$$

The next input for VLOOKUP is a reference to the cell range where Excel needs to look for that value and where the value you want it to return is also located.

The lookup value has to be in the left-hand column of your selected range.

If you have a twenty-column table and the value you want to look up is in the third column, then the range you enter here has to start with that third column and the value you're going to return has to be on the right-hand side of the lookup column.

In this case, we've built the table to work just fine with those constraints. We want to look up the value from Column A and return the value from Column B. (But that has tripped me up before, let me tell you.)

$$=VLOOKUP(A9,A1:B6,$$

The third entry in a VLOOKUP is which column in the range of cells you gave in the second entry contains the value you want to pull.

Given the constraints of VLOOKUP the first column contains what you're using for your search. Count from there to find your column number for your result.

In this example, our number is 2 because discount is in the second column in our range.

If you don't need exact matches, you're done. You can close it out with the last paren and hit enter.

Here's our final formula with $ signs added to fix the reference table range:

$$=VLOOKUP(A9,\$A\$1:\$B\$6,2)$$

What I left off of the formula above is a final, optional input, that tells Excel whether it's looking for an exact match (0/FALSE) or an approximate match (1/TRUE).

If it's an exact match, you'll only get a value returned when what you're looking up matches an entry in the table exactly.

If it's an approximate match you'll get a result for all entries and your value will be determined based on the table sort and where that value falls in the range of values.

Obviously the VLOOKUP I just used for our discount table is a lot simpler than the IFS equivalent we discussed earlier.

But as I said above, I run into issues using VLOOKUP because I want to use it on unsorted data or on data that has the value I want to pull to the left of the lookup value in my table. So for me personally it's easier to write an IFS function with a lot of inputs than it is to rearrange my data.

Just think of nested IF functions as the way to do VLOOKUP without all the pesky rules. But because there are no rules, you have to do a lot more of the heavy lifting up front.

A few more points:

Excel cautions that numbers or dates stored as text may produce unexpected results and so may text entries that have inconsistent usage of spaces or quote marks.

If the data table you're using for your lookup values is large or complex, be very, very careful that the results you get are what you expect. And absolutely be sure to sort your data table in ascending order.

Also check, double-check, and check again.

And one final point.

With an IF function to change the IF formula to adjust for whether you want your criteria to be "a customer spent $25 or more" versus "a customer spent over $25" you adjust the formula from >= to >. With VLOOKUP, you'll need to adjust your *lookup table* not your formula. So instead of $25.00 in the table, we'd have $25.01 for a situation where customers get the discount if they spend over $25 as opposed to $25 or more.

Okay. That's it for our top ten functions. On to Base Functions.

Base Functions

The functions I'm putting in this category of "base functions", which is not a category that exists anywhere except right here, are those statistical or mathematical functions that are used as the base for the other IFS functions. Functions like COUNTIFS, SUMIFS, etc. We already covered SUM, but now we're going to cover the functions that let you take an average, count the number of values you have, take a minimum value, or take a maximum value as well as their iterations.

First up, the AVERAGE function.

The AVERAGE Function

Notation: AVERAGE(number1, [number2],…)

Excel Definition: Returns the average (arithmetic mean) of its arguments, which can be numbers or names, arrays, or references that contain numbers.

AVERAGE is listed as a Statistical function by Excel, but when I think about taking an average I generally think of it along with addition and division. I add up my values and then divide by how many there are.

Also, the definition above is slightly confusing when I read it, so I'm going to rewrite it to clarify.

Let's write it as this: The AVERAGE function returns the average (arithmetic mean) of its arguments. The arguments can be numbers like 1, 2, 3, or 4. Or the arguments can be a named range, an array, or a cell reference as long as the cells or range referenced include numbers.

(If you try to apply AVERAGE to a range of cells with just text in them the result you get is the #DIV/0! error message.)

What the AVERAGE function does is it takes the sum of a range of numbers and then divides that sum by the number of entries in the range that had a numeric value.

For example, if I have the values 1, 2, 3, 4, and 5 in a range of 5 cells from A1 through A5 and I write

=AVERAGE(A1:A5)

Excel will add those values to get 15, divide that total by 5, and return a value of 3.

If I include Cell A6, a blank cell, in that range, and write it as =AVERAGE(A1:A6), I get the same result even though I now have six cells in my range, because AVERAGE only looks at those cells that have values in them.

Likewise, if I have the word "test" in Cell A6 I will still get a result of 3 because only five of the cells in my range had numeric values.

This is very important. Because it may not be what you wanted.

To fix this when you have a cell in your range that should be included but where the value is blank instead of zero, you need to put a zero in that cell or it will not be included in your calculation.

In our example above, putting a zero in Cell A6 changes our average to 2.5 from 3 because we're now dividing 15 by 6 instead of 5.

AVERAGE will, of course, also work on values that you enter directly in the formula. So

$$=AVERAGE(1,2,3,4,5)$$

would return a value of 3. (But doing this is not recommended, as discussed in the best practices chapter.)

The AVERAGEA Function

Notation: AVERAGEA(value1, [value2],…)

Excel Definition: Returns the average (arithmetic mean) of its arguments, evaluating text and FALSE in arguments as 0; TRUE evaluates as 1. Arguments can be numbers, names, arrays, or references.

If you need to take an average from a range that has non-numeric values in it and you need those cells included when calculating the average, you can use AVERAGEA to do so. (It doesn't fix the issue of a blank value, but it does fix the issue of dealing with text entries.)

As it says in the definition, AVERAGEA treats text entries and FALSE values as having a value of 0 and TRUE values as having a value of 1 when calculating the arithmetic mean.

If it's important to include the cells that have text in them, use AVERAGEA. If you want to exclude those cells, use AVERAGE.

For example, if I have four cells and they have the numeric values 10 and 6 and then the text values "This" and "That" in them, AVERAGEA and AVERAGE will return different results.

AVERAGE returns a value of 8 because it adds the 10 and 6 and only divides by 2 ignoring the cells that had text in them.

AVERAGEA returns a value of 4 because it adds the 10 and 6 plus zero for the cell with "this" in it and zero for the cell with "that" in it and then divides by 4.

Another interesting use for AVERAGEA is that because it assigns a value of 1 to TRUE outcomes and a value of 0 to FALSE outcomes, you can use it with the logical arguments like AND and OR or the IFS function to determine the average outcome of a scenario.

For example, if I want to know what percent of the time my customers are both from Alaska and buy Widgets, I could use AVERAGEA in connection with an IF function. (I could do the same with COUNTIFS, but for now we're just going to look at IF and AVERAGEA for this.)

There are two formulas I'd need. The first, assuming the State is in Column A and the Product is in Column B, assigns TRUE or FALSE to each row depending on whether the result is Alaska and Widgets or some other combination.

=IF(AND(A2="Alaska",B2="Widgets"),TRUE,FALSE)

The second uses AVERAGEA to come up with an average value for those results using the TRUE and FALSE values. Assuming they're in Column C and Rows 2 through 8:

=AVERAGEA(C2:C8)

Note that the AVERAGEA function here has to start in the second row (Cell C2) because otherwise it would include the header row in its calculation since it counts text entries.

In my sample worksheet my result of that second formula was .28574 which meant that approximately 29% of the time the entries in Rows 2 through 8 were for customers who were both in Alaska and bought Widgets.

One thing to be careful of if you're going to try to use AVERAGEA in conjunction with TRUE/FALSE statements to get a percentage result:

I initially tried an iteration of this where it was Alaska & Widgets TRUE, Alaska FALSE, and then all other entries blank to try to get the percent of Alaskan customers who bought Widgets, but AVERAGEA wanted to count those blank results and I wasn't able to find a simple workaround for it using the IF function and AVERAGEA.

(Even if you have a blank cell sometimes Excel doesn't think you do. To find out whether it truly thinks a cell is blank and therefore worth ignoring, you can use the ISBLANK function in reference to a cell and see if you get back a TRUE or FALSE result.)

I even tried copy and paste special-values to remove the formula itself and Excel still insisted that those cells had a value in them even though they were completely blank.

This is a good reminder to check your results and make sure the value you're getting back makes sense. Also, if you can't accomplish a task with one approach, there may well be another. Don't get stuck on one solution if it isn't working.

The COUNT Function

Notation: COUNT(value1, [value2],…)

Excel Definition: Counts the number of cells in a range that contain numbers.

The COUNT function is a very basic function. What COUNT does is it allows you to count how many cells within your specified range contain a number or a date.

(It basically gives you the number that AVERAGE uses to divide its results. And, yes, that does mean that AVERAGE will include a date in a range as part of its average.)

For example, a range of three cells that contain the values 1, 12/31/10, and "one" will be counted as 2 because the first two entries (1 and 12/13/10) are considered numbers, but the last entry ("one") is not.

If you have a cell that shows a numeric value due to a formula, so the cell contents are actually =SUM(2,3) but the cell displays 5, that will be counted as well.

Excel will also count a numeric value (1) that is formatted as text.

Also, for a cell to be counted it can only contain a number or date. For example, "1 day" would not be counted since it includes the number 1 but also the text "day".

The COUNT function itself is very simple to use. For example,

$$=COUNT(A1:A5)$$

will count the number of cells in the range from Cell A1 through Cell A5 that contain a number or date.

You could also write a function such as =COUNT(1,2,3) and it would count the number of numbers or dates in the list within the parens. In this case, three.

If you don't want to limit your count to just numbers and dates, then you need to use COUNTA. The COUNTA function allows you to count how many cells within your specified range are not empty. So not just those that contain dates and numbers, but those that contain anything.

Be careful, however, because COUNTA will also count any cell that has a function in it even if that function is not currently displaying a value. (And using copy and then paste special – values to replace that function may not clear the cell enough for COUNTA to ignore it. You have to make sure that a cell is truly blank for it to not be counted.)

There is also a function, COUNTBLANK, which counts empty cells, but be sure to test it with your data since there is some overlap between what COUNTA and COUNTBLANK will count. Both count cells with "" in them.

The MIN Function

Notation: MIN(number1, [number2],…)

Excel Definition: Returns the smallest number in a set of values. Ignores logical values and text.

Another useful Statistical function is the MIN function. This one takes a range of values or list of numbers and returns the smallest value.

You could say

$$=MIN(1,2,3)$$

and it would return a value of 1 or

$$=MIN(-1,0,1)$$

and it would return a value of -1, but the real power of this function is when you use it on a range of cells.

So, for example, let's say you want to know the lowest test score from a class that had 125 students in it and where all of the test scores were recorded in Column C. You would simply write the function as

$$=MIN(C:C)$$

and it would return for you the lowest test score in the range.

According to Excel, if you reference a range and ask Excel to return the minimum value and there are no numbers in the range it will return a value of zero.

Also, if the range contains an error value such as #DIV/0! the function will return that error value. In this case, #DIV/0!

If there are dates in the range it will use those as well. Most current dates fall in the range of about 40,000-50,000 so that will only be relevant if your minimum values lie within that range.

But that does also mean that MIN can be used to pull the oldest date from a range of values. (Just remember to format the result as a date if you do that.)

The function MINA is much like MIN except that it will consider logical values and text in determining the minimum value. If you have a range that has TRUE and FALSE values in it, TRUE will be treated as a 1 and FALSE will be treated as a zero. Basic text entries such as "try" are also treated as zeros.

The MAX Function

Notation: MAX(number1, [number2],…)

Excel Definition: Returns the largest value in a set of values. Ignores logical values and text.

MAX is the counterpart to MIN. Where MIN looks for the smallest value in the range, MAX looks for the largest value in the range.

So =MAX(1,2,3) will return a value of 3 because that's the largest number in the list of provided values. Once again, though, the optimal use of MAX is by applying it to a cell range, such as an entire column or row.

$$=MAX(4:4)$$

would return the maximum value in Row 4 of your worksheet, for example.

If there are no numbers in the specified range, MAX will return a value of 0.

If there is a cell that has an error message within the range, MAX will return that error message.

MAX ignores text entries and does not include logical values like TRUE or FALSE in its determination.

As with MIN, MAX will also work with dates. It will return the latest date in the series but formatted as a number so you have to change the formatting.

Also, just like with MIN and MINA, MAX has a counterpart, MAXA, which will incorporate logical values into its determination. TRUE values are treated as a 1 and FALSE values are treated as a 0. Also, text entries are treated as zeros.

Logical* Functions

Now let us cover Logical Functions like the AND function we already discussed.

I have that little asterisk there because I'm also including one function, NA, in this section that Excel places in the Information category instead. But I think these five functions all fit together and are good to review before we cover the rest of what I think of as the IF-related functions.

The OR Function

Notation: OR(logical1, [logical2],…)

Excel Definition: Checks whether any of the arguments are TRUE, and returns TRUE or FALSE. Returns FALSE only if all arguments are FALSE.

The OR function is similar to the AND function except it doesn't require that all of the conditions are met to return a TRUE value. With OR if one of the conditions in the list is met, then the value is TRUE.

Say, for example, I want to identify all of my customers who are in the states of Florida, Georgia, and North Carolina because I have a special promotion running in those states. I could write that as

=OR(A1="Florida",A1="Georgia",A1="North Carolina")

and if the value in Cell A1 is any of those (Florida, Georgia, or North Carolina), Excel would return a value of TRUE.

If none of the conditions were met, Excel would return a value of FALSE.

(Very random side comment to make, but important: Hopefully when you're reading this book the quote marks you see used in the formulas are what are called straight quotes. Meaning they have no curl to them, they are straight up and down. The default in Word and other programs is to turn quote marks into what are called smart quotes which curl around the text they're quoting. If you ever copy a formula from somewhere like Word into Excel and it has smart quotes instead of straight quotes, that formula will not work until you replace those smart quotes with straight quotes. So just be advised that can be an issue at times. I've run into it with Excel as well as with SQL.)

Okay. Back to the OR function. This is one I rarely use as a standalone, but it is nice to use it with an IF function. So say I was running a 50% off price promotion in those three states, I could write an IF function that says,

=IF(OR(A1="Florida",A1="Georgia",A1="North Carolina"),C1*.5,C1)

or an IFS function that says

=IFS(OR(A1="Florida",A1="Georgia",A1="North Carolina"),C1*0.5,
TRUE,C1)

to give a 50% discount to any customer in one of those three states.

Like with AND, you can use text criteria (like above), numeric criteria, or cell references. So

=OR(A1=C1,A1=C3)

would check to see if the value in Cell A1 was the same as the value in Cell C1 OR the value in Cell C3. And

=OR(A1=5,A1=10)

would check to see if the value in Cell A1 was equal to 5 OR 10.

The TRUE Function

Notation: TRUE( )

Excel Definition: Returns the logical value TRUE.

When I was working on this guide I found myself occasionally needing a cell to return a value of TRUE or FALSE to test some of the different functions. Simply typing TRUE into the cell didn't always work, so I found myself using TRUE and its counterpart, FALSE.

If you use it, be sure to include the parens ( ) or Excel may think you're trying to reference a named range. (It works with a space between the parens like I have here or without a space between them.)

You should also be able to just type TRUE and get the same result, but that didn't always seem to work for me.

According to Excel, TRUE and FALSE exist primarily for compatibility with other spreadsheet programs. FALSE is just like TRUE except you type =FALSE( ) instead.

The NA Function

Notation: NA( )

Excel Definition: Returns the error value #N/A (value not available)

You can use the NA function to mark empty cells. This avoids the issue of inadvertently including empty cells in your calculations.

A friend of mine suggested including it in this guide because he recently had a scenario where he was generating results using an IF function and then graphing those results. When his results generated an empty cell or a null value Excel tried to include those entries in the graph. He found that using NA fixed that problem, because Excel does not graph #N/A values.

To do this, you could write something like:

$$=IF(A1>10,5,NA(\ ))$$

In this case, if A1 is greater than 10, Excel returns a value of 5 but if it isn't Excel returns a value of #N/A.

Be sure to use the empty parens as I did in the example above or Excel won't recognize it as the NA function.

Also, be careful using this one because it will make some calculations return a value of #N/A.

The NOT Function

Notation: NOT(logical)

Excel Definition: Changes FALSE to TRUE, or TRUE to FALSE.

This next one, the NOT function, is one I'm including only because Microsoft themselves highlight it as useful.

Also, it is related to the AND and OR functions. But the fact of the matter is that my psychology background tells me that using a negative to build a function is a bad idea and I would encourage you to find another way to accomplish your goal if you're ever tempted to use the NOT function.

At its most basic, the NOT function returns the opposite result. So

$$=NOT(FALSE)$$

returns a value of TRUE. And

$$=NOT(TRUE)$$

returns a value of FALSE.

But you're never going to use it that way.

Where you might want to use it is to evaluate whether your criteria were met.

So let's say that I have two conditions that must be met for someone to be given a bonus. They have to have been employed for over 12 months and they have to have generated over $25,000 in sales.

I could use a NOT function to ask if that happened. So, for the first criteria, was my employee's time with the company in Cell B5 greater than 12 months?

To do this with a not function, I'd write

$$=NOT(B5<12)$$

to get a result of FALSE when the employee had not been there at least 12 months and a result of TRUE if they had.

See how I had to do less than 12 there to get the right result?

I could have just as easily used an IF function instead and written

$$=IF(B5>12,TRUE)$$

to get the same result without the mental gymnastics using the NOT function requires.

In the Excel help text for this function, they give their own bonus scenario and then write a really ugly looking formula to calculate the bonus. It looks like this:

$$=IF(AND(NOT(B14<\$B\$7),NOT(C14<\$B\$5)),B14*\$B\$8,0)$$

But let me flip that around for you by removing the NOT function and switching the less than signs to greater than signs. If I do that I get:

$$=IF(AND(B14>=\$B\$7,C14>=\$B\$5),B14*\$B\$8,0)$$

It returns the same result as using the NOT function but with a lot less headache. (Just be sure to test that border case of equals to B7 and B5 to make sure you get it exactly right…I had initially written it as > instead of >=, a common problem I have to watch out for.)

Bottom line with the NOT function: If you're ever tempted to use it ask yourself if there isn't a different and simpler way to do what you're trying to do. I'm not going to say that there's absolutely no possible use for this function, but I am pretty confident in saying that ninety-nine times out of a hundred you should be able to find an alternate way of doing your calculation that doesn't require you to use the NOT function.

But for that remaining one in a hundred scenario, now you know how to use it.

IF Functions

Alright. Now we're back to a powerful set of functions, what I refer to collectively as the IF Functions.

We needed the base math functions and the logical functions that we just discussed as tools to help with understanding and working with these more advanced IF functions, but the functions we're about to discuss are ten times more powerful in my opinion than any of what we just covered.

In Excel 2019, Excel introduced MINIFS and MAXIFS to what it already had, which was SUMIFS, AVERAGEIFS, and COUNTIFS. About all they're missing at this point is MEANIFS and MEDIANIFS.

SUMIFS, AVERAGEIFS, and COUNTIFS are upgraded versions of SUMIF, AVERAGEIF, and COUNTIF that can be used in place of those earlier functions.

There never was a MINIF or MAXIF.

The reason I bring this up is because of backwards compatibility. Do not do what I did which is when SUMIF came out use it in a complex worksheet that your client then can't use because they're still on an old version of Excel.

Be sure before you use these highly valuable functions that you can use them in the setting you need to use them in. If not, you can recreate what they do with the underlying function and nested IF functions and maybe a cascading series of steps.

I'm not going to walk through that here, though, because this book is about Excel 2019. So I am going to assume that you are only working in Excel 2019 or with others who are also working in Excel 2019 or newer versions and so have full access to these functions.

I'm also not going to cover SUMIF, AVERAGEIF, or COUNTIF because their "plural" cousins can do everything they can. (I did cover them in *50 Useful Excel Functions* if that's really an issue. Also, Excel's help function is great. The principle for how they work is the same, but each one is limited to just one IF condition and the order of the inputs is likely different.)

Okay. Now that we have that out of the way. At a very high level what these functions do is they perform a calculation (SUM, AVERAGE, COUNT, MIN, or MAX) on a range of values when a set of criteria have been met.

So they only SUM when the customer is from Alaska and bought Widgets. Or they only take the MIN value when the transaction occurred after January 1, 2020.

Essentially they combine IF and the underlying function into one nice little bundle.

That's the bulk of what we're about to walk through in this section. I have also included the basic IF function as well as IFNA and IFERROR, the latter two of which let you suppress ugly error messages in your results.

Alright? Let's dive in with IF.

The IF Function

Notation: IF(logical_test, [value_if_true], [value_if_false])

Excel Definition: Checks whether a condition is met, and returns one value if TRUE, and another value if FALSE.

We're not going to spend a lot of time on the IF function in this book because the IFS function should be able to replace it and if you're new to Excel I encourage you to learn the IFS function instead.

But I'm so grounded in using the IF function and other people you work with may be as well, that it deserves a quick pass.

So the IF function at its most basic lets you set up an IF-THEN-ELSE or IF-THEN-OTHERWISE set of conditions just like the IFS function did.

A basic IF function requires less inputs than the basic IFS function. Let's take the shipping example we used for IFS

$$=IFS(A1>=25,0,TRUE,A1*0.05)$$

That was saying that if the value in A1 is greater than or equal to 25, our shipping cost should be zero, otherwise it should be 5% of the value in A1.

With IF that same formula is:

$$=IF(A1>=25,0, A1*0.05)$$

We don't need that extra TRUE in there to tell Excel this is the last condition. But where IFS shines compared to IF is in the more complex nested functions.

Let's take that final sample from IFS that we used:

$$=IFS(A8>=A3,B3,A8>=A2,B2,TRUE,0)$$

That was saying that if the value in Cell A8 is greater than or equal to the value in Cell A3 then return a value of B3. ELSE if the value in A8 is greater than or equal to A2 return a value of B2. OTHERWISE return a value of 0.

I wrote that with the ELSE and the OTHERWISE in the descriptions because every time it's an ELSE if you're working with a basic IF function you need to put in a new IF function in your formula. Like so:

$$=IF(A8>=A3,B3,IF(A8>=A2,B2,0))$$

See that I have two IF functions in there? And that I had to close it out with two closing parens, one to close the first IF function and one to close the second IF function?

Okay. So those are some simple examples of IF versus IFS. If you're new to Excel just learn IFS.

But if you do enough in Excel you may run into a very complex IF function written by someone like me who has used them for years. And if you need to troubleshoot that function I want to give you a few tips on how to approach that.

Here's an incredibly complex nested IF function:

$$=IF(A22>\$A\$2,IF(A22>\$A\$3,IF(A22>\$A\$4,$$
$$IF(A22>\$A\$5,IF(A22>\$A\$5,\$B\$5),\$B\$4),\$B\$3),\$B\$2),0)$$

(This is an example written in what I find the harder format for nested IF functions because each new IF function is added in the middle of the formula rather than the end which makes it much harder to see where each IF function actually starts and ends..)

What I do if I have to troubleshoot a mess like this is remove everything except the first IF function. So I take that mess up there and I make it:

$$=IF(A22>\$A\$2,"THEN X",0)$$

Everything in the middle is irrelevant until I make sure that the first part works. If it does, then I drop that part of the formula away and check the next part with everything that isn't part of *that* IF function removed.:

$$=IF(A22>\$A\$3,"THEN X",\$B\$2)$$

And so on and so on until I've found the part that was written incorrectly Does that make sense?

Remember when working with nested IF functions: slow and steady wins the race. Take it one step at a time. Test your possible outcomes. Don't get frustrated. Draw a diagram if you have to.

Okay, now on to COUNTIFS.

The COUNTIFS Function

Notation: COUNTIFS(criteria_range1, criteria1, [criteria_range2, criteria2],…)

Excel Definition: Counts the number of cells specified by a given set of conditions or criteria.

COUNTIFS will count the number of times your conditions are met in a selected range of cells. It does not have a calculation range like SUMIFS, AVERAGEIFS, etc. that we're going to discuss after this, because there's nothing to perform a calculation on. It's just counting how many times your conditions are met in the specified range of cells.

If you set more than one condition, the criteria ranges for all of the conditions must be the same size. To set just one condition only provide one criteria range and criteria.

You may run into COUNTIF in older versions of Excel or when only one condition is being used, but with COUNTIF and COUNTIFS the order of the inputs are identical so that shouldn't trip you up.

If you reference multiple conditions, your criteria do not have to be of the same type. Criteria can use numeric values (24 or "24"), cell references (A1), expressions (">42"), or text ("how").

Cell references and numbers do not need to be in quotation marks, but expressions and text references do.

For example:

=COUNTIFS(A1:A5,B2)

says to count how many times the values in Cells A1 through A5 are the same as the value in Cell B2.

$$=COUNTIFS(A1:A5,"YES")$$

says to count how many times the values in Cells A1 through A5 are the text YES. It will only count those instances where the full value in the cell matches the value given in the quotes. So a cell that says YES, PLEASE would not be counted. Nor would one that has YES followed by an extra space. It has to be an exact match unless you use wildcards, which we'll cover in a moment.

$$=COUNTIFS(A1:A5,">20")$$

says to count how many cells between Cell A1 and Cell A5 have a numeric value greater than 20. Note that even though the criteria is related to a number value that it's still shown in quotes because it's an expression. (If you had =COUNTIFS(A1:A5,20), which looks for any cells with a value equal to 20, you wouldn't need the quotes but you could still use them.)

If you want to reference a cell for your criteria but you also want to use a greater than or less than symbol, you need to combine the two using an ampersand (&).

For example

$$=COUNTIFS(A1:A5,">="&G2)$$

would count how many times the cells in the range from Cell A1 to Cell A5 contain a value that is greater than or equal to the value in Cell G2.

You can also use wildcards with the COUNTIFS function if your condition relates to a text value.

The asterisk (*) represents any number of characters or spaces. If you simply wanted to count any cell that contains text you would write that as

$$=COUNTIFS(A1:A5,"*")$$

It can also be used in combination with other letters to, for example, count any entry where there is an e. You would write that as

$$=COUNTIFS(A1:A5,"*e*")$$

The asterisks on either side of the e say to look for any cells where there is an e anywhere. If it were just on one side or the other then Excel would only look for words that starts with an e (e*) or ended with an e (*e).

If you want to count entries of a certain text length you can use the question mark (?) as a wildcard. It represents one single character. So

$$=COUNTIFS(A1:A5,"???")$$

would count all cells in the range from Cell A1 through A5 where the entry is three letters or spaces long. (It doesn't work with numbers.)

If you actually need to find an asterisk or question mark you can do so by using the tilde (~) before the mark you need. So ~? or ~* will look for an actual question mark or an actual asterisk

Always test different scenarios to make sure the count is counting everything you want it to but also not more than you want it to. (And be sure you've covered all possible scenarios in your testing, a mistake I know I've made at least once.)

Those were instances that would all work with COUNTIF or COUNTIFS because there was only one condition that needed to be met. Let's walk through a couple of scenarios that use multiple criteria now.

To count based upon multiple criteria, you simply include additional ranges and additional criteria for each one.

When you do so, the criteria range for all of your conditions must be the same size. So if your first cell range is A1:B25, then your other cell ranges must also be two columns wide and 25 rows long.

Ranges do not have to be adjacent, but they do have to be the same size.

The way the count is performed is it looks at all first cells in each of the criteria ranges and sees if the criteria for the first cell in each range is met.

If so, that entry is counted. If not, it isn't. It then moves on to the second cell in each of the criteria ranges and checks to see if all of the second cells meet the specified criteria. And so on and so on.

Each time all of the criteria are met, Excel counts that as 1.

Let's walk through an example to see this in action. I've created a table that has columns for State and Total Purchases for six customers and I want to count how many of my customers are both in Alabama (AL) and spent $250 or more. State is in Column A, Total Purchases is in Column B. The data is in Rows 2 through 7 with the header row in Row 1.

The function we need is:

$$=COUNTIFS(A1:A7,"AL",B1:B7,">=250")$$

Here it all is:

	A	B	C	D
1	State	Total Purchases		Customers From AL Who Spent At Least $250
2	AL	$ 275.00		3
3	AL	$ 250.00		Cell D2: =COUNTIFS(A1:A7,"AL",B1:B7,">=250")
4	AZ	$ 110.00		
5	AL	$ 95.00		
6	AR	$ 250.00		
7	AL	$ 300.00		

Our answer is 3 even though there were four potential purchases from AL and four purchases for $250 or more. Only three purchases met both conditions.

Let's break that down.

The first criteria range is A1 through A7. (We could have just as easily used A2 through A7 but it doesn't matter in this case if I include the header row since it won't meet my count criteria.) Those are the entries with our State values in them.

We told Excel we wanted to count any entry where the state is "AL".

The second criteria range is B1 through B7. That's our Total Purchases.

And we told Excel that for that range we wanted to count any time when a value was greater than or equal to $250. That's written as ">=250".

(Since this is a number and not a cell range we don't need the ampersand to combine the two.)

Excel then started with Cells A2 and B2 and determined whether both conditions were met. In this case, yes, so that first observation was counted. It continued onward like that to the end. Cells A5 and B5 only met one condition so were not counted. Same with Cells A6 and B6.

But Cells A3 and B3 as well as A7 and B7 did meet both conditions so were counted to give a total count of 3.

Remember, it's always a good idea to test your results against your data. So if I had a thousand rows of data I was using this formula on, I might write it to just cover ten rows first so I could test that it was working as expected before expanding to a sample size too big for me to judge easily. (Although with most of these you could use the filter options to filter your data to the same criteria you're using in your formula and then count, average, sum, etc. the results to double-check. That's another option.)

Okay. On to SUMIFS.

The SUMIFS Function

Notation: SUMIFS(sum_range, criteria_range1, criteria1, [criteria_range2, criteria2],...)

Excel Definition: Adds the cells specified by a given set of conditions or criteria.

SUMIFS allows you to sum the values in a range when multiple conditions are met. It can also work with just one condition if you only provide one criteria and one criteria range.

The first input is the range of cells that contain the values you want to add together. The second input is the range of cells that contain the values for your first criteria. The third input is the criteria itself. And then you just keep adding range of cells and condition that needs to be met until you have all of your criteria.

(Be careful if you ever do need to work with SUMIF which was this function's precursor, because the inputs are provided in a different order in SUMIF versus SUMIFS and SUMIF had less restraints than SUMIFS does.)

You can enter up to 127 conditions that need to be met before your values will be summed.

When using SUMIFS your sum range and the criteria ranges you use need to be the same size. They do not need to be next to one other or in any specific order on the worksheet, but they do need to cover the same number of rows and columns each.

SUMIFS can use a number (22 or "22"), an expression ("<13"), a text-based condition ("YES"), or a cell reference (H1) for the sum criteria. For anything except a single number or a cell reference, be sure to use quotation marks around your criteria.

You also don't have to use the same type of condition for each range. So you can use an expression for your first condition, a cell reference for your second, and a text-based condition for your third.

For text-based criteria, you can also use wildcards. The asterisk (*) represents any number of characters, the question mark (?) represents a single character, and the tilde (~) is used to distinguish when you're actually searching for an asterisk or question mark.

(See the COUNTIFS discussion for more detailed examples of all of the above.)

Here is a simple SUMIFS function with two conditions:

=SUMIFS(A1:A25,B1:B25,"USD",C1:C25,">10")

This would sum the values in Cells A1 through A25 if the value in the corresponding cells in Cells B1 through B25 contain "USD" and the values in Cells C1 through C25 are greater than 10. For Cell A1 it would look to Cells B1 and C1, for Cell A2 it would look to Cells B2 and C2, and so on and so on.

SUMIFS is one of the functions that I use the most.

For example, I use it in my budget worksheet to sum the amount I still owe on my bills each month.

I'll list all of my bills due for the month in Column A, whether I pay them with cash or with a credit card in Column B, the amount due in Column C, and I'll put an X when the bill is paid in Column D.

The SUMIFS formula I use is then:

=SUMIFS(C1:C10,B1:B10,"CASH",D1:D10,"")

That says sum the values in Column C if the values in Column B are "CASH" and Column D is blank. That lets me know how much cash I need in my bank account before those bills hit. As far as Excel is concerned Cash and CASH are the same. It is not case-sensitive.

The other place I use this is with my payables from publishing. I am usually owed money at any given time in about five different currencies and from about ten different sources. I have a worksheet where I sum the amount owed in each currency that I haven't yet been paid using a formula similar to the one above. In this case the formula for my USD payments is:

=SUMIFS(B$3:B$91,D$3:D$91,"USD",E$3:E$91,"")

This says to sum the values in Cells B3 through B91 if the values in Cells D3 through D91 are USD and the values in those cells in Column E are blank. I use Column E to check off when I receive a payment, so once payment is received that cell is no longer blank for that particular row.

I have a formula like this for each of the currencies I'm owed money in (CAD, AUD, INR, EUR, GBP, etc.) which is what the $ signs help with. This way I can just copy the formula to however many rows I need and all I have to update is the currency abbreviation.

Or even better yet, I can use a cell reference for that USD, say K2, and then when I copy the formula down it just references that same column but the new row so the currency abbreviation updates without any more effort from me.

$$=SUMIFS(B\$3:B\$91,D\$3:D\$91,K2,E\$3:E\$91,"")$$

That's just two examples of the power of SUMIFS. If you start to think about it, there are any number of places you can use it.

The AVERAGEIFS Function

Notation: AVERAGEIFS(average_range, criteria_range1, criteria1, [criteria_range2, criteria2],…)

Excel Definition: Finds average (arithmetic mean) for the cells specified by a given set of conditions or criteria.

The AVERAGEIFS function works just like SUMIFS except it takes an *average* of the values when a specified criteria is met. And just like SUMIFS and SUMIF, the order of the inputs in AVERAGEIFS differs from the order of the inputs in AVERAGEIF, so keep that in mind if you ever run into AVERAGEIF.

The inputs for the function are the range of cells that contain the values you want to average followed by the range of cells for your first condition and then the first condition parameters. If you want to use multiple criteria you then list the next range of cells and the next condition and so on and so on up to a total of 127 times.

Your average range and criteria range(s) must all be the same size and shape.

Your criteria do not have to be of the same type and can reference numeric values (24 or "24"), cells (A1), expressions (">42"), or text ("how").

Cell references and numbers do not need to be in quotation marks, expressions and text references do.

As with SUMIFS and COUNTIFS, you can use wildcards for text-based criteria. See the COUNTIFS description for examples.

For a value to be included in the average calculation, all of the conditions you specify must be met.

Be careful with empty cells, blanks, or text values where numbers are expected as these may generate an error message rather than a calculation or may impact the calculation.

M.L. Humphrey

(See the Excel help screen for the function for a full listing of the errors and adjustments that Excel makes. Always check a formula against a small sample of data to make sure you're getting the result you want.)

AVERAGEIFS evaluates TRUE values as 1 and FALSE values as 0.

The function will not work if the values in the average_range cannot be translated into numbers.

An example of using AVERAGEIFS might be if you were looking at student grades and wanted to see average score across teacher name and student gender to identify potential gender bias and/or overall score bias across teachers.

To do this, I'm going to build a table that has Test Score in Column A, Teacher Name in Column B, and Gender in Column C. Next, I'll build a table that has F and M in the header row on either side of a listing of the teacher names.

Finally I can then use AVERAGEIFS to pull into the second table the average score for female (F) and male (M) students for each teacher.

Here it is:

	A	B	C	D	E	F	G	H	I	J	K
1	Score	Teacher	Gender								
2	50	Smith	F								
3	49	Barker	M			F		M			
4	68	Vasquez	F			80.25	Smith	84.50			
5	75	Smith	M			90.00	Barker	68.67			
6	90	Barker	F			68.00	Vasquez	76.00			
7	94	Smith	M								
8	93	Barker	M		Cell F4:	=AVERAGEIFS($A$1:$A$13,$B$1:$B$13,G4,$C$1:$C$13,$F$3)					
9	91	Smith	F		Cell H4:	=AVERAGEIFS($A$1:$A$13,$B$1:$B$13,G4,$C$1:$C$13,$H$3)					
10	76	Vasquez	M								
11	82	Smith	F								
12	64	Barker	M								
13	98	Smith	F								

By putting the F and M values in Cells F3 and H3 to match the values in the Gender column in Column C I was able to reference those values with my formula. Same with the teacher last names in Column G.

The formula used in Cell F4 (for female students of Teacher Smith) is:

=AVERAGEIFS($A$1:$A$13,$B$1:$B$13,$G4,$C$1:$C$13,$F$3)

What that's saying is, average the values in Cells A1 through A13 where the values in Cells B1 through B13 are equal to the teacher name in Cell G4 and the gender of the student listed in Cells C1 through C13 is equal to the value in Cell F3.

334

By using the $ signs in the formula I can then copy the formula down to the other two rows in that table without making any other changes.

I did have to adjust the reference to $F$3 when I then copied the formula over to Column H for the male side and make that $H$3.

But by using $G4 I didn't have to adjust the reference to the teacher name when I copied it over.

Done. (Not statistically robust because we don't have enough data to really draw any sort of conclusion at all, but you can see how it could be interesting with enough data and really doesn't take all that much time to create.)

Don't forget, too, that AVERAGEIFS can be used with a single condition as well. So you could use it to calculate the average customer order amount for each state if you had a list of states, for example.

=AVERAGEIFS(A1:A1000,B1:B1000,"CO")

Would take the average of the values in Cells A1 through A1000 where the value in Column B was "CO".

(If you're ever trying to do a quick double-check of your values with AVERAGEIFS you can select the cells that it should be averaging and look on the bottom right side of your Excel screen and you should see values for Average, Count, and Sum for the selected cells. If Excel doesn't see your entries as numbers it will only show a count value.)

That's AVERAGEIFS, now on to MINIFS.

The MINIFS Function

Notation: MINIFS(min_range, criteria_range1, criteria1, [criteria_range2, criteria2],…)

Excel Definition: Returns the minimum value among cells specified by a given set of conditions or criteria.

The MINIFS function is a new function in Excel 2019. It works just like COUNTIFS, SUMIFS, and AVERAGEIFS except its purpose is to return the minimum value in a range of cells.

The inputs into the function are similar to the other functions we already discussed. The first input is the range with the values where your minimum value will be found. The next input is the range for your first condition. The third input is the condition. And so on and so forth up to 127 conditions.

As with the other functions, your min_range and criteria ranges need to all be the same size.

Your criteria do not have to be of the same type and can reference numeric values (24 or "24"), cells (A1), expressions (">42"), or text ("how"). Cell references and numbers do not need to be in quotation marks, expressions and text references do. And you can use wildcards for text-based criteria.

See the COUNTIFS description for examples of the various criteria types and wildcards.

Also, be sure your ranges are properly aligned. In the help section for this one they show an example where the ranges are not aligned and the function still works anyway because the ranges are the same size.

Also, the function will return a value of zero if there are not matches to the conditions you set, so be careful on that one because I can see a scenario where you might think zero was a legitimate result and it turns out that the zero result was just because the formula was written wrong.

So when would you use this? Well, let's go back to our grades by teacher and gender example and apply MINIFS instead of AVERAGEIFS.

	A	B	C	D	E	F	G	H	I	J	K
1	Score	Teacher	Gender								
2	50	Smith	F								
3	49	Barker	M			F		M			
4	68	Vasquez	F			50.00	Smith	75.00			
5	75	Smith	M			90.00	Barker	49.00			
6	90	Barker	F			68.00	Vasquez	76.00			
7	94	Smith	M								
8	93	Barker	M			Cell F4:	=MINIFS($A$2:$A$13,$B$2:$B$13,$G4,$C$2:$C$13,$F$3)				
9	91	Smith	F			Cell H4:	=MINIFS($A$2:$A$13,$B$2:$B$13,$G4,$C$2:$C$13,$H$3)				
10	76	Vasquez	M								
11	82	Smith	F								
12	64	Barker	M								
13	98	Smith	F								

The formula in Cell F4 becomes:

=MINIFS($A$2:$A$13,$B$2:$B$13,$G4,$C$2:$C$13,$F$3)

That's basically the same as the formula we used for AVERAGEIFS except we swapped out the function. What's interesting here is that we can see that for Barker, the minimum score for his female students is 90. That highlights a flaw in this data, which is that there is just one female student in Barker's class. And with Vasquez we can see that the averages and the minimums are the same as well and that's because there's only data for two students for Vasquez in the entire table, one male and one female.

Next we'll do the same for MAXIFS.

The MAXIFS Function

Notation: MAXIFS(max_range, criteria_range1, criteria1, [criteria_range2, criteria2],...)

Excel Definition: Returns the maximum value among cells specified by a given set of conditions or criteria.

MAXIFS was another new function added to Excel 2019. It works just like MINIFS except that it returns the maximum value in the range that meets the specified conditions.

Everything that held true for SUMIFS, AVERAGEIFS, and MINIFS also holds true for MAXIFS. The max_range and criteria_ranges need to be the same size and should be aligned correctly. If you have more than one condition they don't need to be the same type. You can use wildcards with text conditions. Criteria can reference numeric values, cells, expressions, or text.

Here is an example of applying MAXIFS to that same range of student scores that we applied it to for AVERAGEIFS and MINIFS:

	E	F	G	H	I	J	K
3		**F**		**M**			
4		98.00	**Smith**	94.00			
5		90.00	**Barker**	93.00			
6		68.00	**Vasquez**	76.00			
7							
8	**Cell F4:**	=MAXIFS($A$2:$A$13,$B$2:$B$13,$G4,$C$2:$C$13,$F$3)					
9	**Cell H4:**	=MAXIFS($A$2:$A$13,$B$2:$B$13,$G4,$C$2:$C$13,$H$3)					

The formula used in Cell F4 this time is:

=MAXIFS($A$2:$A$13,$B$2:$B$13,$G4,$C$2:$C$13,$F$3)

This time the values we see in the analysis table we built are the maximum scores for each gender for students in each teacher's class.

Again this serves to highlight the fact that for Barker there is only one female student and for Vasquez there is only one male and one female student.

This is noticeable when comparing the results across all three functions we've applied to the data.

In this table the Average column uses AVERAGEIFS, the Min column uses MINIFS, and the Max column uses MAXIFS. (And because of how I built the table I could just write each formula once and copy it down the rest of that column.)

Teacher	M/F	Average	Min	Max
Barker	F	90.00	90.00	90.00
Barker	M	68.67	49.00	93.00
Smith	F	80.25	50.00	98.00
Smith	M	84.50	75.00	94.00
Vasquez	F	68.00	68.00	68.00
Vasquez	M	76.00	76.00	76.00

Again, not a large enough data set to say anything about, but if it were a large data set, this is an excellent and easy way to compare grades across gender and teacher. It could as easily be used for sales performance by salesperson by month, product performance, etc.

Once you master one of these advanced IF functions you see that they all work pretty much the same way and so you can pick whichever one best suits your needs and be comfortable using it.

Okay. On to a few more "IF" functions that are a little different and more for cleaning things up than anything else, IFNA and IFERROR.

The IFNA Function

Notation: IFNA(value, value_if_na)

Excel Definition: Returns the value you specify if the expression resolves to #N/A, otherwise returns the result of the expression.

The IFNA function is one that I rarely use because I'm so comfortable with using IF functions that I just quickly write an IF function that does the same thing, which is to suppress that pesky #N/A result that sometimes occurs with IF functions.

The way IFNA works is that you tell it a function to perform and if the result of that function is the #N/A error then instead of returning that error you can specify what Excel returns instead.

(I say function here, but the Excel help text calls it an argument.)

The easiest way to show how this works is to walk you through an example.

Let's say I have a list of my books I've published and how much I've spent on ads for those books each month. I also have a list of how much I've earned for each book each month. And I decide I want to combine those two sets of information to calculate a profit/loss per month for each book.

I can use the TEXTJOIN function to create an entry for both data sets that combines month-year-title into one column and then use VLOOKUP to look up the amount I spent on ads for each title in each month and bring that into the sales worksheet.

But when VLOOKUP can't find an entry—so in months where I had book sales but no ad spend, for example—Excel returns a value of #N/A.

When that happens within a column of data you can no longer click on that column and see its summed value. This would prevent me from easily checking that I'd captured all of my ad costs.

But I can easily fix this issue using the IFNA function.

If my original formula was:

=VLOOKUP(D:D,'Advertising Spend By Series'!E:F,2,FALSE)

(That's saying look for the value in Column D of this worksheet in Column E of the Advertising Spend by Series worksheet and then pull the value from Column F, but only if the two values are an exact match.)

The revised formula using IFNA is:

=IFNA(VLOOKUP(D:D,'Advertising Spend By Series'!E:F,2,FALSE),0)

That looks complicated, but it's not. All I did is wrap the IFNA function around what I already had for VLOOKUP.

Replace the VLOOKUP portion with an X and you have:

=IFNA(X,0)

Basically, if there's a value for VLOOKUP to return then return that value, otherwise return a zero.

I chose to return a value of zero, but you could easily have it return a text statement instead.

If you are going to have it return text, be sure to use quotation marks around the text you want returned. So if I wanted "No Match" returned instead of a zero, I'd use:

=IFNA(VLOOKUP(D:D,'Advertising Spend By Series'!E:F,2,FALSE),"No Match")

If you don't want anything returned, so you just want an apparently blank cell, then leave that second argument blank. You'll still need to use the comma, so it should look like this:

=IFNA(VLOOKUP(D:D,'Advertising Spend By Series'!E:F,2,FALSE),)

That will return a value of "" in that cell instead of the #N/A error message.

And that's it. It looks a little complicated because we were working with a VLOOKUP function, but it's really very simple.

Just take the formula you already have that's giving you the #N/A results, type IFNA(between the equals sign and that first function, go to the end, add a comma, put in the result you want returned when there's an #N/A result (if any), and then add a closing paren. Done.

Just keep in mind, of course, that you will not see an #N/A result if you use this function, which could hide from you valuable information about your calculation or your data.

Also, it's particular to just that type of error. Other error messages, such as #DIV/0!, will still be displayed.

If you want to suppress all error messages, then you need to use IFERROR which we'll discuss next.

The IFERROR Function

Notation: IFERROR(value, value_if_error)

Excel Definition: Returns value_if_error if expression is an error and the value of the expression itself otherwise.

The IFERROR function is just like the IFNA function except that it will return your specified value for any error message, not just the #N/A error message. Error messages suppressed by the function include: #N/A, #VALUE!, #REF!, #DIV/0!, #NUM!, #NAME?, and #NULL!

So be sure before you use it that you are okay with suppressing all of those error messages. For example, the #REF! error message usually will tell you when you've deleted a cell that was being referenced by a formula. That for me isn't something I would like to hide. If I've made that mistake, I want to know it.

But if you have a range of cells with a formula in them that's returning, for example, the #DIV/0! error because you're currently dividing by zero, which is an issue I've run into in some of my worksheets, this might be a good option.

Your other option is to use a simple IFS function instead.

For example, I might use

$$=IFS(P1=0,"",TRUE,J1/P1)$$

in one of my worksheets, because it returns a #DIV/0! error until P1 has a value and that annoys me. IFERROR would work the same in that situation. I could use

$$=IFERROR(J1/P1,)$$

instead. Note that I left the second argument, the value_if_error empty which will return a blank cell as long as dividing the value in Cell J1 by the value in Cell P1 produces an error message.

To do that I still had to include the comma, though.

My temptation in using either IFNA or IFERROR is to have them return zeroes or empty cells, but I would recommend that if you're using IFERROR in a crucial situation that you have it return a text entry instead so that you always know when there's an error message that's being suppressed. So

$$=IFERROR(J1/P1,"No Value")$$

is probably a better choice than

$$=IFERROR(J1/P1,)$$

because you will know for a fact that the formula generated an error message and won't think that the value in that cell calculated as zero.

Note above that I used quotes around the text I wanted to have Excel display in the place of my error message, just like I did with IFNA.

Lookup Functions

Alright, so that was our IF functions. Now on to another set of functions that are potentially useful, the Lookup Functions.

A quick note: If you're feeling like this is all a bit of a struggle you might want to skip this section for now because functions like INDEX and MATCH fall into what I think of as an advanced intermediate category. It might help to go read about the rest of the math functions and the date functions first, which are very easy to use, and then come back to this section later when you're more grounded in working with functions overall.

But I put this section here because I think the Lookup Functions have the most potential after the top ten functions and the IF functions to provide value.

VLOOKUP, which we already covered, is probably the most celebrated of these functions, but there are others you can use, and if you master all of them you will save yourself tremendous amounts of effort.

So let's start with VLOOKUP's counterpart, HLOOKUP.

The HLOOKUP Function

Notation: HLOOKUP(lookup_value, table_array, row_index_num, [range_lookup])

Excel Definition: Looks up a value in the top row of a table or array of values and returns the value in the same column from a row you specify.

HLOOKUP is basically the horizontal equivalent to VLOOKUP. Where VLOOKUP scans down a column to match your value and then pulls a result from another column in the row where the match was made, HLOOKUP scans across a row to match your value and then pulls a result from another row in that column where the match was made.

So it's a transposed version of VLOOKUP.

VLOOKUP is the much more popular of the two options because of how most people structure their data. But let's say I have a table of data with month across the top and vendor across the left-hand side and I want to extract how much was earned on a specific vendor in a specific month. I could do that using HLOOKUP.

Here's an example data table and result for looking up March and then pulling the fourth row of data which corresponds to ACX:

	A	B	C	D
1		January	February	March
2	Amazon	$100.00	$107.00	$114.49
3	Createspace	$37.00	$39.59	$42.36
4	ACX	$23.50	$25.15	$26.91
5	Con Sales	$10.00		
6				
7	March, ACX	$ 26.91		
8	Cell B7:	=HLOOKUP("March",B1:D5,4,FALSE)		

The formula I used was:

=HLOOKUP("March",B1:D5,4,FALSE)

That's saying look for an exact match to the word March in my data table contained in Cells B1 through D5 and then return the result for the fourth row in the data table.

Let's break this down further.

The first entry in any HLOOKUP formula is going to be what you're looking up. This can be a numeric value, a text string, or a cell reference. In the example above, because I wanted to look up a specific text value, I had to use quotation marks.

With text entries, you can also use the wildcards that Excel has for text lookups. A question mark means any one character and an asterisk means any number of characters. So "*April" would search for any text string that has April at the end whereas "?April" would only search for any text string that has one character before ending in April.

The second input into the HLOOKUP function is where you're going to search. That's the table array. The first row of that table array is where what you're searching for needs to be. The table array then has to have the row with the values you want to return somewhere below the search row.

I used B1:D5 here but I could have as easily used A1:D5 for the cell range.

The third input is which row in your table to pull the result from.

If you provide a negative number, you'll get an error message. If you provide a value that is larger than the size of the range you specified, you will also get an error message.

A value of 1 that will return either the value you were looking up (for an exact match) or the closest possible value (for an approximate match), which can be especially useful if you're trying to find the closest result to a specific value.

The fourth input is TRUE or FALSE to tell Excel what type of search it's performing. With HLOOKUP (as with VLOOKUP), there are two options for what you're searching for. You can search for an exact match (FALSE) or you can search for an approximate match (TRUE).

If you choose to search for an approximate match, then your data in the lookup row needs to be sorted in ascending order for HLOOKUP to work properly. If you're looking for an exact match (like in the example above) then the order of the entries doesn't matter.

(You can sort data in a row using the Sort option in the Data tab by clicking on Options when the Sort dialogue box appears and choosing to sort from left to right.)

When looking up values Excel treats uppercase and lower case entries as the same. It is not case sensitive.

If Excel can't find a match for an exact match search you will get an #N/A result.

You will also get an #N/A error if you ask for an approximate match but the lookup value you specify is smaller than the smallest value in the table.

If you do get an error message, check your spelling, that your table range is correct, and that your row references are correct. If that all looks good, then you can look at the help function for HLOOKUP to see which error message you received and what that might mean.

Where VLOOKUP to me seems to be best used for looking up values in a table, like a discount table, I see HLOOKUP as most useful when you want to extract data from an existing summary table like in the example I gave above. But the two do operate on the same principles, so if you understand how to use one you should be able to use the other as well.

If you go to the Excel help for HLOOKUP or VLOOKUP you may be a little confused because at the top it suggests that you use XLOOKUP instead. But if you try to type XLOOKUP into your worksheet, you'll find that Excel doesn't act like that's a function. That's because XLOOKUP is not actually available in Excel 2019. It's currently only available in Microsoft 365. And if like me you like to own your software after a one-time fee and not be someone's guinea pig, then you don't have Microsoft 365 so that little comment they put there is a bit of a moot point.

But know that some day in a future version of Excel there will likely be a function you can use called XLOOKUP that is a better version of HLOOKUP and VLOOKUP because it works in any direction and returns exact matches by default. Won't that be nice to have someday? But not today, at least not in Excel 2019.

The SWITCH Function

Notation: SWITCH(expression, value1, result 1, [default_or_value2, result2],…)

Excel Definition: Evaluates an expression against a list of values and returns the result corresponding to the first matching value. If there is no match, an optional default value is returned.

In the meantime, we do have the SWITCH function which was added to Excel 2019. From what I can tell looking at the examples they give it allows you to make a calculation and then provide one of up to 126 different answers based on the result.

The examples that Excel provides for how to use this function are about providing the day of the week for a specific date. But the TEXT function does that better. They use:

$$=SWITCH(WEEKDAY(A2),1,"Sunday",2,"Monday",3,"Tuesday","No$$
$$Match")$$

I can do the same thing with:

$$=TEXT(A2, "dddd")$$

So bad examples. Let's set that aside and think of some other option for how to use SWITCH. I think I would want to use it in a setting where I couldn't provide that response otherwise. My mind goes to my days of learning BASIC computer programming language when I was little and how you'd walk someone through a little choose your own adventure game.

M.L. Humphrey

Maybe I could set it up to ask someone a question and if they give me the right answer I give them one response. If they give me the wrong answer I give them another. Like this:

=SWITCH(A1,100,"Congratulations, that's correct.","Sorry, try again.")

That works. This is saying if the value in Cell A1 is 100 then put in this cell "Congratulations, that's correct." If it isn't, then put in this cell "Sorry, try again."

You could combine this with protecting the cells that use SWITCH so that users can't see what the answer is that's driving the response and basically use it to create self-directed quiz.

That's one option. What other use can we put this to?

What if we want to assign a salesperson to each account based upon letter of the alphabet? You could use SWITCH for that as well. I'm not going to write out the whole alphabet, but let's try a few letters. Here's the ugly, never want to do it again version which would require you to go into the function to swap things around each time someone left the company or joined it:

=SWITCH(LEFT(A1,1),"a","Jones","b","Smith","c","Carter","Harvey")

What that's saying is take the first letter of the value in Cell A1 and if that letter is an "a" assign it to Jones, if it's a "b" assign it to Smith, if it's a "c" assign it to Carter, and if it's any other letter assign it to Harvey.

We can transform that into a build-it-once, work-with-a-data-table-after-that version:

=SWITCH(LEFT(A1,1),G2,H2,G3,H3,G4,H4,H5)

Without context that second version is incomprehensible, but let's walk through it with reference to the version above where everything is in the formula itself.

All I've done in the second formula is put the values "a" and "Jones" in Cells G2 and H2, respectively. And then done the same thing for the remaining values, building a table that any user could see and interact with easily.

Either option would be a pain to build the first time out. But with the second one if I need to make edits I could make them to the data table not the formula.

Another thought. When I was trying to figure out why you'd use this I found someone mentioning that it's easier than using nested IF functions, which is probably true, but now that IFS exists, I don't think it's necessarily easier than IFS.

350

Comparing the two, think of this one as not using the branching paths that IFS and nested IF functions do but more just a straight line list of alternatives.

Also, know that this function can take up to 126 values, although that would be quite a challenge to write the first time through.

Okay. On to another Excel function that you may or may not ever use but probably exists for a good reason, CHOOSE.

The CHOOSE Function

Notation: CHOOSE(index_num, value1, [value2],...)

Excel Definition: Chooses a value or action to perform from a list of values, based on an index number

At its most basic, CHOOSE lets you pick a result from a list of values. So if the index_num is 2 then it picks the second value in your list. If it's 3 it picks the third value in the list. Which sounds pretty boring.

For me the power of CHOOSE lies in how it interacts with other functions, which is why I think the Excel help examples for this one vastly underplay what it can do. That's because the examples all use a fixed number for the index_num entry and the power in this function lies in having that index_num field be a calculation.

Let's walk through it and I'll show you what I mean.

The first input is an index_num that tells you which of the values to pick from a list. If it says 1, it picks the first value. If it says 2, it picks the second value. This number cannot be less than 1 nor can it be greater than the number of values you list in the function or else you'll get a #VALUE! error message.

You can, however, have a fraction for this value and Excel will truncate the value. So 2.33 becomes 2 and chooses the second listed option.

The rest of the function are your "values" or chosen outcomes. So:

$$=CHOOSE(2,23,43,54)$$

returns a result of 43. My index_num is 2 and the second value I provided was 43. If I change that 2 to a 5, I'll get an error. If it's less than 1 I get an error. If it's 3.45 that becomes 3 and my result is 54.

So far, not something we really feel a need for, right?

What if instead of that 2, though, I used an IF function? Or a SWITCH function? Or the WEEKDAY function to give me a day of the week?

Here's a goofy little use of this:

$$=CHOOSE(WEEKDAY(F1),"Sunday is my fun day","Just another manic Monday","Tuesdays are boring","Wednesday, humpday")$$

This returns a saying for whatever the day of the week is for the date in Cell F1. Because the WEEKDAY function returns a number for the day of the week, we can then match that up with a saying for each day. (Who says uses of Excel always have to be serious?)

The only constraint there is that the index value you use in the first input needs to be a number from 1 to 254 and you need to have enough values after that to cover any index value your calculation comes up with. There's no last entry or default value that gets returned like with SWITCH or IFS.

We can also rewrite this one to replace the individual values with cell references:

$$=CHOOSE(WEEKDAY(F1),G2,G3,G4,G5)$$

In this case I've put the individual sayings in Cells G2 through G5. Much easier to work with after the fact.

So what's the difference between SWITCH and CHOOSE? They seem awfully similar, right?

SWITCH lets you specify specific results that return a chosen value. It's not limited to numeric results.

CHOOSE is a little less flexible. The index_num has to be a number. But it's easier to write if you're working with a numbered list and there are more values allowed.

One final note, your value inputs can be cell ranges as well. In the help text they use A1:A10, B1:B10, and C1:C10 as one set of values in a CHOOSE function formula. This is useful for when you nest CHOOSE within another function like SUM.

The TRANSPOSE Function

Notation: TRANSPOSE(array)

Excel Definition: Converts a vertical range of cells to a horizontal range, or vice versa.

The TRANSPOSE function is one that you probably won't use very often, but it does come up. So let's walk through what TRANSPOSE does. It takes a series of entries that are in a column and displays them in a row instead or takes a series of entries that are in a row and displays them in a column.

You can do this with more than one row and/or column at a time. It will basically flip those entries so that what was in columns is now in rows and what was in rows is now in columns.

TRANSPOSE is a special kind of function that Excel introduced called an array formula. There are two key things to remember when working with array formulas.

First, you need to select a range of cells where your results will go *before* you start typing your formula in or it won't work.

Second, you need to use Ctrl + Shift + Enter when you're done entering your formula or it also won't work properly.

These two steps are what, for me, distinguish array formulas from other formulas. (That and the fact that the values they return appear in a range of cells instead of a single cell, of course because array formulas return multiple results.)

Let's walk through an example:

Let's say that in Cells A1 through A6 you have typed the numbers 1 through 6 and now you want those values across a row instead of in a column.

Go to where you want to put those values and highlight the entire range of cells where you want to put them. It needs to be the same size as the cells you're transposing, so in this case six cells.

I'm going to highlight Cells E6 through J6 for this.

Keeping those cells highlighted, start typing your formula which is

=TRANSPOSE(A1:A6)

Finish with Ctrl + Shift + Enter.

If you've done it right, the numbers 1 through 6 will now also appear in Cells E6 through J6.

If you click on one of those cells, the formula in the formula bar should look like this for every one of those cells:

{=TRANSPOSE(A1:A6)}

Those squiggly brackets indicate an array formula.

Any change to the original cell range A1 through A6 will also change the value in the corresponding Cells E6 through J6. So if I replace 1 in Cell A1 with 10, that will also update Cell E6.

Now, the other option if you just want to change the orientation of your data is to copy and then use Paste Special-Transpose. To do this, select the cells you want to copy, click in the first cell where you want to paste that data (making sure enough cells are empty so you're not over-writing anything), and then right click, and under Paste Options choose the Transpose option. (The one with two little two-box grids with an arrow pointing between them in the bottom right corner of the clipboard image. For me, right now, that's the fourth image choice.)

You might wonder, if you can just copy and Paste Special-Transpose, why would you want to use this TRANSPOSE function instead? The key difference is that when you use the TRANSPOSE function your data it is still linked to the original source. That is not true with Paste Special-Transpose.

Also, you can pair TRANSPOSE with another array formula that would normally return results in a column to immediately return them in a row instead.

Basically, which option (function or pasting) is the better choice will depend on why you needed to do that. If you just wanted to transform a row of data into a column or vice versa, which is my usual reason for doing this, then Paste Special – Transpose is the easiest choice. If you're wanting to change the orientation of data that's output from an array formula or you want to copy data from one source and paste it to another in a different orientation while keeping the two sources linked, then the TRANSPOSE function will be the better option.

Just remember that when you use it it's an array formula so has to be set up and completed in a different manner than a normal function does.

The INDEX Function

Notation: INDEX(array,row_num, [column_num]) or
INDEX(reference, row_num, [column_num], [area_num])

Excel Definition: Returns a value or reference of the cell at the
intersection of a particular row and column, in a given range.

The INDEX function can take two forms. It can be an array formula and return a range of values like we just saw TRANSPOSE do, or it can serve as a basic lookup formula and return a value from a specified column and row within a specified table.

When you open the help pane for this function it links to a video which gives a very nice overview of both ways of using the INDEX function, so I'd encourage you to watch that. But I'm going to walk through it here, too, so you don't have to if you don't want to.

At its most basic, the reference version

$$=\text{INDEX}(\text{reference, row\_num, [column\_num], [area\_num]})$$

looks for a specific value in a specified position in a table. (To me this is much like how VLOOKUP and HLOOKUP work except it's not looking for a match to a value but a specific *location*.)

The first argument you provide in this version is the table you want to look in.

Let's say you have student grades for a series of tests and the data table is in Cells A2 through E7 with the actual data in Cells B3 through E7. Like so:

	A	B	C	D	E
1		Semester 1			
2		Test 1	Test 2	Test 3	Test 4
3	Student A	82	87	94	92
4	Student B	88	81	84	83
5	Student C	65	68	64	63
6	Student D	98	98	98	99
7	Student E	86	88	84	83

If you want to extract from that table the grade on the third test for Student B, you could write either of the two following formulas using the INDEX function:

$$=INDEX(A2:E7,3,4)$$

or

$$=INDEX(B3:E7,2,3)$$

The difference between these two is the range of cells I told Excel to use for the reference data table. In the first one, Cells A2 through E7, I included the header row and column with the student names. In the second, Cells B3 through E7, I just included the results.

That's the first input into the INDEX function. The data range to use.

The second input is which row *in that range* to pull the data from. *This is not the actual row number in the worksheet.* This is which row *in your chosen range* to pull from.

So when I include the header row, Student B's data is in the third row of the data range. When I don't include the header row Student B's data is in the second row of the data range.

The third input is which column *in that range* to pull the data from. Same concept. Because in the first example I included the student names column, then to pull data for the third test we need to look at the fourth column in the data range. But in the second example where I only included the results, we pull from the third column.

There is a fourth input option that the INDEX function can use. It is very well demonstrated in that video that I referenced above, but I'll walk through it here as well.

The fourth input option works when you have more than one data table to look up values in. To use this option, the first input for the function has to include more than one data range. If you include more than one range in that first input then you can use the fourth input option for INDEX to tell Excel which of the multiple ranges you provided it should use.

(If you have not provided multiple ranges and specify a number for this fourth input you will get a #REF! error.)

Let's say that you teach the same group of students for two different semesters and so have test results for both of those semesters for the same students. Like this:

	A	B	C	D	E
1		Semester 1			
2		Test 1	Test 2	Test 3	Test 4
3	Student A	82	87	94	92
4	Student B	88	81	84	83
5	Student C	65	68	64	63
6	Student D	98	98	98	99
7	Student E	86	88	84	83
8					
9		Semester 2			
10		Test 1	Test 2	Test 3	Test 4
11	Student A	88	92	93	96
12	Student B	90	83	85	85
13	Student C	62	62	62	62
14	Student D	65	65	68	66
15	Student E	91	92	93	95

And now you want to pull the test score for the same student for the third test for each semester.

First, let's pull the same data we pulled above, but with the INDEX formula set up to pull from either table, and specifying which table to use.

We can rewrite both formulas to include both table ranges and to pull from the first table like so:

$$=INDEX((A2:E7,A10:E15),3,4,1)$$

or

$$=INDEX((B3:E7,B11:E15),2,3,1)$$

Now we can modify both of those formulas to pull a value from the second table instead by changing the value of the last input in the function:

$$=INDEX((A2:E7,A10:E15),3,4,2)$$

or

$$=INDEX((B3:E7,B11:E15),2,3,2)$$

Of course, the way I would actually use this is not by manually going in and changing that final number each time. I would instead build a table that pulls in values from each semester. Like this:

	I	J	K	L
8		Test 3 Results		
9				
10			Semester	
11			1	2
12	Student A	1	94	93
13	Student B	2	84	85

The formula I used here in Cell K12 is:

$$=INDEX((\$A\$2:\$E\$7,\$A\$10:\$E\$15),(\$J12+1),4,K\$11)$$

M.L. Humphrey

That says that there are two tables of data to pull from with the given cell ranges and that the row to use is equal to the number in Column J plus 1. The column in each table to use is the fourth one, and that the table to pull from is the table number in Row 11.

I can then just copy that formula into all four cells and it will populate my table for me by looking in each of the semester grade tables for each student.

That to me has some potential value in extracting information from multiple tables to create a summary table.

The other potential value of the INDEX function is in its ability to pull an entire row or column of data out of a table. That is done by treating it as an array formula.

Remember from looking at the TRANSPOSE function that there are a few key things you need to do to treat a function as an array formula. (At least in Excel 2019.)

You have to select a range of cells not just one cell beforehand and then you have to use Ctrl + Shift + Enter after you've created the formula.

So let's go back to our two tables of data and let's extract all of the test scores for Student A using INDEX as an array formula, one row per semester, like this:

	I	J	K	L	M	N	O
16			Semester				
17	Student A	1	1	82	87	94	92
18		1	2	88	92	93	96

In Columns I, J, and K and Rows 17 and 18 I create a simple table with my semester number and my student row number so that I can use cell references to do this.

Once I've done that I highlight Cells L17 through O17 and then in L17 put the array formula:

=INDEX(($B$3:$E$7,$B$11:$E$15),J17,0,K17)

I finish by using Ctrl + Shift + Enter.

That's saying there are two tables and that I should pull the values from the table number listed in Cell K17. And I should then pull the row number listed in Cell J17. In this case, my table ranges are both just the data, so no need to adjust that value by adding one.

I just want the row of data, so for the column value I list 0.

360

I then repeat that same process with Cells L18 through O18 to pull grades for the same student for the second semester.

(I will note here that you can't just copy and paste that second formula down like you would with a normal formula. It took a little fiddling to get it to copy down properly for me.)

In the same way that we extracted a row from a data table, you can also extract a column. Just make the row value 0 and provide a column value instead. Also, make sure that you highlight the number of cells needed for that specific column at the start.

And, to circle back to our TRANSPOSE function, if you wanted to return the column values as a row, you could pair the INDEX function with the TRANSPOSE function. So you could highlight five cells within a row and then use:

$$=TRANSPOSE(INDEX((\$B\$3:\$E\$7,\$B\$11:\$E\$15),0,3,1))$$

to pull the third column of data from the table of data contained in Cells B3 through E7 and put it in a row.

Keep in mind that these are still formulas, so if you change your source data you will change the values that you've pulled from the table. To lock any values into place use Paste Special – Values.

The MATCH Function

Notation: MATCH(lookup_value, lookup_array, [match_type])

Excel Definition: Returns the relative position of an item in an array that matches a specified value in a specified order.

What MATCH is going to do for you is look in a range of cells, either a row or a column that you specify, and it is going to return for you the position of a specific value that you're looking for within that range.

You can also have it return the position of the closest value to what you're looking for rather than an exact match.

Note that this is a *position* (i.e. location) that you're getting back. It will tell you that that value you wanted is in the seventh row of the specified range. Or the third column of the specified range.

In and of itself, that's not going to do much for you. But where this becomes incredibly powerful is when you combine the MATCH function with other functions, like the INDEX function, to specify a row number or a column number.

So thinking back to what we did with INDEX, I can go back to that same table I had for student grades and I can use MATCH to look up the row number for each student and then combine that with the INDEX function to pull those student's grades on a specific test. Like so for Student A:

=INDEX(($A$2:$E$7),MATCH("Student A",$A$2:$A$7,0),4)

where I know that Column A in the table range has my student names in it.

The MATCH portion here is saying to find an exact match to "Student A" in Cells A2 through A7. That value is then used in the INDEX portion to say look in the cell range from Cells A2 through E7 and pull the value from the nth row where n is the value returned by the MATCH function and the 4th column.

I could go a step further and create a data table with all of my student names and then replace that "Student A" entry with a cell reference.

Pretty cool, huh? It requires a little twisting of your mind to get it to work, but this is incredibly powerful if you can do that.

A few things to know:

MATCH will look for a numeric value, a text value, or a logical value. It can also work with cell references.

There are three match types you can specify. Using a 0 means an exact match. Using a negative 1 means MATCH will find the smallest value that is greater than or equal to the specified lookup_value. Using a positive 1, so just 1, means MATCH will find the largest value that is less than or equal to the lookup_value.

If you use -1 or 1, you need to sort your data or it won't work properly; it will return a value of #N/A. For -1, sort your data in descending order. For 1, sort your data in ascending order.

Excel's default is to treat MATCH as if you've specified 1 as your match type, so be very very careful using MATCH since the default match type requires a specific sort order.

(I will note here that with all of these lookup functions I far prefer to use them for exact matches, because it's less likely I'll mess something up that way, but there are very good reasons to use them without wanting an exact match. You just have to be more careful.)

Keep in mind, too, that MATCH is not returning a row or column number. It is returning the *relative* row or column number *within your specified range of cells* which works perfectly in a scenario like the one above where we're using it in conjunction with the INDEX function, but would not work so well with say, macros.

Also, for text, MATCH does not distinguish between upper and lowercase letters.

If there is no match, MATCH will return a result of #N/A.

One of the reasons I included this function was because I saw an interesting use of the INDEX function when paired with the MATCH function that used MATCH and INDEX to pull in rank order of 34 different variables for a list of individuals. I'm not going to walk through it here because parsing it out would take about two pages of text, but just suffice it to say that you can get very complex results by using two simple functions like these together.

Statistical Functions

Phew. Okay. That's the end of the Lookup Functions that we're going to cover. Now we get to blaze through a bunch of other functions that will be generally useful but are more focused on one specific calculation.

We're going to start with functions that Excel classifies as statistical functions, then we'll move on to the rest of the math functions, and then we'll wrap up with the text and date and time functions.

If you have a particular way in which you plan to use Excel that focuses more in one of these areas than another, this is the time to start skipping around.

This section will cover medians, modes, ranked values, linear forecasts, frequencies, and how to calculate the nth-largest or nth-smallest value in a range.

The MEDIAN Function

Notation: MEDIAN(number1, [number2],…)

Excel Definition: Returns the median, or the number in the middle of the set of given numbers.

A calculation of the average of a range of values is very useful and very commonly used, but it can sometimes give very misleading results. That's where MEDIAN and MODE come in. They provide a better picture when your data is skewed in some way.

For example, writing income is highly skewed. (As is acting income.) There's someone out there making $100,000 a month and a lot of other someones out there making $10 a month. If you average those incomes you'll see an average of $10,000 a month, which looks really good. But the reality is that it's either be that one person making $100,000 a month or be everyone else making $10 a month. (It's not quite that bad. But it's close.)

An average won't show this, but the median will.

So if you don't know the nature of your data, it's always a good idea to take both the average and the median and compare them.

If the data is evenly distributed (spread out nicely) then they'll give you similar results. But if it's skewed, like in my example above, you'll have vastly different outcomes.

MEDIAN pretty works just like AVERAGE. All you do is use the function and give Excel the range of cells that contain you values. So

$$=MEDIAN(A1:A9)$$

will find the middle value out of the range of values in Cells A1 through A9.

It's that simple.

If you give Excel a range that has an even number of values, so there isn't just one middle value, Excel will average the two middle values and return their average. So

$$=MEDIAN(1,2,3,4)$$

will return 2.5 which is the average of the middle two values, 2 and 3.

(Be careful with this. Because =MEDIAN(1,100) would return a value of 50.5 which is very misleading since it's nowhere close to any actual potential value in the data. In general, it's a good idea to chart or visually inspect your data so you can see when situations like this exist.)

Median also works on logical values (TRUE, FALSE) that are typed directly into the argument. So =MEDIAN(TRUE,TRUE,FALSE) will return a value of 1 and =MEDIAN(FALSE,FALSE,TRUE) will return a value of 0. But if you reference a range with TRUEs and FALSEs in it you'll get a #NUM! error. I'm not sure how much good it does you that you can type it into the function directly, but that's the way it works.

(If you do ever have a set of TRUE/FALSE results, you can always convert them to ones and zeros using an IF function and then take the median of the ones and zeros.)

The MODE.SNGL Function

Notation: MODE.SNGL(number1, [number2],…)

Excel Definition: Returns the most frequently occurring, or repetitive, value in an array or range of data.

As we discussed above, AVERAGE doesn't work well if your data has a high skew to it. So if most people score really low and there are just a few people who score really high then looking at an average is going to mislead you about how the average person will do. MEDIAN can sometimes be a better measure because it looks at the result in the exact middle.

But MEDIAN also has a flaw. And that's that it's not very good with data that has spikes that aren't near the middle of your data range. When that happens, sometimes it's best to look at the mode of your data. Excel 2019 has two options for doing this, MODE.SNGL and MODE.MULT.

MODE.SNGL is very simple to use.

$$=MODE.SNGL(A1:A10)$$

will calculate the mode for a range of values in Cells A1 through A10.

What MODE.SNGL basically does is count each value in your range and then returns the outcome with the highest count. But it has a flaw which is that if two values occur equally, it will only return the first of them because it can only return one value.

MODE.MULT which we'll talk about next can be used instead to find when there are multiple values that occur equally frequently.

The MODE.MULT Function

Notation: MODE.MULT(number1, [number2],…)

Excel Definition: Returns a vertical array of the most frequently occurring, or repetitive, values in an array or range of data. For a horizontal array, use TRANSPOSE(MODE.MULT(number1,number2,…))

The MODE.MULT function allows Excel to return more than one value when it calculates the mode for a range of values. So if you have multi-modal data (meaning there are multiple bumps in your data), using MODE.MULT will return those multiple values where MODE.SNGL can't.

Now, there is a trick to using it because it is an array formula.

To use MODE.MULT you need a range of values that you're going to use for your mode calculation and a range of cells where you're going to put the result of that calculation.

Highlight the range of cells where you want your results to be displayed. You need to highlight enough cells to allow Excel to provide all possible values. (This is why plotting your data is a good idea. If you've plotted your data and seen that it has two equal-sized bumps in it, then you would know to highlight two cells. Otherwise you can guess and Excel will just return an #N/A value for the cells it didn't use.)

In the example at the end of this section, I highlighted Cells D5 through D8. Next, type in your formula. In the example below I typed:

$$=MODE.MULT(A1:A10)$$

to take the mode of the values in Cells A1 through A10.

Then, and this is crucial because it won't work otherwise, instead of typing Enter, you need to type Ctrl + Shift + Enter.

You'll know you've done it right, because when you click back into the cell the formula will have little brackets around it. Like this:

$$\{=\text{MODE.MULT}(A1:A10)\}$$

That exact same formula will appear in all of the cells you highlighted, not just the top one. And it will calculate the multiple modes in your data.

MODE.MULT also has a flaw. And that's that if you have one value that appears 99 times and another that appears 100 times, it will only return the value that appears 100 times even though they're almost identical results.

So let's put it all together to show AVERAGE, MEDIAN, MODE.SNGL, and MODE.MULT with a data set that is deliberately built to be multi-modal.

I've created a set of forty values that repeat the pattern 1, 3, 3, 3, 3, 30, 30, 30, 30, 500 four times. Here's a count table of those results and a graph of the values:

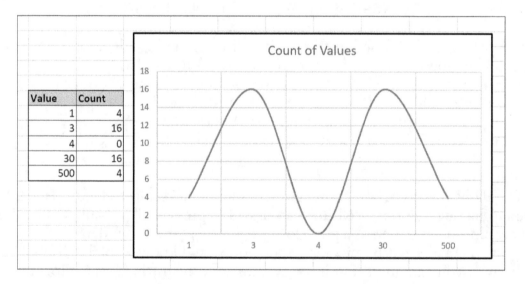

Value	Count
1	4
3	16
4	0
30	16
500	4

You can see from this graph that the v~alue of 3 and the value of 30 are the most commonly occurring values. They each occur 16 times in the data. The values of 1 and 500 each occur four times in the data. Those are the only possible outcomes: 1, 3, 30, 500.

Now, here are the calculations of the average, the median, the singular mode, and the multiple mode.

AVERAGE	63.3	=AVERAGE(A1:A40)
MEDIAN	16.5	=MEDIAN(A1:A40)
MODE.SNGL	3	=MODE.SNGL(A1:A40)
MODE.MULT	3	{=MODE.MULT(A1:A40)}
	30	{=MODE.MULT(A1:A40)}
	#N/A	{=MODE.MULT(A1:A40)}
	#N/A	{=MODE.MULT(A1:A40)}

See the wide range of values you get?

Average is skewed higher than most outcomes because of the four 500 values in the data.

Median falls nowhere near an actual result that anyone will get because I have an even number of observations so it's showing the average between the two closest observations of 3 and 30. Despite that it does show a more realistic result than average in this case.

The single mode misses that 30 is just as likely an outcome as 3.

The multiple mode shows that the two equally frequent most common outcomes are 3 and 30 but it completely misses showing that 1 and 500 are possibilities as well. (Also, if either 3 or 30 were smaller by even one occurrence, it wouldn't show for MODE.MULT either. They have to be exactly equal in occurrence.)

So they all have their flaws.

That's why it's always a good idea to plot out your data to see what kind of patterns there are and to use multiple approaches to the data. (For example, this count table isn't the best for showing those outliers at 500 but a histogram would definitely show it.)

The RANK.EQ Function

Notation: RANK.EQ(number, ref, [order])

Excel Definition: Returns the rank of a number in a list of numbers: its size relative to other values in the list; if more than one value has the same rank, the top rank of that set of values is returned.

In recent versions, Excel has taken what used to be the RANK function and designated it as RANK.EQ so that it can also have a RANK.AVG function. Both functions tell you the rank of a specified number within a range of values, but they each do it a little differently.

We'll start with RANK.EQ since that's the equivalent to the old RANK function.

The first input into the function is the number you're analyzing.

The next input is the overall range of numbers you want to compare it to. (The number can be pulled from the reference range and probably will be in most instances.)

The final input, order, tells Excel which way to rank things, from the highest number down or from the lowest number up. If you omit it, which you can, or use a zero (0), then Excel will rank based on descending order. If you use a one (1) or any other number other than zero, Excel will rank based on ascending order.

The sort order of the data in your reference range does not matter.

I placed the values 1 through 15 in Cells J1 through J15 and had Excel rank the 6 in that range using:

=RANK.EQ(6,J1:J15,0)

This returned a value of 10 regardless of how the reference range was sorted. (Because if you start at 15 and count down, 6 will be the 10th value in the list.) Same with:

$$=RANK.EQ(6,J1:J15)$$

It also returned a value of 10. But

$$=RANK.EQ(6,J1:J15,1)$$

returned a value of 6 regardless of how the reference range was sorted because it was counting from 1 upward.

Be careful when using RANK.EQ if you have duplicates in your reference range. RANK.EQ assigns the same rank to duplicate values but then does not assign the next rank(s) to any value until it has skipped past the number of duplicates.

So if I have the numbers

$$1, 2, 2, 3, 4$$

and use an ascending rank order they would be ranked

$$1, 2, 2, 4, 5$$

respectively. If I used a descending rank order they would be ranked:

$$5, 3, 3, 2, 1$$

See how there are two ranks of 2 in that first example and two ranks of 3 in that second example? And how Excel skipped the rank of 3 in the first example and the rank of 4 in the second example?

If you have a tie like this the help text for the function gives a correction factor you can use.

Or you can use RANK.AVG which works just like RANK.EQ except it will average the ranks that would've been assigned to the tied values and return the average instead of the best rank.

So in the example above you'd have 1, 2.5, 2.5, 4, 5 or 5, 3.5, 3.5, 2, 1 as your result depending on the sort order.

The SMALL Function

Notation: SMALL(array, k)

Excel Definition: Returns the k-th smallest value in a data set. For example, the fifth smallest number.

The SMALL function will look at a range of values and return the kth smallest value in the range where k is the number you specify.

It's pretty straight-forward. The first input is the cell range you want to use and the second input is a number representing the position in the range you're interested in.

If you want the smallest value in Column A (and didn't want to use MIN for some reason), you could use

$$=SMALL(A:A,1)$$

to return it. But more likely you're going to want something like the 10th smallest value which would be:

$$=SMALL(A:A,10)$$

Your array can also cover more than one row or column. So:

$$=SMALL(A1:B5,3)$$

would return the 3rd smallest value in Cells A1 through B5.

Technically, you could also use SMALL to return the *largest* value in an array if you knew the number of values in the array. Depending on your data this could be done with the COUNT function like so:

=SMALL(A1:B5,COUNT(A1:B5))

But, better yet, there's the LARGE function which does exactly what the SMALL function does but for the k-th largest value in a data set.

With either LARGE or SMALL, if you use a value for k that is larger than the count of the numeric values in the range, you will get a #NUM! error message as your result. So if I had text in one of the cells above and used COUNTA instead of COUNT that wouldn't have worked.

The FORECAST.LINEAR Function

Notation: FORECAST.LINEAR(x, known_ys, known_xs)

Excel Definition: Calculates, or predicts, a future value along a linear trend by using existing values.

Excel provides a couple of interesting functions that are designed to forecast future values based on existing data. We're just going to cover the basic linear forecast function, FORECAST.LINEAR, here but you can also use an exponential smoothing forecast option, FORECAST.ETS for when your data isn't linear and/or has seasonality to it.

The FORECAST.LINEAR function replaced the old FORECAST function.

Now, one thing to note right up front is that this function assumes a linear trend in your data. So the plotting example I used in *Excel 2019 Intermediate* for scatter plots that involved calculating time to hit the ground when an object is dropped from different heights would not work with FORECAST.LINEAR since that's not a linear relationship.

Which means you should definitely plot your data before you apply this forecast function to it to see if it's following a general linear trend.

The way FORECAST.LINEAR works is you give Excel a table of known x and y combinations and Excel then uses those data points to create the best linear fit through the points.

You then tell Excel your x value that you want to predict y for.

Your x values must be numbers otherwise you will get a #VALUE! error.

You also must provide an equal number of x's and y's that have values. If they don't match up or one is empty you will get a #N/A error message.

If there is no variance in your x values you will get a #DIV/0! error message.

If you want to know the formula Excel uses to do this calculation, it's in the help documentation for the function.

Now let's walk through an example. Here's a data table where I've put number of customers in the store and number of sales in a data table. I've built this data so that for every two customers who walk through the door, the store gets a sale.

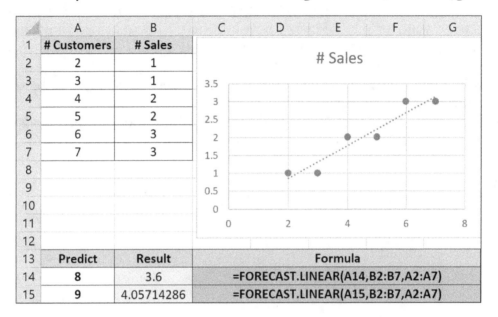

	A	B	C	D	E	F	G
1	# Customers	# Sales					
2	2	1					
3	3	1					
4	4	2					
5	5	2					
6	6	3					
7	7	3					
8							
9							
10							
11							
12							
13	Predict	Result			Formula		
14	8	3.6			=FORECAST.LINEAR(A14,B2:B7,A2:A7)		
15	9	4.05714286			=FORECAST.LINEAR(A15,B2:B7,A2:A7)		

I've also plotted the results so that you can see it is a generally linear progression, although not perfectly linear and I've added a linear trendline to that plot to show the line that Excel is calculating behind the scenes to make its predictions with this function.

Below the table I have used FORECAST.LINEAR to predict the number of sales when there are 8 customers and 9 customers in the store. (Because this is artificial data we know the answer for both should be 4.)

The first formula I used was:

$$=FORECAST.LINEAR(A14,B2:B7,A2:A7)$$

where the value 8 was in Cell A14.

As you can see, the predictions that Excel came up with for 8 and 9 customers were 3.6 and 4.06 because it's trying to draw the best line it can through the data and that best line falls between the actual data points.

Now, one thing to point out here, because it tripped me up the first time I used the function, is that you list all of your *y values* before you list all of your x values. This was backwards to me since every point coordinate I ever remember seeing was written x, y.

Also, if you ever try to use FORECAST.LINEAR for time series data (and I have with FORECAST) understand that your x values are numbers to Excel not dates so 0 is a valid x value. Meaning if you try to predict a prior value from your data range you need to account for 0 representing one of your observations. If 1 is January 2019, then 0 is December 2018.

(This is why it's always good to gut check the results you get to see if they make sense given the data.)

One final note. Even though in the example above I had the data points sorted by x-value, you don't need to do that. Your data can be out of order and Excel will still be able to work with it effectively when using FORECAST.LINEAR.

If you have data where the order matters (like monthly sales data, for example), especially if the data is not linear then considering using FORECAST.ETS instead.

The FREQUENCY Function

Notation: FREQUENCY(data_array, bins_array)

Excel Definition: Calculates how often values occur within a range of values and then returns a vertical array of numbers having one more element than Bins_array.

Earlier we talked about how to use functions to calculate the average, median, and mode, and as part of doing so I pointed out that one of the drawbacks of even MODE.MULT is that it only cares about the most frequently occurring value or values. So if you have a value that appears 29 times and one that appears 28 times, MODE.MULT will only return the value that appears 29 times.

One way to get around this is by building a frequency table which we're going to do using the FREQUENCY function.

The first input into the FREQUENCY function is your data.

We're going to work with a set of values where we have the number 1 one time, the number 3 four times, the number 30 three times, and the number 500 twice. (See below.)

So 3 is the most frequently occurring value but 30 comes in close behind.

(If I were to use MODE.MULT on this data range I would get the result of 3 back, but nothing else. I want more detail than that and that's where FREQUENCY comes in.)

The second input into the function is what's called the bins array. This is how we tell Excel to bucket the results. If we want exact counts of every value in our data range then we can remove duplicates from our initial data set and use those as our bins. That will give a unique count for every value in the table.

If we're okay having values from 0 to 25 grouped together and then up to 50 grouped together, etc. we could tell Excel our bins are 25, 50, and so on.

Below I've taken both approaches. My first table has 1, 3, 30, and 500 as my bins. My second table has 25, 50, 500, and then a blank cell as my bins to cover anything over 500.

FREQUENCY is an array function so you have to highlight all of the cells where you want your results to be displayed before you type the function. You can then type in the function and use Shift + Ctrl + Enter to finish.

This is what we get for both approaches:

	A	B	C	D	E	F	G
1	Values		Bins	Count	Formula		
2	1		1	1	=FREQUENCY(A2:A11,C2:C5)		
3	3		3	4	=FREQUENCY(A2:A11,C2:C5)		
4	3		30	3	=FREQUENCY(A2:A11,C2:C5)		
5	3		500	2	=FREQUENCY(A2:A11,C2:C5)		
6	3						
7	30		Bins	Count	Formula		
8	30		25	5	=FREQUENCY(A2:A11,C8:C11)		
9	30		50	3	=FREQUENCY(A2:A11,C8:C11)		
10	500		500	2	=FREQUENCY(A2:A11,C8:C11)		
11	500			0	=FREQUENCY(A2:A11,C8:C11)		

The formula in the first example where the bins are 1, 3, 30, and 500 is

=FREQUENCY(A2:A11,C2:C5)

And because this is an array formula that is the formula for all of the rows of the table, not just the first one.

The formula in the second example where the bins are 25, 50, 500, and blank is:

=FREQUENCY(A2:A11,C8:C11)

Both formulas are doing the exact same thing. They are counting the number of values that are less than or equal to the first value in each table and then from there up to the second value in the table and so on. The reason the results are different is because of the bins we chose.

So you can use FREQUENCY for precise counts of each value, like we did in the first example, or for counts across a range of values, like in the second example. You just have to structure your bins correctly.

And remember to highlight enough cells when inputting the function to cover the less than and more than portions of the range. In the second example, I had four bin inputs but needed to highlight five cells when I built my table to account for any possible values over 500.

Also, FREQUENCY will ignore blank cells and text, so if you want the FREQUENCY of text values, you can't use it. It only works with numbers.

And remember, this is an array function, so always highlight all of your cells where you want your answers before you input your function and use Shift + Ctrl + Enter when you're done or you won't get the right results.

More Math Functions

Okay. Now on to more functions that Excel categorizes as Math & Trig functions. This section covers functions that round values, take the sum product, provide the square root, etc. I'm pretty sure none of the functions I'm covering here would actually be classified as trig functions but they do exist. So if you need sine and cosine, etc. this is the category they'd fall under in the function library.

The SUMPRODUCT Function

Notation: SUMPRODUCT(array1, [array2], [array3],…)

Excel Definition: Returns the sum of the products of corresponding ranges or arrays.

You use SUMPRODUCT when you have a range of cells that need the values in each position in the range to be multiplied times one another (like number of units and price to get total cost for a specific transaction) and then the results summed (to get total cost, for example).

SUMPRODUCT is incredibly useful when you need it. You could get the same result using a combination of SUM and PRODUCT, but why do that when one little function will do it for you? (I'm not going to cover PRODUCT separately here, but it basically takes whatever values you give it and multiplies them times one another.)

Now, that definition and the use of "array" in the Excel notation for the function probably seem a little intimidating. Don't worry, they're not.

Let's walk through an example with units and price:

	A	B	C	D
1	**Product**	**Units**	**Price**	**Total**
2	Widgets	4	$ 2.25	$ 9.00
3	Whatsits	5	$ 3.50	$ 17.50
4	Whatchamacallits	3	$ 6.00	$ 18.00
5	Whatnots	2	$ 4.00	$ 8.00
6				$ 52.50

What we have here is a list of products bought by a customer. We have product name, number of units bought, and price paid per unit.

In Column D I've calculated the total to the customer the old-fashioned way. I've taken Units times Price for each row and then totaled those values to get the total for the customer in Cell D6.

Now let's use SUMPRODUCT for that same calculation:

8	Calculated Result	Formula
9	$ 52.50	=SUMPRODUCT(B2:B5,C2:C5)

In Cell A9 I've made that same calculation but with the SUMPRODUCT function:

$$=SUMPRODUCT(B2:B5,C2:C5)$$

That says, take the values in Cells B2 through B5 and the values in Cells C2 through C5 and then multiply B2 times C2, B3 times C3, etc. and add together the results to return a total.

A few things to be aware of. The ranges you input into the function need to be the same size for this to work. If they aren't you will get a #VALUE! result instead.

Also, be sure that the ranges you choose have numbers in them and not text. Excel will treat non-numeric values as zeros and any number times zero is...zero.

And, while the example I used above had values in two columns you are not limited to just two columns of values. (Just be sure the cells you select should be multiplied by one another and then added. So I could've had another column in there for sales tax, for example.)

You can also use SUMPRODUCT with values that are in rows instead or columns or in a combination of rows and columns. The key is that the ranges you specify have to be the same dimension, so the same number of columns and rows. (And obviously it needs to make sense.)

Okay, now let's talk about absolute value.

The ABS Function

Notation: ABS(number)

Excel Definition: Returns the absolute value of a number, a number without its sign.

The ABS function essentially converts any number you have into a positive number. I could see this being useful if you are calculating, say, a ratio of two numbers and it doesn't matter whether one or both of those numbers is negative, you just want the ratio as a positive number.

So, for example, if I had -6 in Cell A1 and 2 in Cell A2 and wanted the ratio of those two numbers as a positive value, I could use:

$$=ABS(A1/A2)$$

or

$$=ABS(A1)/A2$$

Either way my result would be 3. If I had just divided those two numbers without using ABS the result would have been -3.

That's pretty much it.

(Interestingly enough, if you have numbers stored as text a function like SUM or PRODUCT will not work on them, but ABS still does.)

The POWER Function

Notation: POWER(number, power)

Excel Definition: Returns the result of a number raised to a power.

POWER is a function that will let you raise any number to any power. But as a reminder first, you don't need a function to do powers. You can just use the little caret symbol (^) and input your power that way. So

$$=3^2$$

returns the value of three squared which is 9.
And

$$=9^{.5}$$

returns the value for the square root of 9 which is 3.

As you can see with these examples, you use whole numbers to take a number to a power and decimals to take the root of a number.

You can also use negative powers to indicate that the number is part of the denominator. (So $=3^{-2}$ is the same as 1 divided by three squared or 1/9.)

The caret works with cell references, too. So

$$=A1^{A2}$$

would take the value in Cell A1 and raise it to the power of the value in Cell A2.

But you can also use the POWER function for this, so let's cover it.

It's very simple. The first value is the number you want to take to a power, the second number is the power you want to use.

So three squared would be

$$=POWER(3,2)$$

And the square root of 9

$$=POWER(9,.5)$$

The power can also be a negative number which, as mentioned above, puts the value in the denominator. So

$$=POWER(3,-2)$$

is the same as 1 divided by 3 squared.

You can also put a complex calculation or a cell reference in for either of the inputs:

$$=POWER(A1,A2)$$

for example.

Just like you learned in math class, if the power is 0 then the result is 1.

If you are specifically taking the square root of a value, you can use the SQRT function instead. And the SQRTPI function will take the square root of the product of a number and pi.

Also, if you're working with natural logarithms, the EXP function will return the value of e raised to a given power. This means that you can also use $=EXP(1)$ to derive the value of e if you need it.

The PI Function

Notation: PI( )

Excel Definition: Returns the value of Pi, 3.14159265358979, accurate to 15 digits.

The PI function is another function that can make life simpler when working with complex formulas. If you need to do a calculation that involves the number pi, 3.14 etc. etc., using the PI function will return that value for you accurate up to the 15th digit.

So, for example, the area of a circle can be calculated using pi times the square of the radius. Let's assume radius is in Cell A1.

I could write

$$=PI( )*(A1^2)$$

to make that calculation.

Note that when I use the function PI I need to include those opening and closing parens to let Excel know that's what I'm doing. You don't put anything in them, though.

If you just want the value of pi in a cell type

$$=PI( )$$

in that cell and hit enter.

(Also, you don't need that space in between the parens. It will work with or without it.)

The LOG Function

Notation: LOG(number, [base])

Excel Definition: Returns the logarithm of a number to the base you specify.

The LOG function does just what it says, it returns the logarithm of a number to the specified base. The default is to assume that you're working with base 10. So if you don't provide a second value in the function and just write

$$=LOG(10)$$

it will assume that the base you meant it to use is base 10. That means the answer you'll get is 1. Because 10 to the what power gives you 10? 1
That's why

$$=LOG(1000)$$

is 3. Because 10 to what power gives you 1000? 3
If you want to work with a different base than 10, say 2, you just put that into the function as your second argument. So

$$=LOG(32,2)$$

is asking what power you have to take 2 to to get 32. (That's a mouthful of 2's isn't it?)Answer, 5.
For natural logs you can use the EXP function with the LOG function. Like so:

$$=LOG(86,EXP(1))$$

This will return for you the power to which you have to take *e* to get a value of 86, which is approximately 4.45.

Excel also has the LN function which is built to work with natural logs where

$$=LOG(86,EXP(1))$$

and

$$=LN(86)$$

will return the same result.

There is also the LOG10 function for base 10 where

$$=LOG10(100)$$

and

$$=LOG(100)$$

will return the same result.

The FACT Function

Notation: FACT(number)

Excel Definition: Returns the factorial of a number, equal to 1*2*3*...*Number.

The FACT function returns the factorial of a number which is used in calculating permutations. So

$$=FACT(3)$$

will give you a value of 6 which is equal to 3 times 2 times 1. And

$$=FACT(4)$$

will give you a value of 24 which is equal to 4 times 3 times 2 times 1.

If you try to use a number that is not a whole number with the FACT function Excel will truncate it to a whole number. So

$$=FACT(4.567)$$

returns the same value as =FACT(4)

(Note that's a truncation not rounding. 4.567 became a 4 not a 5.)

Also, keep in mind that you can't have a factorial of a negative number and that the factorial of zero is returned as a value of 1 since that's standard practice when working with factorials.

The COMBIN Function

Notation: COMBIN(number, number_chosen)

Excel Definition: Returns the number of combinations for a given number of items.

You can use factorials to calculate the number of combinations in a given population, but Excel has provided two functions that will do this for you.

The COMBIN function calculates the number of combinations given a population size and sample size without repetition. So with the numbers 1, 2, and 3 you can have 12 as a possible combination but not 11.

The inputs to the COMBIN function are your population size and your sample size. So

$$=COMBIN(3,2)$$

is asking how many combinations of 1, 2, and 3 you can have if you choose two at a time and don't repeat. The answer is 3 for 12 or 21, 23 or 32, and 13 or 31.

If you do want to allow for repetition then the function to use is COMBINA. It has the same inputs, population size and sample size, but

$$=COMBINA(3,2)$$

returns a value of 6 because with repetitions you can also have 11, 22, and 33 as possible combinations.

Text Functions

Excel has a number of text functions that can come in handy. Functions that let you transform text to upper or lower case, select just a portion of an entry, and transform certain values to their text equivalent. You can also use text functions to search for a specific result which is useful when combined with other functions as well as if you ever venture into using macros.

Let's cover some of those now.

The UPPER Function

Notation: UPPER(text)

Excel Definition: Converts a text string to all uppercase letters.

The UPPER function has a very simple purpose, and that is to take a text entry and convert it to all uppercase letters.

So, for example,

$$=UPPER(\text{“test”})$$

will return TEST. Or, if you had the word "test" in Cell B2 and you wrote

$$=UPPER(B2)$$

it would also return the value TEST.

You cannot reference more than once cell at a time using UPPER. However, you can combine the UPPER function with other functions to return a result that is in upper case letters.

For example,

$$=UPPER(TEXTJOIN(" ",1,A1:A2))$$

would return the text in Cells A1 and A2 with a space between them and all in upper case letters.

If you want all lower case letters, you can use the LOWER function. And to have a text string where the first letter of each word is capitalized and the rest is in lower case, use PROPER.

The LEFT Function

Notation: LEFT(text, [num_chars])

Excel Definition: Returns the specified number of characters from the start of a text string.

The LEFT function allows you to extract the left-most portion of a text string.

This can be a useful function if you only want a portion of a standardized entry. For example, for a driver's license number that starts with a two-digit year, then a dash, then the license number, to extract the year portion, you could use

$$=LEFT(B2,2)$$

assuming the value was in Cell B2. That would give you just the year portion of that license number.

Note that the definition says it works on a text string, but I was able to also get it to work on a number. So

$$=LEFT(1234,2)$$

returns 12.

You can accomplish the same thing with Text to Columns using Fixed Width, but LEFT is a better option when all you want is that one portion of the entry and you don't need the rest of it.

Other identifiers that might be similarly structured include customer identification numbers and social security numbers.

The number of characters specified must be greater than or equal to zero.

If the number of characters you specify is greater than the length of the text entry, Excel will return the full text entry.

If you omit the number of characters, Excel will extract the left-most character only. So

$$=LEFT(\text{``test''})$$

will return a result of t.

The RIGHT function works exactly like the LEFT function but it returns the specified number of characters from the end (or right-hand side) of the text string.

For languages such as Chinese, Japanese, and Korean you may need to use LEFTB or RIGHTB functions instead and specify the number of bytes rather than the number of characters. This also applies for the next function we're going to cover, the MID function, where you'd use MIDB.

The MID Function

Notation: MID(text, start_num, num_chars)

Excel Definition: Returns the characters from the middle of a text string, given a starting position and length.

The MID function works much like the LEFT and RIGHT functions except it extracts characters from the middle of an entry. Because of this, it requires one more input, the start number. So you have to tell Excel which character in your string should be the first character pulled and then how many characters you want after that.

For example, for a social security number if you want the middle two digits of the value stored in Cell B2 you would use

$$=MID(B2,5,2)$$

assuming the number was written as XXX-XX-XXXX.

Be sure to count each space, dash, etc. in your determination of the start number.

If your start number is greater than the number of characters in your referenced text, Excel will return an empty text entry.

If you ask for more characters to be returned than exist, Excel will return what there is. So

$$=MID("advice",3,7)$$

will returned "vice" even though that's only four characters.

Your start number must be equal to or greater than 1. Your number of characters must be equal to or greater than zero.

The TEXT Function

Notation: TEXT(value, format_text)

Excel Definition: Converts a value to text in a specific number format.

The TEXT function is an interesting one, because it really has two completely different uses, one for formatting and one for extracting a name for day of the week or month from a date.

I'm going to cover the usage here that interests me and that's the second one, it's ability to extract the name for the day of the week or the month from a date.

(If you're interested in its other use, check out the help section which goes into incredible detail on all the possibilities. Just be careful because it's possible to format your entries in ways that do not make sense at all using TEXT.)

Okay.

So using TEXT you can take a date, like 4/4/2018, and you can have Excel return for you the name of the day of the week or the month associated with that date. So Wednesday or April in this case.

I find that very useful, and recently used it when I was trying to create a table with day of the week across the top but only had dates to work with.

To extract the name of the day of the week, use

=TEXT(A1,"dddd")

or

=TEXT(A1,"ddd")

Assuming the date is in Cell A1 that will give you the full name for the day of the week (Tuesday) in the first example or the abbreviated day of the week (Tue) in the second example.

To extract the name of the month, use

$$=\text{TEXT}(A1,\text{"mmmm"})$$

or

$$=\text{TEXT}(A1,\text{"mmm"})$$

That will give you the full month (January) in the first example or the abbreviated month (Jan) in the second example.

The LEN Function

Notation: LEN(text)

Excel Definition: Returns the number of characters in a text string.

The LEN function returns a numeric value representing the number of characters in a text string. (Note that for some languages like Japanese, Chinese, or Korean that you may instead need the LENB function which returns the number of bytes in a text string.)

You can use LEN with text directly in the function or with a cell reference. The count includes spaces as well as actual characters. So

$$=LEN("One\ day")$$

will return a value of 7 for the o-n-e-space-d-a-y in "one day".

I could also type my text in Cell A1 and then use

$$=LEN(A1)$$

to get the same result.

If there is a formula in a cell that is referenced by LEN, it will count the number of characters in the result of the formula not the formula itself. (Which is good.)

If a cell is empty or has a "" value, LEN will return a value of zero.

You might be asking yourself when you would use this function.

One possibility is when you want to remove standardized text from a longer text string.

You could pair LEN with a function like LEFT, RIGHT, or MID to extract the remainder of your text.

For example, let's say I have the following entries:

12,500 units

5,122 units

312 units

And I want just the numbers without the space or "units" included. Assuming that first value is in Cell A1, I could use

=LEFT(A1,LEN(A1)-LEN(" units"))

and then copy that formula down the next two rows to extract just the numbers from those entries.

This works because all of the entries have the same text at the end, " units" that I want to remove.

Because the number of units isn't the same between each one, that is probably the only way to trim that off using a function. (You could also use the Text to Columns option on the Data tab as an alternative way to split the number from the units, but it would then require deleting the column of data you don't want so would require an additional step.)

Another function you could use for tasks similar to LEN is SEARCH. SEARCH will tell you the number of the character in a text string at which the text you care about first appears, moving from left to right.

The EXACT Function

Notation: EXACT(text1, text2)

Excel Definition: Checks whether two text strings are exactly the same, and returns TRUE or FALSE. EXACT is case-sensitive.

The EXACT function compares two text strings to see if they're exactly the same or not. I've used a simple IF function to do the same thing before, but this is easier to write.

What I've needed it for in the past was to see if two sets of data that I was trying to compare had entries in the same order. I used to use some advertising reports where the entity providing me with data would insert new ads in the midst of the old data and if I tried to compare an old report to a new report I'd end up comparing results for Ad 10 with results for Ad 35.

To fix that I would sort the report and then check that I had the ads lined up properly using an IF function that looked something like this:

$$=IF(B2=P2,"","ERROR")$$

That's saying, do the text values in Cell B2 and Cell P2 match? If so, good. If not, tell me there's an error.

But I could have used the EXACT function instead and written:

$$=EXACT(B2,P2)$$

If the two values match it returns a value of TRUE. If they don't it returns a value of FALSE.

The function is case-sensitive, but will ignore any differences in formatting.

Once you have your TRUE and FALSE values you can then filter for the ones that have an issue or use search or just scan the list.

Date & Time Functions

Alright. On to the date and time functions. If you're not going to use them much you can probably skip what I'm about to discuss, but since it's tripped me up a few times when I needed to work with dates I wanted to be sure to cover some quirks to how dates are treated in Excel.

Excel actually encodes each date as a number starting with the number 1 for the date January 1, 1900 and then moving forward one number at a time for each subsequent date. You can test this by typing the number 1 into a cell and then formatting that cell as a date. As soon as you format that cell as a date you will see January 1, 1900 in that cell. This is important for a few reasons.

First, it means that Excel does not do well with dates prior to 1900. I learned this the hard way on a work project that had dates back to the 1700s when I found that Excel had converted those 1700s and 1800s dates to 1900s dates after they were imported from a SQL database into Excel. So it's something to keep an eye on if you're working with older dates.

Second, because Excel encodes dates as numbers this means that simple addition and subtraction works on dates in Excel. If you want a date fifteen days in the future, you just add 15 to the current date. So say that date is stored in Cell A1, then you'd write =A1+15 and Excel would return a date for you that is 15 days past the date in Cell A1. If you wanted a date that was 14 days *prior* to that date then you would write =A1-14.

As long as the dates remain in the range of January 1, 1900 to December 31, 9999 you're fine.

This also means that Excel converts hours, minutes, and seconds into decimals. So .5 is the equivalent of 12 hours, .041667 is a single hour, .000694 is a minute, and .00001157 is one second.

Third, the fact that dates are encoded as numbers means that any date functions that mention a serial_number as the input are actually telling you to input the date that you want to use.

Now, to put a wrinkle in this, if someone is using a Mac instead of a PC and Excel 2008 for Mac or earlier what I said above about the date range covered by Excel is not accurate. In that case Excel actually started with the date January 2, 1904 and moved forward from there. This was fixed in Excel for Mac 2011. The dates should convert automatically when moving between the two, but be careful if you're working with someone who has a Mac version of Excel.

One option to avoid these kinds of issues with dates that are out of range or dates that appear as one date in one version and another date in another version is to store your dates as text instead of dates unless you need them to be dates for calculation purposes.

(This may also be a good time to point out that Excel is not necessarily the ideal option for handling large amounts of complex data. It's great for basic usage and calculations but when you really get into data it's probably time to use something else. For example, I've worked with R, Stata, and SQL databases when dealing with large amounts of data.)

Also…

Best practice when dealing with dates in Excel is to enter the four-digit year. So if I want January 1, 2019 it is best to enter that date as 1/1/2019 so that Excel knows exactly what date I want. If you leave off the first two numbers of the year, so use 1/1/19 instead, Excel will convert that to a four-digit year using the following logic:

As of now, numbers 00 through 29 are interpreted as the years 2000 through 2029. Numbers 30 through 99 are interpreted as the years 1930 through 1999.

To avoid this being an issue as we approach 2029, I'd recommend that you always try to enter four digits for every year so that this is never an issue for you.

(And if you want to read up on all of this more it's under the Excel help topic "change the date system, format, or two-digit year interpretation.")

Good times.

Okay, then. Now that we have a basic understanding of how dates are handled by Excel, let's look at some date-related functions.

The DATE Function

Notation: DATE(year, month, day)

Excel Definition: Returns the number that represents the date in Microsoft Excel date-time code.

I don't use the DATE function regularly but we need to discuss it first because in the help text for most of the date and time functions Excel has a caution that dates used in each function should be created using the DATE function or as results of other formulas or functions. The implication is that if you don't do this your results may not be fully accurate.

In general, I don't think you'll have an issue using a date you've typed in. For example,

1/1/11

1-1-11

1/1/2011

1-1-2011

January 1, 2011

all work as long as you keep in mind what we discussed above about how Excel handle dates.

But if it's vitally important that your date calculations be accurate then maybe use the DATE function.

So how does it work?

For the most basic usage, you input a value for year, month, and day and Excel turns it into a numeric value representing a date. For example:

$$=DATE(1900,1,1)$$

will return a value that displays as 1/1/1900 and is automatically formatted as a date.

There are, however some definite quirks with this function. The worst one is that if you input a year value between 0 and 1899, Excel will *add* that value to 1900 to calculate your year.

It's the most ridiculous thing I've ever seen, but that's how it works. (An error message would've been better in my opinion.)

So

$$=DATE(1880,1,1)$$

which you would hope returns a date of January 1, 1880 will actually return a date of 1/1/3780.

A reminder that if you're going to work with dates in Excel you must drill into your head that they only work between the years of 1900 and 9999. Also, a good reason to always have your dates display with a four-digit year so you can see when this happens, because 1/1/80 looks like it could be 1/1/1880 like you intended even though it's actually 1/1/3780.

With the DATE function if you put in a year that's less than 0 or past 9999 you do get an error message, the #NUM! error.

DATE can do more than just create a date from your inputs. It can also take an existing date and by adding values to year, month, and day create a new date. For this reason, you can enter any value you want for month and for day.

If the value for month is greater than 12, Excel will add that number of months to the first month in the year specified. So

$$=DATE(1900,14,1)$$

returns a date of February 1, 1901, which is two months into the next year. And

$$=DATE(1900,38,1)$$

returns a date of February 1, 1903, which is two months into the year three years from 1900.

If you enter a negative value for month, Excel will subtract "the magnitude of that number of months, plus 1, from the first month in the year specified."

I find that wording horrible.

What you have to keep in mind is that when you go backwards, Excel includes the value of zero as a legitimate value. So if I use

$$=DATE(1905,-2,1)$$

Excel returns a date of October 1, 1904 which is *three* months prior to January. To get a date of December 1, 1904, I have to use

$$=DATE(1905,0,1)$$

The same thing happens with days of the month. If you're going negative you have to adjust by 1 because of the fact that Excel will take a value of 0 as the value for one day prior and then work from there.

I'd be very careful using DATE to go backward for this very reason. It's far too easy to mess up if you're not paying attention, so check, double-check, triple-check your results.

Now let's walk through the more complex usage for DATE and the reason all the craziness exists.

The DATE function can be used in conjunction with other functions or basic math to create new dates.

So, for example, you can create a date five years from now by taking a date that's in Cell A1 and combining that with the DATE function as well as the YEAR, MONTH, and DAY functions to extract the values for year, month, and date, respectively. This is more precise than adding 365 times 5 days to that date because it won't be impacted by something like leap year.

What does that look like?

Assuming your date is stored in Cell A1 and you want a date five years from that date, you would write:

$$=DATE(YEAR(A1)+5,MONTH(A1),DAY(A1))$$

That's saying, take the year from the date in Cell A1 and add 5 to it. Then take the month from the date in Cell A1 and the day from the date in Cell A1, and build a date with those values.

If Cell A1 was January 1, 2015 you would now have a date of January 1, 2020.

If we had instead used five times 365 days and added that to the date in Cell A1, so =A1+1825, we would end up with a date in 2019, specifically December 31, 2019, because of the existence of a leap year in that date range.

So use DATE if you want to create a new date x number of years or months in the future. Use math if you want to create a date x number of days in the future.

Also, just to note that if I had wanted to use the date directly in the formula instead of a cell reference, I would need to use quotation marks to do so, like this:

$$="1/1/2015"+(365*5)$$

(I've sort of cheated here by using a date that has the same month and day because I suspect the required format for that date entry will vary across country depending on whether you're in a month/day country or a day/month country.)

Alright, now that we used it in an example let's actually walk through the YEAR function.

The YEAR Function

Notation: YEAR(serial_number)

Excel Definition: Returns the year of a date, an integer in the range 1900-9999.

The YEAR function extracts the four-digit year from a date.

If this matters for you, the dates are treated as Gregorian dates. Even if they're displayed as some other date type, the year that YEAR will return is the Gregorian-equivalent year for that date.

It's very simple to use. You have a date in a cell and then you use YEAR to reference that cell. So

$$=YEAR(A1)$$

will return the year of the date in Cell A1.

If you reference a date stored as text or written in a text format and formatted as text, Excel will still be able to extract the year for you. Assuming, of course, that the date is a valid date to Excel, so has a year value between 1900 and 9999.

If Excel doesn't recognize the date as a valid date, then it will return a #VALUE! error.

You can also enter the date directly into the function, like so:

$$=YEAR("January 1, 2010")$$

$$=YEAR("1/1/2010")$$

$$=YEAR("1-1-2010")$$

Each of the above will return a value of 2010.

Remember to use the quotation marks or you'll get a #NUM! error message.

Just like the YEAR function extracts the year from a date, the MONTH function extracts the month (as a number between 1 and 12), and the DAY function extracts the day of the month (as a number between 1 and 31).

Also, assuming time of day information is available, the HOUR function extracts the hour (as a number from 0 to 23 because it uses military time), the MINUTE function extracts the minute (as a number from 0 to 59), the SECOND function extracts the second (as a number from 0 to 59).

The WEEKDAY Function

Notation: WEEKDAY(serial_number, [return_type])

Excel Definition: Returns a number from 1 to 7 identifying the day of the week of a date.

The WEEKDAY function is another one that's similar to what we just discussed. But this function identifies the day of the week for a specific date. So does it fall on a Monday? A Wednesday? A Sunday? The WEEKDAY function lets you figure that out.

By default the WEEKDAY function returns a number for the day of the week, so a number between 1 and 7, where 1 is equal to Sunday and 7 is equal to Saturday and each day in between is assigned a number value within that range. So

$$=WEEKDAY(A1)$$

where A1 has January 1, 2019 in it and that date is a Tuesday, will return a value of 3.

You could also write that as

$$=WEEKDAY("1/1/2019")$$

or

$$=WEEKDAY("January 1, 2019")$$

If you don't like having Sunday be your first day, you can use the return_type input variable to define a different start point for numbering the days of the week.

Using a return_type value of 2 will assign a value of 1 to Monday instead of Sunday and will then number each day of the week from there ending with a value of 7 for Sunday. So

$$=WEEKDAY("1/1/2019",2)$$

will return a value of 2 instead of the default value of 3.

Using a value of 3 for return_type assigns a value of 0 to Monday on through to a value of 6 for Sunday. So

$$=WEEKDAY("January 1, 2019",3)$$

would return a result of 1 since Monday is 0 which makes Tuesday 1.

If you look in the help text for the function you'll see that there's an option for every single day of the week to be your starting point using values from 11 through 17 for return_type.

One way to use this function is to check what day of the week it is and then have different reactions based on that result. So let's say you run an amusement park and you want to have one set of prices, $24.95, for weekday attendees and another price, $29.95, for weekend attendees.

You could write

$$=IF(WEEKDAY(A1,11)<6,24.95,29.95)$$

That's saying that using a numbering system where Monday is 1 and Sunday is 7 that if the number of the week is 1 through 5 (or Monday through Friday) then assign a cost of $24.95. If it's not, assign a cost of $29.95.

Done. Works.

The WEEKNUM Function

Notation: WEEKNUM(serial_number, [return_type])

Excel Definition: Returns the week number in the year.

The WEEKNUM function is much like the WEEKDAY function except it returns what week of the year a date falls in. So

$$=WEEKNUM("January 1, 2019")$$

will return a value of 1 because that day is in the first week of the year, no matter how you slice or dice it. But, interestingly,

$$=WEEKNUM("December 31, 2019")$$

returns a value of 53 even though there are only 52 weeks in a year.

This is driven by how Excel defines a week.

The default is for Excel to define a week as starting on a Sunday and only including dates for that year. So in 2019 the first week of that year is considered to be January 1st, a Tuesday, through to January 5th, a Saturday. Week 2 of 2019, if you're using the default return type, starts on January 6th, a Sunday. That means that the final days of the year, December 29th through December 31st, fall in the 53rd week of the year.

Under the default, dates in December will always be assigned to their year even if that means that the WEEKNUM result you get back is 53. However, you can use the return_type input option to change how Excel defines a week.

The values of 11 through 17 can be used to start a week on any day from Monday (11) through Sunday (17) but they still keep dates within their year meaning you can still have a week number 53.

There is, however, an option, return_type 21, which follows the ISO 8601 standard for week numbering which is used in Europe. The ISO approach keeps weeks together even if they cross years. It will take the first week of the new year that has a Thursday in it and will then start the week from the Monday of that same week, even if the Monday falls in the prior year. So

$$=WEEKNUM("12/31/2018",21)$$

will return a value of 1, since under the ISO methodology the first week of the year is from December 31, 2018 through January 2, 2019.

Using the return_value of 21 you will never have a week 53 in your results. But you will have end-of-December dates that are assigned to the first week of the next year.

So choose wisely if you use this one.

Also, if you don't want to be bothered to include a return_value of 21 for the WEEKNUM function in order to use the ISO standard, you can just use the ISOWEEKNUM function instead.

The EDATE Function

Notation: EDATE(start_date, months)

Excel Definition: Returns the serial number of the date that is the indicated number of months before or after the start date.

The EDATE function takes any given date and gives the date x number of months from that date. So, for example, where the date in Cell B1 is June 15, 2018 and I'm telling Excel to add six months I could just use

$$=EDATE(B1,6)$$

which gives me a date of December 15, 2018, six months later.

Now, one thing to keep in mind with EDATE is that it will initially return the serial number for the date, so you need to format that cell as a date or your result will be a number. 43449 in this example.

EDATE also works with negative numbers for the number of months. So =EDATE(B1,-6) will give the date six months before the date in Cell B1; in this example that's December 15, 2017.

Note that EDATE returns the exact same date of the month each time, regardless of how many days are in each of the months in between. If for some reason your date is February 29th and you move in a twelve-month increment it will return the 28th.

Also, any month value you use that's not an integer will be truncated not rounded. (So 5.89 would be treated as 5 not 6.)

The EOMONTH function is similar to the EDATE function except it provides the last day of the month x months from your specified date, so December 31, 2018 in our first example above.

The **NETWORKDAYS.INTL** Function

Notation: NETWORKDAYS.INTL(start_date, end_date, [weekend], [holidays])

Excel Definition: Returns the number of whole workdays between two dates with custom weekend parameters.

The NETWORKDAYS.INTL function is a more sophisticated version of NETWORKDAYS and was introduced with Excel 2010. It allows you to take a starting date and an ending date and calculate the number of whole workdays between them, excluding any dates that you classify as holidays.

It's an improvement on NETWORKDAYS because it allows you to specify what constitutes a weekend.

Let's walk through an example. It's December 15, 2020 and I want to know how many workdays there are between now and the end of the year, let's say January 4, 2021.

Let's first just look at the calculation without holidays excluded:

=NETWORKDAYS.INTL("December 15, 2020","January 4, 2021")

The result it gives me is 15.

If I look at my calendar I can see that it's including the 15th as well as January 4th because otherwise there would be three workdays the first week (the 16th, 17th, and 18th) and then five workdays in each of the next two weeks. Only by counting December 15th and January 4th can we get the result of 15.

Not exactly *between* those two dates. It's *inclusive* of the dates you include in your function. Good to know, right?

Now I want to add holidays, but because of the way that NETWORKDAYS.INTL is built, I have to deal with the weekend issue first. For now I'm just going to use a Saturday/Sunday weekend which requires a value of 1. We'll come back to this in a minute.

I don't want to include Christmas or New Year's in the calculation. The easiest way to do this is to have a separate data table where all the holidays to exclude are listed and then use a cell reference.

In this case, I put the dates in Cells C1 and C2, which then gives me:

=NETWORKDAYS.INTL("December 15, 2020","January 4, 2021",1,C1:C2)

where the 1 is my weekend designator and the C1:C2 is my cell range that includes my holidays.

The result I get now is 13 because December 25, 2020 falls on a Friday as does January 1, 2021.

If I don't want the first and last days included, I can combine the function with some basic math and just subtract 2 from my calculated number of days:

=NETWORKDAYS.INTL("December 15, 2020","January 4, 2021",1,C1:C2)-2

In the examples above I used a cell range for my holidays, but how do you include more than one date within the function itself? You have to use curly brackets around your holiday date entries. Like so:

=NETWORKDAYS.INTL("December 15, 2020","January 4, 2021",1,{"12/25/20","1/1/21"})-2

Also note that for every date I listed in the formula above that I had to put quotes around it for Excel to recognize it as a valid date.

Now let's circle back to that third input, the weekend value.

When you get to this point in inputting your values, you will see a dropdown menu of options you can use to specify what days Excel should consider weekends.

Using numbers 11 through 17 allow a single-day weekend and numbers 1 through 7 allow two-day weekends of any consecutive two days in a week.

So let's say that I get off Thursdays and Fridays each week. It looks like this:

=NETWORKDAYS.INTL("December 15, 2020","January 4, 2021",6)

because 6 is the value to use for a Thursday/Friday weekend.

(Interestingly, the result is still 15, but it's using different dates to get there.)

If I expand the function to include my two holidays (which both happen to fall on a Friday), I get this:

=NETWORKDAYS.INTL("December 15, 2020","January 4, 2021",6,{"12/25/20","1/1/21"})

and my result is *still 15*.

Remember with a standard weekend it was 13 because the holidays fell on a workday, but because the holidays in this scenario fall on our "weekend" they've already been excluded from our count of workdays and don't need to be excluded again.

So there you have it. That is how NETWORKDAYS.INTL works.

It also has a counterpart WORKDAY.INTL that calculates what the date will be (January 4, 2021, for example) a specified number of workdays in the future or the past.

Just be advised that unlike NETWORKDAYS.INTL that WORKDAY.INTL does *not* include the present or the final day in its calculation so they are not directly interchangeable.

Other Functions

That's it for this guide to functions. There are many, many more functions in Excel. Chances are there's at least one I didn't cover here that you will eventually need. But hopefully you now have a good understanding of how the functions work and can use Excel's help to find and structure any function you do need.

I hope this has also given you a taste of the potential power and breadth of Excel. It's a tremendous program that can do so, so much. (You don't have to master all of it, though, to get value from it, so don't feel like you have to keep digging and digging if what you already know now meets your needs.)

Next I want to discuss the various error messages and what they mean and what to do when your formula isn't working.

When Things Go Wrong

As you start to work with formulas, chances are you're going to run into some errors. I certainly do and I've been at this a long time.

You might see a #/DIV0! or a #REF! or a #VALUE! or a #N/A or a #NUM! error. It happens. Sometimes you'll realize exactly what you did, but at other times it's going to be a puzzle.

So let's me see if I can help a bit.

#REF!

If you see #REF! in a cell it's probably because you just deleted a value that that cell was referencing. So if you had =A1+B1+C1+D1 in a cell and then you deleted Column C that would create a #REF! error. Excel won't adjust the formula and drop the missing value, it will return this error message instead.

To see where the cell generating the error was in your formula, double-click in the cell with the #REF! message. This will show you the formula, including a #REF! where the missing cell used to be.

So you'll see something like =A1+B1+#REF!+D1 and you'll know that the cell you deleted was used as the third entry in that formula.

If it's something like the example I just gave you where you just need to delete that cell reference, do so. Turn it into =A1+B1+D1. But you may also realize that your formula now needs to reference a different cell. If so, replace the #REF! with that cell reference. Hit enter when you've made your changes and you're done.

#VALUE!

According to Excel, a #VALUE! error means you typed your formula wrong or you're referencing a cell that's the wrong type of cell.

If you're using dates, see if the date is left-aligned. If it is, then chances are Excel is treating the date as a text entry not a date entry. That means subtraction won't work on it.

Same with numbers. If you use SUM and get this error on a range of numbers make sure that they're formatted as numbers and not text. (This shouldn't be a common problem, but could be if you've imported a data file from elsewhere.)

It can also mean that you have non-standard regional settings and that your minus sign is being used as a list separator (rather than the more standard, at least in the U.S., comma).

Or it can mean that you're referencing a data source that is no longer available like another workbook that was moved.

#DIV/0!

This is a common error to see if you've written a formula that requires division. If I input the formula =A1/B1 and there are no values in Cells A1 and B1, Excel will return #DIV/0!

You need a numeric value for your denominator to stop this from happening. (The numerator can be blank, but not the denominator.)

I usually use IF functions to suppress the #DIV/0! when I have a data table where values haven't been input yet. So I'll write something like =IF(B1>0,A1/B1,"").

Just be sure if you do that that the IF condition makes sense for your data. (In the example I just gave, any negative number would also result in a blank cell.)

#N/A

According to Excel, an #N/A error means that Excel isn't finding what it was asked to look for. In other words, there's no solution. This occurs most often with the VLOOKUP, HLOOKUP, and MATCH functions. You tell it to look for a value in your table and that value isn't in your table.

This can be valuable information that perhaps points to a weakness in your data or your function. For example, it could indicate that the data in your lookup table is in a different format from the data in your analysis table. Or that there are extra spaces in the entries in one or the other table

But if you know this is going to happen and don't want to see the #N/A in your results, you can use the IFNA function to suppress that result and replace it with a zero, a blank space, or even text.

#NUM!

According to Excel, you will see this error when there are numeric values in a formula or function that aren't valid. The example Excel gives involves using $1,000 in a formula instead of 1000, but when I just tried this to validate it Excel wouldn't even allow me to use that formula, it wanted to fix the formula for me as soon as I hit Enter. So this may be more of an issue in older versions of Excel.

Excel will also return this error message if an iterative function can't find a result or if the result that would be returned by the formula is too large or too small. (If you're running into this error for those reasons chances are you're doing some pretty advanced things, so we're not going to worry about that here.)

Circular References

Excel will also flag for you any time that you write a formula that references itself. (I do this on occasion without meaning to.)

For example, if in Cell A5 you type =SUM(A1:A5), Excel will display a dialogue box when you hit Enter that says "Careful, we found one or more circular references in your workbook that might cause your formulas to calculate incorrectly."

Say OK and then go back to the cell with the formula and fix the issue.

Keep in mind that sometimes a circular reference error can be generated by an indirect circular reference, so you're referencing a cell that's referencing another cell and it's that other cell that's the issue.

If you can't figure out the cause and Excel doesn't "helpfully" start drawing connections on your worksheet to show it to you, in newer versions of Excel you can go to the Formulas tab and under Formula Auditing click on Trace Precedents to see what values are feeding that cell.

(Usually when this happens I know exactly what I did and it's just a matter of getting Excel to stop trying to fix it for me so I can make the correction myself.)

Too Few Arguments

I also on occasion will try to use a function and get a warning message that I've used too few arguments for the function. When that happens check that you've included enough inputs for the function to work. Anything listed that isn't in brackets is required. So =RANDBETWEEN(bottom, top) requires that you enter values for both bottom and top but =CONCATENATE(text1, [text2],...) only requires one input.

If that's not the issue, make sure that you have each of the inputs separated by commas and that your quotation marks and parens are in the right places.

General Wonkiness

Sometimes everything seems fine but the formula just doesn't seem to be giving the right answer. If it's a complex formula, break it down into its components and make sure that each component works on a standalone basis.

You can also double-click on the cell for a formula and Excel will color code each of the separate components that are feeding the formula and also highlight those cells in your worksheet. Confirm that the highlighted cells are the ones you want.

For formulas you copied, verify that none of your cell ranges or cell references needed to be locked down but weren't. (I do this one often.) If you don't use $ to lock your cell references, they will adjust according to where you copied that formula. If that's what you wanted, great. If it isn't, fix it by going back to the first cell and using the $ signs to lock the cell references and copying and pasting again or by changing the cell references in the location you copied the formula to so that it works.

And, as we've seen here, sometimes there are choices you can make with a function that impact the outcome, like whether you remembered to sort the input range.

If you're working with a function you're not familiar with, open the Excel Help for the function and read through it. That will often give a list of common issues encountered with the function.

Conclusion

That's it for this guide. There are many more functions that I did not cover here. Excel is incredibly broad in what it can do, but also incredibly specialized at times.

If you can think of it, chances are there's a way to do it in Excel. So don't be afraid to go to Insert Function and poke around to see what's possible.

(And if there isn't a function for what you want, you can always learn how to write your own macros in Excel. Although be careful with those. And don't look to me for that one.)

If you have a specific issue or question, feel free to reach out to me. mlhumphreywriter@gmail.com. I'm happy to help.

Good luck with it! Remember, save your raw data in one place, work on it in another, take your time, check the individual components of complex formulas, check your threshold cases, and Ctrl + Z (Undo) is your friend.

APPENDIX A: CELL NOTATION

If you're going to work with functions in Excel, then you need to understand how Excel references cells.

Cells are referenced based upon their column and their row. So Cell A1 is the cell in Column A and Row 1. Cell B10 is the cell in Column B and Row 10. Cell BC25232 is the cell in Column BC and in Row 25232.

If you want to reference more than one cell or cell range in a function then you can do so in a couple of ways. To reference separate and discrete cells, you list each one and you separate them with a comma. So (A1, A2, A3) refers to Cells A1, A2, and A3.

When cells are touching you can instead reference them as a single range using the colon. So (A1:A3) also refers to Cells A1, A2, and A3. Think of the colon as a "through".

You don't have to limit this to a single row or column either. You can reference A1:B25. That refers to all of the cells between Cell A1 and Cell B25. That would be all cells in Column A from Cell A1 through Cell A25 as well as all cells in Column B from Cell B1 through Cell B25.

When you note a range best practice is for the left-hand cell that you list (A1) to be the top left-most cell of the range and the right-hand cell you list (B25) to be the bottom right-most cell of the range.

You can also reference an entire column by using the letter and leaving off any numbers. So C:C refers to all cells in Column C.

And you can do the same for a row by leaving off the letter. So 10:10 refers to all the cells in Row 10.

If you ever reference a cell in another worksheet or another workbook, this also needs to be addressed through cell notation.

For a cell in another worksheet, you put the sheet name as it appears on the worksheet tab followed by an exclamation point before the cell reference. So Sheet1!B1 is Cell B1 in the worksheet labeled Sheet 1.

For another workbook you put the name of the workbook in brackets before the worksheet name. So [Book1]Sheet2!$D$2 refers to Cell D2 in the worksheet labeled Sheet 2 in the workbook titled Book 1.

(I should note here that I think it's a bad idea to reference data in another workbook due to the odds that the formula/function will break as soon as that other workbook is renamed or moved to a new location and that I generally don't think it's worth doing.)

Now, before you start to panic and think you need to remember all of this and that you never will, take a deep breath. Because when you're writing a formula you can simply click on the cells you need when you need them and Excel will write the cell notation for you.

It's just useful to know how this works in case something doesn't work right. (And even then you can still use Excel to show you what each cell reference is referring to. Just double-click on the formula and Excel will color code the cell references in the formula and put a matching colored border around the cells in your worksheet.)

INDEX

CONTROL SHORTCUTS

The following is a list of useful control shortcuts in Excel. For each one, hold down the Ctrl key and use the listed letter to perform the command.

Command	Ctrl +
Bold	B
Copy	C
Cut	X
Find	F
Italicize	I
Next Worksheet	Page Down
Paste	V
Print	P
Prior Worksheet	Page Up
Redo	Y
Replace	H
Save	S
Select All	A
Underline	U
Undo	Z

ABOUT THE AUTHOR

M.L. Humphrey is a former stockbroker with a degree in Economics from Stanford and an MBA from Wharton who has spent close to twenty years as a regulator and consultant in the financial services industry.

You can reach M.L. Humphrey at:

mlhumphreywriter@gmail.com

or at

www.mlhumphrey.com